# ROBERT J. MARZANO

# TAMMY HEFLEBOWER

# Teaching & Assessing 21st Century Skills

**Marzano Research Laboratory**
Powered by Solution Tree

THE **CLASSROOM** STRATEGIES **SERIES**

555 North Morton Street
Bloomington, IN 47404

888.849.0851
FAX: 866.801.1447

email: info@marzanoresearch.com
marzanoresearch.com

Visit **marzanoresearch.com/classroomstrategies** to download the reproducibles in this book.

Printed in the United States of America

Library of Congress Control Number: 2011928938

ISBN:   978-0-9833512-0-7 (paperback)

       978-0-9833512-1-4 (library binding)

15 14 13 12 11          1 2 3 4 5

Vice President of Production: Gretchen Knapp

Managing Production Editor: Caroline Wise

Copy Editor: Sarah Payne-Mills

Proofreader: Elisabeth Abrams

Text Designer: Raven Bongiani

Cover Designer: Amy Shock

# MARZANO RESEARCH LABORATORY DEVELOPMENT TEAM

**Staff Writer/Editor**

Lindsay A. Carleton

**Staff Writer/Researcher**

Julia A. Simms

**Marzano Research Laboratory Associates**

| | |
|---|---|
| Tina Boogren | David Livingston |
| Bev Clemens | Beatrice McGarvey |
| Jane K. Doty Fischer | Margaret McInteer |
| Maria C. Foseid | Diane E. Paynter |
| Mark P. Foseid | Debra Pickering |
| Tammy Heflebower | Salle Quackenboss |
| Mitzi Hoback | Tom Roy |
| Jan Hoegh | Phil Warrick |
| Sharon Kramer | Kenneth Williams |

# ACKNOWLEDGMENTS

Marzano Research Laboratory would like to thank the following reviewers:

Nancy R. Bunt
Program Director, Math & Science Collaborative
Allegheny Intermediate Unit
Homestead, Pennsylvania

Linda Carmichael
Gifted Intervention Specialist
Hastings Middle School
Upper Arlington, Ohio

David Doerfler
Pre-Algebra Teacher
North High School
Edmond, Oklahoma

Stephen Elrod
Third-Grade Teacher
Wake Forest Elementary School
Wake Forest, North Carolina

Ursula Kirchner
Chemistry Teacher
South Lakes High School
Reston, Virginia

# CONTENTS

*Italicized entries indicate reproducible pages.*

# ABOUT THE AUTHORS

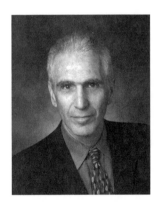

Robert J. Marzano, PhD, is the cofounder and CEO of Marzano Research Laboratory in Denver, Colorado. Throughout his forty years in the field of education, he has become a speaker, trainer, and author of more than thirty books and 150 articles on topics such as instruction, assessment, writing and implementing standards, cognition, effective leadership, and school intervention. His books include: *Designing and Teaching Learning Goals and Objectives, District Leadership That Works, Formative Assessment and Standards-Based Grading, On Excellence in Teaching, The Art and Science of Teaching, and The Highly Engaged Classroom.* His practical translations of the most current research and theory into classroom strategies are internationally known and widely practiced by both teachers and administrators. He received a bachelor's degree from Iona College in New York, a master's degree from Seattle University, and a doctorate from the University of Washington.

Tammy Heflebower, EdD, is vice president of Marzano Research Laboratory in Denver, Colorado. She is a consultant with experience in urban, rural, and suburban districts throughout North America. Dr. Heflebower has served as a classroom teacher, building-level leader, district leader, regional professional development director, and national trainer. She has also been an adjunct professor of curriculum, instruction, and assessment courses at several universities. Dr. Heflebower has served as president of the Nebraska Association for Supervision and Curriculum Development and president-elect for the Professional Development Organization for Nebraska Educational Service Units. She was president-elect of the Colorado Association of Education Specialists and legislative liaison for Colorado Association of School Executives. Her articles have been featured in the monthly newsletter *Nebraska Council of School Administrators Today*, and she is a contributor to *The Teacher as Assessment Leader* and *The Principal as Assessment Leader*. Dr. Heflebower holds a bachelor of arts from Hastings College in Hastings, Nebraska, a master of arts from the University of Nebraska at Omaha, and an educational administrative endorsement from the University of Nebraska–Lincoln. She also earned a doctor of education in educational administration from the University of Nebraska–Lincoln. To learn more about Dr. Marzano's and Dr. Heflebower's work, visit http://marzanoresearch.com.

To book Dr. Marzano or Dr. Heflebower for professional development, contact pd@solution-tree.com.

# ABOUT MARZANO RESEARCH LABORATORY

Marzano Research Laboratory (MRL) is a joint venture between Solution Tree and Dr. Robert J. Marzano. MRL combines Dr. Marzano's forty years of educational research with continuous action research in all major areas of schooling in order to provide effective and accessible instructional strategies, leadership strategies, and classroom assessment strategies that are always at the forefront of best practice. By providing such an all-inclusive research-into-practice resource center, MRL provides teachers and principals the tools they need to effect profound and immediate improvement in student achievement.

# INTRODUCTION

*Teaching and Assessing 21st Century Skills* is part of a series of books collectively referred to as the *Classroom Strategies Series*. The purpose of this series is to provide teachers as well as building and district administrators with an in-depth treatment of research-based instructional strategies that can be used in the classroom to enhance student achievement. Many of the strategies addressed in this series have been covered in other works such as *The Art and Science of Teaching* (Marzano, 2007), *Classroom Management That Works* (Marzano, 2003), and *Classroom Instruction That Works* (Marzano, Pickering, & Pollock, 2001). Although those works devoted a chapter or a part of a chapter to particular strategies, the *Classroom Strategies Series* devotes an entire book to an instructional strategy or set of related strategies.

As the 21st century unfolds, the pace of change in the world is accelerating while education in the United States remains stagnant or, at best, progresses in isolated pockets. Concern over the effects of an inadequate education system on the nation's economy and innovative potential is growing, and it seems a crisis point is near—a point when the negative aspects of the education system will outweigh the benefits. The consequences of a poorly educated population would be dire, and in order to correct this trajectory, every level of the education system will have to undergo massive changes. Teachers and administrators must lead this cultural shift, which is perhaps as important and massive as the industrial revolution. In *Teaching and Assessing 21st Century Skills*, we present a model of instruction and assessment based on a combination of cognitive skills (skills students will need to succeed academically) and conative skills (skills students will need to succeed interpersonally) necessary for the 21st century.

We begin with an overview of the major changes in the 21st century and how those changes have affected the education system and overall student achievement. In the second chapter, we review the research and theory behind the cognitive and conative skills addressed in the model. Although you might skip this chapter and move right into those that provide recommendations for classroom practice, you are strongly encouraged to examine the research and theory as they are the foundation for the entire book. Indeed, a basic purpose of *Teaching and Assessing 21st Century Skills* and others in the *Classroom Strategies Series* is to present the most useful instructional strategies that are based on the strongest research and theory available.

Because research and theory can provide only a general direction for classroom practice, *Teaching and Assessing 21st Century Skills* (and each book in the series) goes one step further to translate that research into applications for the classroom. Specifically, this book addresses three cognitive skills (analyzing and utilizing information, addressing complex problems and issues, and creating patterns and mental models) and two conative skills (understanding and controlling oneself and understanding and interacting with others).

## How to Use This Book

*Teaching and Assessing 21st Century Skills* can be used as a self-study text that provides an in-depth understanding of how to gear instruction toward 21st century students. At the end of chapters 3 through 8, you will find comprehension questions. It is important to complete these questions and then compare your answers with those in appendix A (page 193). Such interaction provides a review of the content and allows you to examine how clearly you understand it.

Teams of teachers or entire faculties that wish to examine the topic of 21st century skills in depth may also use *Teaching and Assessing 21st Century Skills*. When this is the case, teacher teams should answer the questions independently and then compare their answers in small- and large-group settings.

# Chapter 1

# THE STATUS OF THE 21ST CENTURY

The specific skill set that students will need to succeed in the 21st century has been a topic of interest in education since at least the early 1990s. In 1991, the United States Department of Labor formed the Secretary's Commission on Achieving Necessary Skills (SCANS) and charged it with the task of examining "the demands of the workplace and whether our young people are capable of meeting those demands" (U.S. Department of Labor, 1991, p. vii). The commission's 1991 report, *What Work Requires of Schools*, contrasted the old requirements for success in America, defined as "a strong back, the willingness to work, and a high school diploma," with what students need in the new American workplace, defined as "a well-developed mind, a passion to learn, and the ability to put knowledge to work" (p. 2). The report criticized schools, saying that "despite their best efforts, most schools have not changed fast enough or moved far enough" to prepare students for the demands of the new workplace (p. 4). It also defined the criteria for success in the workplace in terms of five competencies and three foundational requirements. This was one of the first efforts to define 21st century skills and the role that schools should play in teaching them.

The ideas articulated in the SCANS report led to a variety of efforts over the next decades to define what was needed for success in the modern world. Many of these efforts focused on the interests of the organization doing the work. For example, the National Communication Association worked on defining speaking and listening skills, the International Society for Technology in Education focused on effective uses of technology, and the American Library Association outlined information literacy standards for students. These efforts were precursors to the Partnership for 21st Century Skills's more comprehensive 2002–2003 project to define 21st century skills in terms of a "unified, collective vision for education and a framework for action" (Partnership for 21st Century Skills, 2003, p. 2). Composed of business and education organizations, the partnership's goal was to close the gap between "the knowledge and skills most students learn in school and the knowledge and skills they need in typical 21st century communities and workplaces" (p. 3).

In a 2003 report titled *Learning for the 21st Century*, the Partnership for 21st Century Skills outlined six key elements of 21st century learning. Those elements eventually grew into the *Framework for 21st Century Learning*, published first in 2007 and updated in 2009. The framework identified 21st century student outcomes in four broad areas: (1) core subjects and 21st century themes, (2) learning and innovation skills, (3) information, media, and technology skills, and (4) life and career skills. It also recommended a foundation of "critical systems necessary to ensure student mastery of 21st century skills" (Partnership for 21st Century Skills, 2009, p. 7): standards and assessments, curriculum and instruction, professional development, and learning environments.

## Why Do We Need 21st Century Skills?

In response to these efforts and others like them, a logical and important question educators should ask is "Why do we need a new set of skills for the 21st century?" Ken Kay (2010) listed two fundamental reasons that our students need these new skills: (1) the world is changing and will continue to change dramatically throughout the 21st century, and (2) schools are not keeping up with these changes. Others agree that these are important reasons K–12 educators need to rethink what they teach and how they teach it (see Darling-Hammond, 2010; Dede, 2010; Gardner, 2010; Hargreaves, 2010; Johnson & Johnson, 2010; Lemke, 2010).

### The World Is Changing

The 21st century world will change in many ways.  One of those with immediate implications for K–12 education is the change relevant to jobs and careers. Kay (2010) highlighted the fact that the types of jobs available in America are shifting from manufacturing and industrial jobs to service-sector occupations. Computers now perform most routine, rule-guided tasks, and information and communications technologies enable extensive interaction among people from many cultures in the global marketplace. Instead of completing routine, task-based assignments, employees must now set goals, solve problems, work effectively with a wide variety of customers and colleagues, and make decisions without direct supervision. Kay observed that these functions require skills that were not necessary for most manufacturing and industrial jobs in the 20th century.

Bernie Trilling and Charles Fadel (2009), board members at the Partnership for 21st Century Skills, also made this point:

> This monumental shift from Industrial Age production to that of the Knowledge Age economy—information-driven, globally networked—is as world-changing and life-altering as the shift from the Agrarian to the Industrial Age three hundred and fifty years ago. (p. 3)

Tony Wagner (2008) agreed:

> In the twenty-first century, mastery of the basic skills of reading, writing, and math is no longer enough. Almost any job that pays more than minimum wage—both blue and white collar—now calls for employees who know how to solve a range of intellectual and technical problems. (p. xxii)

Wagner described 20th century work as what people did "with their hands—not with their heads—and so they didn't need . . . analytical skills in their daily life" (p. xxiv). He noted that "increasingly, the only decent jobs that remain in this country will go to those who know how to continuously improve products or services or create entirely new ones—the knowledge workers of the twenty-first century" (p. 256).

Wagner (2008) also conducted a series of interviews with CEOs and managers in various industries; these interviews highlight the skills employers are looking for in the 21st century.

Clay Parker, CEO of BOC Edwards Chemical Management Division, said:

> Our business is changing, and so the skills our engineers need change rapidly, as well. We can teach them the technical stuff. But for employees to solve problems or to learn new things, they have to know what questions to ask. And we can't teach them how to ask good questions—how to think. The ability to ask the right questions is the single most important skill. (Wagner, 2008, p. 2)

Christi Pedra, CEO of Siemens Hearing Instruments, said:

> When you're in a sales and marketing environment, it's really important that you understand your customer. I've found that the best way to understand people is to ask questions. I ask questions all day long. If I ask the right questions, I get information that allows me to be more successful in a variety of ways. (Wagner, 2008, p. 5)

Mark Maddox, human resources manager at Unilever Foods North America, said:

> Twenty-five years ago, management was 16 percent of the labor force, and administrative support was 12 percent; today management is 5 percent, and support 3 percent. . . . Today we practice self-direction and continuous improvement and teamwork. (Wagner, 2008, pp. 18–19)

Michael Jung, a senior business consultant, noted that this new knowledge-based economy will surely create a different kind of worker: "I think the most successful worker will not merely adapt to working conditions that are given to him but be able to adapt in a way that creates a position that fits his own profile" (Wagner, 2008, p. 40). Finally, Ted McCain and Ian Jukes (2001) said that lifelong learning was now essential due to the rapidly changing nature of information in the 21st century:

> In the past, when information had a much longer shelf life, learning was something that was done once in your youth. Then you were done with learning for life. In the good old days, what you learned in your youth prepared you for your single career. Today, learning has become a lifelong process. Given the rapidly changing nature of our world, people of all ages must constantly learn and relearn what they need to know. What they learned yesterday may no longer be valid in tomorrow's world. Tomorrow, they will have to learn again because today's information will already be out of date. (p. 89)

## U.S. Schools Are Not Keeping Up With the Changing World

The second reason for a focus on 21st century skills is that the United States is not keeping up with the rapid global changes. Here we consider three indications: (1) dropout rates, (2) lack of student engagement, and (3) achievement gaps.

### *Dropout Rates*

To highlight the high dropout rate in America, Wagner (2008) cited statistics showing the United States' graduation rates (for high school and college) compared with the graduation rates in other countries. He found:

The high school graduation rate in the United States—which is about 70 percent of the age cohort—is now well behind that of countries such as Denmark (96 percent), Japan (93 percent), and even Poland (92 percent) and Italy (79 percent). . . . The United States now ranks tenth among industrial nations in the rate of college completion by 25- to 44-year-olds. (pp. xix–xx)

Jobs for the Future (2005) reported similar statistics: "For every 10 students who enter eighth grade, only seven graduate high school on time, and only three complete a postsecondary degree by age 26" (p. 2). Tamara Erickson (2008) pointed out that the overall graduation rate for the United States does not tell the whole story, and she pointed to specific groups in California as examples:

California's overall high school graduation rate is about 71 percent, and within that, the graduation rates for African American and Latino students are 57 percent and 60 percent, respectively. The Los Angeles and Oakland unified school districts graduate *fewer than half* of their incoming freshmen within four years. (pp. 15–16)

This means that not only does the United States have an overall problem with students dropping out, but it also has severe problems with dropouts from specific socioeconomic and ethnic groups.

### Lack of Student Engagement

Dropout rates and student engagement are inextricably linked. Cheryl Lemke (2010), the president and CEO of the Metiri Group, made this point, citing "the current lack of student engagement in American schools that has contributed to an extremely high dropout rate nationally; nearly 30 percent of students who begin their ninth-grade year of high school do not graduate" (p. 246).

Trilling and Fadel (2009) attributed students' current lack of engagement to a "new set of desires and expectations" that 21st century students have developed as a result of their "lifelong immersion in all things digital" (p. 29). They cited a 2009 study of eleven thousand individuals born between 1978 and 1998 that identified "eight common attitudes, behaviors, and expectations" specific to that generation (p. 29). These included (pp. 29–30):

1. Freedom to choose what's right for them and to express their personal views and individual identity

2. Customization and personalization, the ability to change things to better suit their own needs

3. Scrutiny—detailed, behind-the-scenes analysis so they can find out what the real story is

4. Integrity and openness in their interactions with others and from organizations like businesses, government, and educational institutions

5. Entertainment and play to be integrated into their work, learning, and social life

6. Collaboration and relationships to be a vital part of all they do

7. Speed in communications, getting information, and getting responses to questions and messages

8. Innovation in products, services, employers, and schools, and in their own lives

According to Trilling and Fadel (2009), students who expect to encounter these eight elements throughout their lives do not respond well to "a one-size-fits-all factory model and one-way broadcast approach to learning" (p. 30).

Wagner (2008) asserted that "boredom continues to be a leading cause of our high school dropout rate" (p. xxv) and that "motivation and our nation's dropout rate go hand in hand" (p. 114). He challenged the assumption that students drop out because they lack the necessary skills to succeed in school, citing a study by the Bill & Melinda Gates Foundation that found "poor basic skills in reading, writing, and computation were not the main reason for the high dropout rate: It turns out that *will*, not *skill*, is the single most important factor" (p. 114).

### Achievement Gaps

Kay (2010) noted the presence of achievement gaps in the United States and the effect those gaps have on the nation as a whole: "Nationally, Black, Hispanic, and disadvantaged students perform worse than their peers on national assessments . . . dragging down the collective capacity of the future workforce" (p. xviii). According to Kay, these gaps, combined with the high dropout rate, endanger the economic competitiveness of the United States and demonstrate that our schools are not effectively adapting to the dramatic changes in the world today.

Wagner (2008) cited the gap in achievement between "white middle-class students' achievement and that of poor, predominantly minority students" as a reason the United States lags behind other countries educationally (p. 200). This achievement gap, he noted, is "well-documented, widely discussed, and [has been] the focus of education reform efforts for the past decade or so" (p. 8). He characterized another kind of achievement gap between what U.S. schools are doing and what they should be doing as "the gap between what even our *best* suburban, urban, and rural public schools are teaching and testing versus what *all* students will need to succeed as learners, workers, and citizens in today's global knowledge economy" (p. 8).

Additionally, Wagner (2008) noted the gap between the knowledge high school students have by graduation and the knowledge they need to be successful in college. He pointed out that "forty percent of *all* students who enter college must take remedial courses" (p. xix). This lack of college readiness among U.S. students is a leading indicator of the United States' poor performance related to other countries. In a 2005 study, researchers interviewed three hundred instructors at two- and four-year colleges. Respondents said that high school had not prepared their students to comprehend complex materials (70 percent), think analytically (66 percent), or apply new learning to solve problems (55 percent) (Peter D. Hart Research Associates/Public Opinion Strategies, 2005). Following are some statistics supporting the position that the United States has fallen behind and is continuing to fall behind other countries.

> Our overall score [on the PISA problem solving test] put us behind twenty-eight other countries—just after the Russian Federation and barely ahead of Portugal. . . . Even the kids we consider to be our most academically talented are not even close to the competition. (Wagner, 2008, p. 74) . . . To be in the top 10 percent of students in the United States, students needed at least a score of 604 . . . but 675 or better in Japan. (Lemke et al., 2004, p. 29, as cited in Wagner, 2008, p. 74)

> On that assessment [PISA] of forty countries, the United States ranked thirty-fifth in mathematics and thirty-first in science. . . . In each disciplinary area tested, U.S. students scored lowest on the problem-solving items. (Darling-Hammond, 2010, p. 35)

> Surveys from the Asia Society and the National Geographic Society have also shown that compared with their peers in other industrialized countries, U.S. high school students lag behind in knowledge of other countries and cultures. And while learning a second language is standard in other industrial countries, only 50 percent of U.S. high school students study a foreign language. (Stewart, 2010, p. 101)

Finally, Wagner (2008) put the problem of faltering U.S. achievement in perspective by noting that "if I'm an employer of a multinational corporation, and I need to hire lots of employees who can solve problems, all other things being equal I'm likely to locate my new facility in a number of other countries before I'd consider coming to the United States" (pp. 74–75).

## Major Frameworks

Our efforts in this book represent one of many attempts to identify a specific set of 21st century skills. Besides the Partnership for 21st Century Skills, a number of other organizations and individuals have outlined what they consider to be the requisite skills for the 21st century.

Chris Dede (2010) compared the following four current conceptual frameworks for 21st century skills:

1.  The Partnership for 21st Century Skills' (2009) Framework for 21st Century Learning

2.  The North Central Regional Educational Laboratory (NCREL) and the Metiri Group's (2003) *enGauge 21st Century Skills* framework

3.  The Organisation for Economic Co-operation and Development's (OECD) (2005) *Definition and Selection of Key Competencies*

4.  The National Leadership Council for Liberal Education and America's Promise's (2007) Essential Learning Outcomes

In his review of these frameworks, Dede (2010) observed that they are "largely consistent in terms of what should be added to the curriculum" (p. 73), but that they also contain some differences. Dede classified these differences as those that allow for more emphasis, and those that allow for more specificity. For example, Dede observed that by including skills in their frameworks like "risk-taking," (NCREL & Metiri Group, 2003, p. 28) or "the ability to act within the big picture" and "the ability to form and conduct life plans and personal projects" (OECD, 2005, pp. 14–15), organizations gave special emphasis to aspects of the framework that they felt were underemphasized.

## The Problem of Defining 21st Century Skills

The pace of progress in the last fifty years has been staggering, and now, in the 21st century, it is only accelerating. For example, in 1974 the first personal computers sold as kits. Prior to that, computers were primarily for military use. In 1982, with the introduction of the mouse and the ability to click, interacting with a computer no longer required the user to type in coded instructions. The 1990s brought smaller, less expensive, and faster computers that could be connected via networks. Today, computers are integrated with every aspect of our society (Hiltz, 2000). Many jobs available today did not exist fifteen years ago. Google was born in 1998 and run out of a garage in California. By 2000, a mere two years later, it had become the world's largest search engine, and the company employed more than forty people. By 2005, there were eight hundred employees in the California office alone. Now, Google employs over 200,000 people worldwide (Google, 2011). That means that 200,000 people now have jobs that did not exist ten years ago.

Clearly, the pace of change in the 21st century is not slowing down. A big-picture view tells us that no matter how forward looking we are, we cannot predict how this new century will unfold. What then should educators do? How can we ensure that students will be successful in a society we cannot comprehensively forecast? Our answer is that, while it is true that all the 21st century skills (or even a majority of those skills) cannot be yet identified, some certainly can. If, at the beginning stages of the 21st century, we are able to identify a small but important set of skills and teach them well, students will be prepared to adapt to the changing conditions of the 21st century. Consequently, we have identified five categories of 21st century skills, divided into two sets: cognitive skills and conative skills.

## Cognitive and Conative Skills

We believe there are five categories of well-researched skills developed in the 20th century that will have great application throughout the 21st century. They are: (1) analyzing and utilizing information, (2) addressing complex problems and issues, (3) creating patterns and mental models, (4) understanding and controlling oneself, and (5) understanding and interacting with others. Virtually all of these are addressed implicitly or explicitly in many of the frameworks already identified in this chapter. For example, all of the frameworks emphasize analyzing and utilizing information, with a focus on the use and management of information and media analysis. With the exception of the Organisation for Economic Co-operation and Development's (2005) framework, all of the frameworks also underscore the importance of addressing complex problems and issues by emphasizing skills like effective reasoning, problem solving, decision making, higher-order thinking, and inquiry. Creating patterns and mental models is necessary to the creative and critical-thinking skills that are highlighted in the Partnership for 21st Century Skills (2009) and enGauge (NCREL & Metiri Group, 2003) frameworks. Understanding and controlling oneself is included in all the major frameworks with varying emphasis on skills such as independent management of goals and time; the ability to self-direct learning, prioritize, and plan for results; and the ability to establish personal needs and boundaries. Understanding and interacting with others appears in all of the major frameworks as well, each framework emphasizing interpersonal and communication skills and cooperation.

These five categories of skills can themselves be organized into two overarching categories: cognitive skills and conative skills (table 1.1).

## Table 1.1: Cognitive and Conative Skills for the 21st Century

| Cognitive Skills | Conative Skills |
|---|---|
| • Analyzing and utilizing information | • Understanding and controlling oneself |
| • Addressing complex problems and issues | • Understanding and interacting with others |
| • Creating patterns and mental models | |

*Cognitive skills* are not unique to the 21st century. Indeed, K–12 education in the United States saw great interest in enhancing cognitive skills, particularly in the latter third of the 20th century. In 1956, Benjamin Bloom and his colleagues developed the *Taxonomy of Educational Objectives*, which offered a hierarchy of cognitive skills and became the staple of curriculum guides and frameworks. Lynn Erickson (2010) pointed out that "through the decades since the publication of Bloom's Taxonomy, there have been attempts to ensure deeper understanding of disciplinary concepts and principles in curriculum designs" (p. 172). Debra Pickering (2010) described one of these attempts:

> In 1983, the Association for Supervision and Curriculum Development (ASCD) hosted a conference at the Wingspread Conference Center in Racine, Wisconsin. It is considered by many to be the event that launched the thinking skills movement in the United States. Throughout the remainder of the 1980s and into the 1990s, leaders in this movement, including Arthur Costa, Robert Marzano, Lauren Resnick, Robert Sternberg, Richard Paul, Barry Beyer, and David Perkins, dominated the literature. But, as with most movements, interest gradually waned as other topics rose to the forefront in the educational literature and at conferences in the new century. (p. 145)

In 2001, Lorin Anderson and David Krathwohl updated Bloom's Taxonomy and stated that knowledge is not just factual and procedural; rather, there are four types of knowledge: (1) factual, (2) conceptual, (3) procedural, and (4) metacognitive. In 2007, Robert Marzano and John Kendall updated the taxonomy even further, identifying cognitive, metacognitive, and self-system skills as critical to the learning process.

What is new to the 21st century is the idea that cognitive skills should take a dominant role in the curriculum. The same might be said of conative skills, although the term *conative* is not as recognizable as *cognitive*.

*Conative skills* refer to one's ability to analyze situations in light of what one knows and how one feels and select appropriate actions. Richard Snow and Douglas Jackson (1993) conceptualized conation as the intersection of cognition and affection in which personality and intelligence overlap to facilitate decision making. A simplified way of thinking about conation is that it is the process of combining what one knows (cognition) with how one feels (affection) and deciding what action to take in light of both. The intrapersonal and interpersonal skills of understanding and controlling oneself and understanding and interacting with others in the 21st century will require students to combine their factual knowledge about topics, such as effective communication techniques, with their assessment of how they are feeling (their emotional responses, for example) and choose the most appropriate course of action.

We believe both cognitive and conative skills will be vital to the success of all citizens living and working in the highly varied and quickly changing knowledge economy of the 21st century. Chapter 2 reviews the relevant research and theory for each category of 21st century skills.

# Chapter 2

# RESEARCH AND THEORY

In chapter 1, we identified a small set of 21st century skills that have been researched and vetted throughout the 20th century and will likely have great utility throughout the 21st century. Five categories of skills were identified and organized into two sets: cognitive skills and conative skills. Cognitive skills include:

1. Analyzing and utilizing information

2. Addressing complex problems and issues

3. Creating patterns and mental models

Conative skills include:

4. Understanding and controlling oneself

5. Understanding and interacting with others

This chapter is a brief but representative review of the research and theory on the cognitive and conative skills addressed in this book.

## Cognitive Skill: Analyzing and Utilizing Information

The 21st century brings increased access to a vast plain of information. The video *InfoWhelm and Information Fluency* (21st Century Fluency Project, 2010) stated that our worldwide collective digital output by 2009 was five hundred exabytes of data. If you wanted to record five hundred exabytes in printed form, you would need enough books to connect Earth and Pluto thirteen times (and printing them would deforest Earth twelve times)!

A major challenge associated with the exponential explosion of information in the 21st century is the lack of information regulation. Currently, anyone can create a website, and anything can be posted on a website. Consequently, erroneous information is often posted. For instance, one website (www .dhmo.org/facts.html) provides extensive information on the chemical properties, hazards, and uses of dihydrogen monoxide, which is "a colorless and odorless chemical compound" (Way, n.d.). Dihydrogen monoxide is the chemical name for $H_2O$ (water), but the site never mentions this fact, instead asserting that it is "a known causative component in many thousands of deaths and is a major contributor to millions upon millions of dollars in damage to property and the environment" (Way, n.d.). Some of the related dangers that the site lists include (Way, n.d.):

- "Death due to accidental inhalation of DHMO, even in small quantities."

- "Prolonged exposure to solid DHMO causes severe tissue damage."

- "DHMO is a major component of acid rain."

While one can admire the cleverness of the site's creator, it would be very easy for an unsuspecting and uninformed student to glean erroneous and useless information from this site.

Alan November (2010a), a leader in the movement for meaningful technology integration in schools, pointed out that "the growing persuasiveness of the Internet will lead to more and more students potentially being manipulated by the media. Too many young people believe that if they see it on the Internet, it must be true" (p. 12). Dede (2010) agreed, noting that students need to be able to evaluate and avoid "off-target, incomplete, inconsistent, and perhaps even biased [resources]" (p. 53).

November (2010a) illustrated this problem with the story of Zack, a high school sophomore who did not understand principles for evaluating the credibility of a website. While doing research for a history project about the Holocaust, Zack found a website of a professor at Northwestern University. Falsely assuming that a recent publication date, a domain name ending in *.edu*, and an authoritative tone were guaranteed signs of true information, Zack believed the professor's claims that concentration camps were not instruments of genocide but simply the German government's system to fight vermin and disease.

November (2010b) attributed these types of deficiencies to the educational community's tendency to equate technology use with information skills. "Technology is only the digital plumbing," said November, and new gadgets will soon replace current ones (p. 276). However, November noted that:

> What will not go away is access to the overwhelming amounts of shifting (and growing) information and global communications. Our planning focus must shift to clearly define what it means to be Web literate and to link our students to authentic audiences around the world and across the curriculum. (p. 280)

Many share November's conclusions on the proliferation of information and the need for students to be taught critical thinking skills. David Considine, an expert in the area of media literacy, stated:

> While more young people have access to the Internet and other media than any generation in history, they do not necessarily possess the ethics, the intellectual skills, or the predisposition to critically analyze and evaluate their relationship with these technologies or the information they encounter. (Considine, 2002, p. 24)

Tony Wagner, founder of Harvard's Change Leadership Group, highlighted the fact that:

> Students can always look up when the Battle of Gettysburg took place, or who General Sherman was, but they can't just Google the causes of the Civil War and make sense of what comes up on the screen. To understand such an issue, you have to know how to think critically, and you need a broader conceptual understanding of American history, economics, and more. (Wagner, 2008, p. 263)

Donald Leu, director of the New Literacies Research Lab at the University of Connecticut, commented:

> In this new world, what becomes critical to our students' literacy future is the ability to identify important problems, gather and critically evaluate relevant information from information networks, use this information to resolve central issues, and then clearly communicate the solution to others. (Leu, 2002, p. 466)

Finally, Bill Sheskey, a faculty member with Curriculum Designers, noted:

> Problem-solving methods are changing because we have instant access to information and an unprecedented ability to collaborate to solve problems. (Sheskey, 2010, p. 208)

Clearly, information available in the 21st century must be critically analyzed to determine its reliability and usefulness and to avoid errors and misconceptions. According to Diane Halpern (1998), most misconceptions are not the result of a failure to think but the result of "bugs in the reasoning process" (p. 449). She points out that many people who believe in paranormal phenomena can explain the reasoning that led to their beliefs, but in their reasoning, they usually confuse correlation (two events happening in close proximity) with causation (one event causing the other). She asserts that thinking-skills instruction should focus on "understanding how cause is determined, recognizing and criticizing assumptions, analyzing means-goals relationships, giving reasons to support a conclusion, assessing degrees of likelihood and uncertainty, incorporating isolated data into a wider framework, and using analogies to solve problems" (p. 452).

Philip Abrami et al. (2008) conducted a meta-analysis on critical thinking that examined 117 studies with 20,698 participants. *Meta-analysis* is a research technique that allows researchers to quantitatively synthesize a series of studies on the same topic. Typically, meta-analyses report their findings using average effect sizes (ESs). An *effect size* tells you how many standard deviations larger (or smaller) the average score for a group of students who were exposed to a given strategy (in this case, critical-thinking instruction) is than the average score for a group of students who were not exposed to a given strategy (in this case, no critical-thinking instruction). In short, an ES tells you how powerful a strategy is; the larger the ES, the more the strategy increases student learning.

As seen in table 2.1 (page 14), ESs are usually small numbers. However, even a small ES can translate into a large percentile gain. For example, the ES of 0.38 that Abrami et al. calculated for a general critical-thinking-skills intervention translates into a 15 percentile point gain. To say this in a different way, a student at the 50th percentile in a class without instruction in general critical-thinking skills would be expected to rise to the 65th percentile if this instruction was provided. (More information about the concepts of meta-analysis and effect size, along with a chart that translates ES numbers into percentile gains, can be found online at **marzanoresearch.com/classroomstrategies** in the document *What Is an Effect Size?*)

In the 2008 Abrami et al. meta-analysis, the authors reported that "the data . . . suggest a generally positive effect of instruction on students' CT [critical thinking] skills" (p. 1119). They further examined the effects of different types of instruction on students' critical-thinking skills and found:

> Improved CT skills and dispositions are associated with how CT instruction is provided. . . . The mixed method, where CT is taught as an independent track within a specific content course . . . had the largest effect. . . . Making CT requirements a clear and important part of course design is associated with larger instructional effects. Developing CT skills separately and then

applying them to course content explicitly works best; immersing students in thought-provoking subject matter instruction without explicit use of CT principles was least effective. (pp. 1120–1121)

Abrami et al. (2008) also found that pedagogy matters: teachers who received training and feedback about their critical-thinking instruction were most effective at improving students' critical-thinking skills. More specific results and effect sizes from the study are reported in table 2.1.

## Table 2.1: Results From Abrami et al. (2008) Meta-Analysis

| Type of Intervention | Number of Effect Sizes | Effect Size | Percentile Gain |
|---|---|---|---|
| **General critical-thinking skills:** "CT skills and dispositions are learning objectives, without specific subject matter content" (p. 1105). | 39 | 0.38 | 15 |
| **Infusion:** "Deep, thoughtful, and well-understood subject matter instruction in which students are encouraged to think critically in the subject. . . . General principles of CT skills and dispositions are made explicit" (p. 1106). | 52 | 0.54 | 21 |
| **Immersion:** "Subject matter instruction is thought-provoking, and students do get immersed in the subject. However . . . general CT principles are not made explicit" (p. 1106). | 48 | 0.09 | 4 |
| **Mixed:** "Students are involved in subject-specific CT instruction, but there is also a separate thread or course aimed at teaching general principles of CT" (p. 1106). | 22 | 0.94 | 33 |

## Cognitive Skill: Addressing Complex Problems and Issues

The second area we have selected as a cognitive skill for the 21st century is addressing complex problems and issues. Life will certainly not get less complicated for individuals during the 21st century. For example, in the past, most people counted on employer-managed retirement pensions (which a reliable Social Security system supplemented) that came at a precise age. The 21st century may not provide such guarantees. Even now, nearly everyone is responsible for planning and saving for their own retirements. This means that people must start investing in individual retirement accounts (IRAs) or 401(k) plans as early as their twenties, and they must manage those investments throughout their careers in order to ensure that they can retire comfortably. Health care, with its myriad insurance plans and treatment options, also exemplifies the complexity of life in the 21st century. Patients must now educate themselves and advocate for their own care as opposed to simply following a doctor's orders. In these and in many other contexts, the effective citizen of the 21st century will need to be able to address complex problems and issues.

### Research on Teaching Problem-Solving Skills

*Problem solving* is the process of accomplishing a goal when obstacles occur (Halpern, 1984; Rowe, 1985; Sternberg, 1987). Robert Marzano and John Kendall (2007) defined problem solving as "the process one engages in to answer questions such as How will I overcome this obstacle? or How will I reach my goal but still meet these conditions?" (p. 51). As an example of addressing the question, How will I overcome this obstacle?, imagine that a person gets up in the morning to drive to work but his car will not start. He must overcome the obstacle of not having his usual means of transportation. As an example of addressing the question, How will I overcome this limiting condition?, imagine that a person wakes up late and has only fifteen minutes to get ready for work instead of her usual thirty minutes. Her typical condition of thirty minutes has been limited. Obstacles occur when something a person would normally use to reach a goal is not available. Limiting conditions occur when something is still available but not in the normal quantity or quality typically required to reach the goal.

Research from a number of perspectives supports the importance of teaching problem-solving strategies. One such perspective is problem-based learning (PBL), sometimes also referred to as project-based learning. PBL has a deeper, more complex goal than traditional instruction. John Barell (2010) noted:

> *Problem-based learning* goes well beyond . . . short-term instructional instances or simple questions. It encompasses a rethinking of the entire curriculum so that teachers design whole units around complex, "ill-structured" problematic scenarios that embody the major concepts to be mastered and understood. By "ill-structured" or "ill-defined" I mean the realistic, authentic problems—such as pollution of the planet and feeding the hungry—that are so complex, messy, and intriguing that they do not lend themselves to a right or a wrong answer. (p. 178)

In a meta-synthesis of meta-analyses, Johannes Strobel and Angela van Barneveld (2009) found that "PBL is significantly more effective than traditional instruction to train competent and skilled practitioners and to promote long-term retention of knowledge and skills acquired during the learning experience or training session" (p. 55).

Within their synthesis, Strobel and van Barneveld (2009) highlighted two meta-analyses that focused specifically on knowledge retention (Albanese & Mitchell, 1993; Dochy, Segers, Van den Bossche, & Gijbels, 2003), and said that in both studies "long-term knowledge retention favored PBL" (p. 54). Strobel and van Barneveld also found that when assessments were performance or skill based or required a combination of knowledge and skill, students taught using PBL scored higher than students taught using more traditional methods of instruction.

While problem solving is a complex construct, there are a few elements that appear to be central to the effective employment of problem-solving strategies. One of those is focus.

### Focus

*Focus* is the process of directing one's attention to a specific issue for an extended period of time. What we refer to as focus is addressed in much of the literature as *attention*.

Edward Titchener (1915) described a number of types of attention, two of which are primary attention and secondary attention. *Primary attention* occurs when stimuli force us to pay attention to them. These stimuli elicit attention because they are very intense, repeated multiple times, sudden, new, or moving. For example, very intense stimuli might include loud sounds, bright lights, strong tastes or smells, extreme temperatures, or intense pain. *Secondary attention* is the "sustained attention that we pay to a task, a lecture, a puzzle . . . an attention that goes against the grain, in which *we* seem to do the forcing, holding our mind by main force upon a tedious and uninteresting subject" (p. 95). This conscious and prolonged secondary attention is closely related to the concept of focus described here.

David Perkins (1981) discussed focus in the context of purpose. He stated that the essence of invention, or creativity, is purpose:

> Purpose is what organizes the diverse means of the mind to creative ends. . . . Invention often occurs not because a person tries to be original,

but because the person attempts to do something difficult. Necessity, the saying goes, is the mother of invention. I would add: not only necessity, but the sort of commitment that leads some people to put "unreasonable" demands on themselves and their products. . . . As Pasteur said, "Chance favors the prepared mind." Discoveries made in, let us say, medical research, aren't made by bricklayers or businessmen or mathematicians. Nor are they made principally by family doctors or journeyman surgeons. They are the accomplishments of just those individuals who have committed their careers to exploring the complexities of medicine. (pp. 100–101)

Perkins (1981) explained that an intense focus on complex material puts an individual in a frame of mind and exposes him or her to information and phenomena that are more likely to lead to meaningful moments of clarity or discovery. He argued:

There will be more creative thoughts and actions in response to such purposes, just as there will be more carpentering thoughts and actions if one is building a birdhouse than if one is assembling a stamp collection. Purpose shapes process. (p. 101)

He also provided some interesting examples of individuals who experienced moments of discovery that seemed sudden but were actually a result of their purposeful and sustained focus on a particular topic:

- **Archimedes**—This Greek mathematician suddenly realized, while in the bathtub, how to determine the volume of a solid object (by measuring how much water it displaced). According to legend, he then went running naked through the streets yelling, "Eureka" ("I have found it!") (Perkins, 1981).

- **Henri Poincaré**—This French mathematician was boarding a bus when he suddenly had a breakthrough: "At the moment when I put my foot on the step the idea came to me, without anything in my former thoughts seeming to have paved the way for it, that the transformations I had used to define the Fuchsian functions were identical with those of non-Euclidean geometry" (as cited in Perkins, 1981, p. 41).

- **Charles Darwin**—This English scientist was reading about theories of population growth and decline when suddenly his theory of natural selection fell into place: "In October 1838, that is, fifteen months after I had begun my systematic enquiry, I happened to read for amusement 'Malthus on Population,' and being well prepared to appreciate the struggle for existence which everywhere goes on from long-continued observation of the habits of animals and plants, it at once struck me that under these circumstances favourable variations would tend to be preserved, and unfavorable ones to be destroyed" (as cited in Perkins, 1981, p. 53).

Focus, as addressed in this book, might be considered the antithesis of *multitasking*.

### Multitasking

The notion of multitasking has a clear appeal in contemporary society. Everyone has much required of them, and people often find themselves doing more than one thing at a time. Some even believe that multitasking is a skill that should be encouraged and developed. Marc Prensky (2001) included the ability to "parallel process and multi-task" in his set of new skills that he said students today "have acquired and perfected through years of interaction and practice" (p. 2). He contrasted today's students with adults and teachers who "learned . . . slowly, step-by-step, one thing at a time" (p. 2). He claimed that teachers "don't believe their students can learn successfully while watching TV or listening to music" (p. 3), because they find themselves unable to do the same. Additionally, he claimed that the reason adults cannot multitask is because "they didn't practice this skill constantly for all of their formative years" (p. 3).

Many statements in favor of multitasking are observation based. For example, Tapscott (2009) observed that today's students are:

> Faster than I am at switching tasks, and better than I am at blocking out background noise. They can work effectively with music playing and news coming in from Facebook. They can keep up their social networks while they concentrate on work; they seem to need this to feel comfortable. I think they've learned to live in a world where they're bombarded with information, so that they can block out the TV or other distractions while they focus on the task at hand. (p. 108)

Certainly the concept of multitasking has attained high visibility. A report from the Kaiser Family Foundation (Rideout, Foehr, & Roberts, 2010) indicated that in 1999, eight- to eighteen-year-olds spent only 16 percent of their media time using more than one type of media concurrently. By 2010, that number had increased to 29 percent of media time spent multitasking. The same study also found that:

> Over the past five years, young people have increased the amount of time they spend consuming media by an hour and seventeen minutes daily, from 6:21 to 7:38—almost the amount of time most adults spend at work each day, except that young people use media seven days a week instead of five. Moreover, given the amount of time they spend using more than one medium at a time, today's youth pack a total of 10 hours and 45 minutes worth of media content into those daily 7½ hours—an increase of almost 2¼ hours of media exposure per day over the past five years. (Rideout, Foehr, & Roberts, 2010, p. 2)

While authors like Prensky contended that the younger generation simply works and thinks differently than adults, and that the real harm comes in insisting they adapt to older ways of operating and thinking, little evidence shows that this is true. At best, studies like Eric Schumacher et al.'s (2001) have found that, for certain tasks that are well practiced, people may be able to perform them at the same time. Vanessa Vega (2009) said: "Since people can only handle one decision making process at a time, the way to handle two simultaneous processes is to make one of them automatic (so it requires no decision making)" (pp. 3–4). Vega also reported on research indicating that multitasking may not be harmful if the two tasks require different processing sources in the brain. She noted, "When different information channels require non-conflicting processing resources, multitasking may not necessarily impair task performance" (p. 5). So while there is some evidence that students' multitasking habits may not be harmful, there is far more evidence to suggest that the brain simply cannot effectively multitask, and there may be long-term deleterious effects of continually asking it to do so. Here we briefly summarize the results of a number of studies on multitasking.

- Joshua Rubinstein, David Meyer, and Jeffrey Evans (2001) found that when the brain switches between tasks, it has to complete two steps every time it switches: goal shifting and rule activation. *Goal shifting* means making the decision to switch to a new task and *rule activation* is the process of turning the rules that applied to the old task off, and activating the rules for the new task. The constant switching can cause performance on all tasks to deteriorate (Clay, 2009).

- Paul Dux, Jason Ivanoff, Christopher Asplund, and Rene Marois (2006) found that delay in task switching is due to our inability to make two decisions at once, resulting in a response selection *bottleneck*. When the brain is forced to respond to multiple stimuli at once, it needs extra time to decide what task to perform first, so tasks end up taking longer than normal.

- Karin Foerde, Barbara Knowlton, and Russell Poldrack (2006) demonstrated that when you focus while learning, you develop a more flexible kind of knowledge than when you learn while multitasking. They summarized their findings by saying that "the presence of distraction can change the way that a task is learned" (p. 11782). Essentially, you learn more effectively while focused.

- Eyal Ophir, Clifford Nass, and Anthony Wagner (2009) found that people who did *not* multitask on a regular basis were better at filtering out distractions, holding information in working memory, and switching back and forth between tasks compared to people who multitasked often. This led them to conclude that constant multitasking behavior actually impairs one's ability to concentrate, focus, and deal with distractions.

- Loukia Loukopoulos, R. Key Dismukes, and Immanuel Barshi (2009) reviewed studies showing that "although humans generally like a certain amount of diversity and challenge in their work to counter boredom, evidence is mounting that prolonged high levels of multitasking cause stress, impairing both health and performance" (p. 13).

- In their 2008 book *iBrain*, Small and Vorgan concluded that "the bottom line is that the brain seems to work better when implementing a single sustained task than when multitasking, despite most people's perception that they are doing more and at a faster pace when they multitask" (Small & Vorgan, 2008, p. 68).

In addition to the research evidence disputing the efficacy of multitasking as a preferable 21st century skill, there is also a great deal of testimonial evidence against it.

- Edward Hallowell (2005) explained that multitasking over time leaves people unable to prioritize and results in distractibility and impatience. Hallowell also pointed out that individuals who multitask often are characterized by a "constant low level of panic and guilt" and are forced to become "increasingly hurried, curt, peremptory, and unfocused, while pretending that everything is fine" (p. 56).

- David Levy, a professor at the University of Washington's Information School, conducted a survey of sixty students majoring in information and found that the majority of them expressed concerns about being too plugged in and about missing social opportunities, exercise, meals, and sleep because of getting lost in the *multitasking blur* (Wallis, 2006).

- Jordan Grafman, a neuroscientist, observed that not only does the quality of a person's output decrease during multitasking, but the lack of mental downtime is also harmful. The inability to unplug creates an unhealthy aversion to silence and reflection (Wallis, 2006).

While interviewing winners of the MacArthur Fellowship, Haberman (2005) observed that most of them do not multitask. The winners said:

- "I don't walk around the street with an iPod or cellphone. . . . Idle time is used by me to think things out."

- "I'm a great believer in daydreaming. . . . I think it's a very powerful private moment that's loaded with information."

- "It is probably true . . . that if I had been listening to music or to Books on Tape, it [the idea that water from comets played a role in creating the earth's oceans] wouldn't have occurred to me. The thing that is so precious, which becomes so hard to get, is uninterrupted time."

- "Nonconnectivity becomes a commodity, something to cherish. . . . You won't hear different, particularly from novelists. You need so much ruminative time to build these elaborate alternate realities. Every novelist is running away from the telephone. Has been for 100 years."

Multitasking, then, in spite of the rhetoric supporting it, is not something that should be encouraged in students, particularly when they are addressing complex problems and issues.

### *Convergent and Divergent Thinking*

In addition to focus, both convergent and divergent thinking appear to have an important role in the problem-solving process. In the context of problem solving, *divergent thinking* refers to generating multiple options for solving a problem. Additionally, when initial solutions do not appear to solve the problem, divergent thinking is required to generate options that go beyond the logic of the options initially generated. For example, if a student needs to solve the problem of getting a ride home from athletics practice, she might use divergent thinking to generate a number of solutions: get a ride with a friend, take the bus, walk, or ride a bike. A student who is applying to universities might use divergent thinking to generate a list of all the universities he might like to attend.

In the context of problem solving, *convergent thinking* refers to following a clear line of logical steps to select a specific option or options that will solve the problem. For example, once the student athlete stops generating options for getting home and starts deciding what her best option is, she is engaging in convergent thinking. Likewise, once the student applying to universities is finished generating a list of possible options, he might engage in convergent thinking to narrow his list of fifteen down to four or five to which he would like to apply.

Divergent and convergent thinking can occur in cycles. Returning to the college-seeking student, once he has been accepted at several universities, he might again engage in divergent thinking to gather all the information available about each university (for example, scholarships offered, major programs at each university, impressions from campus visits). He would then return to convergent thinking by creating a list of pros and cons for each university, which he would then use to figure out which university was right for him.

Ginamarie Scott, Lyle Leritz, and Michael Mumford (2004) empirically established the link between convergent and divergent thinking and problem solving in a meta-analysis of seventy studies. They reported small to large correlations between problem solving and various aspects of both divergent and convergent thinking.

## Cognitive Skill: Creating Patterns and Mental Models

The final category we have included in our set of cognitive skills is creating patterns and mental models. For decades, researchers have recognized the relationship between creating or identifying patterns and comprehension. Neurologist and classroom teacher Judy Willis (2006) explained how the brain uses patterns to make connections between stored knowledge and new information:

> Patterning is the process whereby the brain perceives and generates patterns by relating new with previously learned material or chunking material into pattern systems it has used before. . . . Whenever new material is presented in such a way that students see relationships, they generate greater brain cell activity (forming new neural connections) and achieve more successful long-term memory storage and retrieval. (p. 15)

Graphic organizers, visual models, and visualization and mental rehearsal are all excellent tools teachers can use to help students create patterns.

## Graphic Organizers

The importance of generating patterns is evidenced in the research and theory on graphic organizers. Graphic organizers are visual devices that help students organize information into patterns. David Hyerle espoused perhaps the most well-known approach to graphic organizers. Hyerle stressed that knowledge is made as opposed to given. His theory is called *connectivism*:

> Knowledge viewed as connective is an interpretive process of thinking about the mental relationships we create between things. In a most fundamental way, it is from a connectivist view that we begin to deeply investigate these "things" we call boundaries and relations. (Hyerle, 1991, p. 17)

It is with this idea of recreating and connecting knowledge that Hyerle proposed the use of graphic organizers or Thinking Maps® (Hyerle, 2009). (See page 97 for more information about Thinking Maps.)

Marzano Research Laboratory (Haystead & Marzano, 2009) conducted and synthesized sixty-five studies on the effectiveness of graphic organizers and found an average effect size of 0.29, which translates into an 11 percentile point gain. John Nesbit and Olusola Adesope (2006) performed a meta-analysis on the effectiveness of using concept and knowledge maps—general types of graphic organizers. They examined fifty-five studies involving 5,818 participants and found an average effect size of 0.60, which translates to a percentile gain of 23 points. John Hattie (2009) synthesized a number of meta-analyses on concept mapping and graphic organizers (see table 2.2) and reported an overall effect size of 0.57, which translates to a percentile gain of 22 points.

## Table 2.2: Meta-Analyses on Graphic Organizers

| Synthesis Study | Focus | Number of Studies | Number of Effect Sizes | Effect Size | Percentile Gain |
|---|---|---|---|---|---|
| Haystead and Marzano (2009) | Graphic organizers (all subjects) | 65 | 65 | 0.29 | 11 |
| Nesbit and Adesope (2006) | Concept and knowledge maps | 55 | 67 | 0.60 | 23 |
| Moore and Readence (1984)* | Graphic organizers in mathematics | 161 | 161 | 0.22 | 9 |
| Vásquez and Caraballo (1993)* | Concept mapping in science | 17 | 19 | 0.57 | 22 |
| Horton et al. (1993)* | Concept mapping in science | 19 | 19 | 0.45 | 17 |

| Kang (2002)* | Graphic organizers in reading with learning disabled | 14 | 14 | 0.79 | 29 |
| Kim, Vaughn, Wanzek, and Wei (2004)* | Graphic organizers in reading | 21 | 52 | 0.81 | 29 |

*as reported in Hattie (2009)

## Visual Models

Creating visual models is another aspect of effectively creating and understanding patterns. Mark Sadoski and Allan Paivio (2001) used Paivio's dual-coding theory to explain why visual models are so effective. Paivio postulated that verbal information travels to and is stored in the brain differently than visual (nonverbal) information. So when information is presented using both verbal and visual cues, the information is dually coded in the learner's brain.

According to dual-coding theory, "The organization is sequential in the verbal system and nonsequential (e.g., spatial) in the nonverbal system, resulting in characteristically different constraints on processing" (Sadoski & Paivio, 2001, p. 43). These two systems also use different neural pathways and storage units in the brain. The verbal system is comprised of units called *logogens*, and the nonverbal system is comprised of units called *imagens*.

Sadoski and Paivio (2001) explained that logogens operate according to sequence. Think of how speech and writing work: the letters in words and words in sentences must be in order for any meaning to arise. It is difficult to spell long words backward because the letters are meaningless when not presented in sequence. Imagens, however, work differently. Upon walking into a room, a person does not see the objects in that room in any particular order. One person might notice a chair first while another might notice a window or a clock. All of the visual information is available at once (Sadoski & Paivio, 2001).

These differences do not mean, however, that one system is closed off from another. In fact, the verbal and nonverbal systems can talk to one another. According to Sadoski and Paivio (2001), "We can switch from one form of representation to another, or recode, both within a system (e.g., speech to writing) or between systems (e.g., language to mental images)" (p. 43). Given this structure, it makes sense that information processed through both systems would be better recalled and more easily understood than information processed and stored using only one system.

Richard Mayer's (1997) work researching the effectiveness of multimedia presentations supported the dual-coding theory. Students who received both visual and auditory instruction generated 75 percent more creative solutions to problem-solving transfer tests than students who only received auditory instruction. A previous study had found the same results, leading the authors to conclude that "successful instruction insures [*sic*] that learners build representational connections for creating verbal representations and visual representations, as well as referential connections between these verbal and visual representations" (Mayer & Anderson, 1991, p. 490).

## Visualization and Mental Rehearsal

The research and theory on visualization is also consistent with the dual-coding theory. Visualization involves creating mental images or sequences. Some assert that when we visualize doing something, we stimulate exactly the same brain regions that are stimulated when we actually perform the action. According to Kirwan Rockefeller (2007):

> When people visualize or imagine using various senses, the parts of their brains involved with those senses become active. What this means is that the body and the brain don't know the difference between imagined events and real events. The body and the mind are integrally connected. (p. 28)

Hattie (2009) reported the results of a study (Lavery, 2008) in which teachers used visualization as a metacognitive strategy (students imagined and visualized the consequences of failing to study). The use of visualization led the treatment group to better performance (effect size = 0.44).

The effectiveness of visualization has also been demonstrated in athletics. Athletic visualization usually takes the form of mental rehearsal. Although researchers and sports psychologists use a number of terms to describe mental rehearsal, the concept they are referring to is essentially what Tony Morris, Michael Spittle, and Anthony Watt (2005) described as "the mental creation or re-creation of sensory experiences that appear to the person imagining them to be similar to the actual event" (p. 4). They explained that mentally performing a task or motor process is powerful because "an imaginary event can provoke real-life emotional and physiological responses. With practice, we can manipulate our imagination to preview upcoming events" (p. 4).

George Grouios, in a 1992 review of the research on mental rehearsal, pointed out that "over 300 research studies investigating the MP [mental practice] phenomenon" have shown that "over a wide variety of different tasks subjects improve their physical performance after spending various amounts of time in 'thinking about' or 'imagining' themselves in the act of performing" (p. 42).

Many researchers and theorists have tried to explain why "imagining hitting a perfect tennis forehand, sinking a free throw, or crossing the finish line first can actually help us to successfully complete these tasks" (Morris, Spittle, & Watt, 2005, p. 29). Some theorists have suggested that mental rehearsal and physical practice are functionally equivalent in the brain. These functional equivalence theories (Farah, 1989; Finke, 1980, 1985; Finke & Shephard, 1986; Jeannerod, 1994, 1995) hold that "imagery and perception or imagery and movement recruit common central nervous system structures and processes, but during imagery execution is blocked" (Morris, Spittle, & Watt, 2005, p. 31). Essentially, the only difference between imagining a motor skill and actually doing it is the physical movement; everything else is the same.

Aside from academic studies, the power of visualization can be seen in anecdotal stories, some of which are summarized here.

- In 1959, Liu Chi Kung, an award-winning Chinese pianist, was imprisoned during China's political revolution. For seven years, he was denied access to a piano and was unable to practice. However, upon his release, Liu Chi Kung's performances received higher critical acclaim than they had received before his imprisonment. He attributed this to visualization, saying that every day, in his jail cell, he had mentally practiced his entire repertoire (Berg, 2002).

- Anatoly Sharansky was a computer specialist and human rights activist in the Soviet Union. In 1977, he was falsely accused of spying for the United States and imprisoned for nine years; he spent four hundred days in solitary confinement. While in isolation, Sharansky played chess in his head. He moved both black and white pieces and kept track of all the pieces' positions in his head. After his release, he eventually became an Israeli cabinet member and had the opportunity to play Garry Kasparov, the world chess champion. Although Kasparov beat all the other members of the cabinet and the prime minister, he could not beat Sharansky (Doidge, 2007).

- Morris Goodman was a successful insurance agent in the United States until he crashed his airplane in March of 1981. Breaking his neck in two places and destroying his diaphragm, Goodman was unable to speak, move, or breathe without a ventilator when he awoke in the hospital after the crash. Goodman decided to visualize his body healing, and by Christmas that year, he had learned to breathe on his own; he subsequently learned to sit, stand, and walk. Although it took another five years, he learned to talk again and is now a motivational speaker (Ho, 2009).

- Nikola Tesla would visualize his inventions before he built them. He claimed that he could build an invention in his head, run tests on it, fine-tune it, and check it for wear and tear, all in his head! Only after completing his mental test run would he build the physical prototype (Tesla, 1919/2007).

## Conative Skill: Understanding and Controlling Oneself

People who are aware of their own reactions to situations and are able to control them in a wide variety of situations are more successful than people who are not. This is evident anecdotally when looking at the world around us. In political debates, for example, the person who remains focused and collected in the face of pressure from the other candidate is almost always the victor. Athletes who cannot monitor and control their own behavior are often penalized or even ejected from games. Self-awareness and self-control contribute not only to individual success but to the success of wider groups of people as well. For example, by drawing penalties, an athletic player hurts the performance of the entire team, and a politician who loses a debate because he could not monitor and control his actions properly has hurt not only himself but his supporters.

In the 21st century, this skill is particularly important and must be taught because communication with a wide variety of people, many of whom hold very different opinions and interpretations, is now commonplace. Students must be able to understand multiple interpretations in order to communicate successfully.

### The Role of Interpretations

Self-understanding begins with an awareness of the nature of interpretations. A number of researchers and theorists have commented on the centrality of interpretations to human behavior. John O'Shaughnessy (2009) explained that:

> Interpretation is basic to all our endeavors whether as scientists or as individuals going about our daily lives. . . . Every time we deliberate on events or on our experience, we are interpreting. Interpretation is fundamental since how things are interpreted determines what actions we consider. (p. 1)

Charles Lord and Cheryl Taylor (2009) explained that "people so readily generalize that they often 'know' in advance what they are going to like and what they are going to dislike. They develop assumptions and expectations, which in part determine their future evaluative responses" (p. 827).

Robert Marzano and Jana Marzano (2010) explained that awareness and control of one's interpretation of a given situation empower an individual. For example, an individual who believes a task to be too difficult to accomplish can first acknowledge that hopelessly difficult, is, in fact, an interpretation amenable to alteration. Second, the individual can reinterpret the situation in a more positive light. A change in behavior would follow the change in interpretation. In a study of one program designed to teach this type of metacognitive control over subjects' interpretations, participants reported that the strategy was used in their lives even years after the initial training (Marzano, Zaffron, Zraik, Robbins, & Yoon, 1995).

## Self-Efficacy

Probably the centerpiece of understanding and controlling oneself is developing self-efficacy. At its core, *self-efficacy* is the disposition that an individual has control over his or her life.

Self-efficacy plays a major role in performance. Dale Schunk and Frank Pajares (2005) reported a 1995 study, which found that "despite the influence of mental ability, self-efficacy beliefs made a powerful and independent contribution to the prediction of performance" (p. 93). They also reported a separate meta-analysis, which found that "the average weighted correlation between self-efficacy and work-related performance was $(G)r = .38$, which transforms into an impressive 28% gain in task performance" (p. 92).

Pajares (1996) reported that students with high self-efficacy also demonstrate more persistence and more frequent use of higher-level thinking skills (problem solving, decision making, and the like), as demonstrated by Schunk (1984), who reported that mathematics self-efficacy influenced math performance. Pajares (1996) also found that students' self-efficacy enhanced students' memory performance by enhancing persistence.

Finally, self-efficacy affects *how* students think. Pajares (1996) noted that "students who believe they are capable of performing academic tasks use more cognitive and metacognitive strategies and persist longer than those who do not" (pp. 552–553). Similarly, Paul Pintrich and Elisabeth De Groot (1990) found that "higher levels of self-efficacy ($r = .33$) and intrinsic value ($r = .63$) were correlated with higher levels of cognitive strategy use" (p. 35).

In part, helping students develop self-efficacy involves teaching students optimal ways of thinking. In this section, we consider four ways of thinking that enhance self-efficacy: (1) a growth mindset, (2) resiliency, (3) positive possible selves, and (4) optimism.

### *A Growth Mindset*

Carol Dweck (2000) approached self-efficacy from the perspective of how students view the nature of intelligence. She and her colleagues studied the differences between mastery-oriented students (students who took on challenges and worked persistently despite failure) and students who were not mastery oriented (students who backed away from challenge, displayed minimal effort, and expressed a preference for good grades over genuine learning). They found that the difference between mastery- and nonmastery-oriented students was their differing views on the nature of intelligence. Students who believed that intelligence is a *fixed* or an unchangeable trait tended to back away from challenges and preferred good grades over learning. Students who believed that intelligence is something that can be changed or *grown* with time and effort, however, welcomed challenge and saw failure only as something learned.

Perhaps the most interesting thing about the fixed and growth theories of intelligence is that belief in one or the other is not necessarily permanent. While teachers cannot change students' past experiences, performances, models, or mentors, they can help students develop a growth mindset. Dweck (2000) performed a study in which two groups of students read a passage about figures of notable achievement like Helen Keller and Albert Einstein. In one passage, however, the achievements of these people were attributed to a fixed and superior intelligence while the other attributed the successes of these notable people to hard work and dedication. After reading the passages, both groups of students were asked to choose between several tasks. Some of the tasks were rather simple and required students to simply recall information they likely already knew. Others were more challenging. They were described as being more difficult, and there was a note with these tasks that students might make mistakes but they would also learn something new. The students who had previously read the fixed-theory-based passage were more likely to choose the easy tasks and the students who read the growth-theory-oriented passage were more likely to take on the challenging tasks (Dweck, 2000).

### *Resiliency*

Resiliency is another optimal way of thinking that is related to self-efficacy. Resilient children bounce back after trying circumstances and actually gain new strength and grow through adversity (as many cancer survivors have been shown to do). Resiliency has been studied quite extensively in the last decade. Norman Garmezy first described it in 1974, and since then, researchers have focused both on outside factors that influence a child's resilience and mechanisms that a child develops within him- or herself to become more resilient. Bonnie Benard (2004) characterized a resilient child as one who has high expectations, meaningful life goals, personal agency, and interpersonal problem-solving skills. She also suggested that schools can foster these traits.

Tan Phan (2003) studied eleven Vietnamese-Canadian high school students. These students came from working-class families and lived in low-income neighborhoods in Vancouver. However, they had each overcome racism and adversity and achieved such a high level of academic excellence that each was awarded academic scholarships for his or her undergraduate studies. According to Phan, the students in this study "believed they could 'fight the odds'" (p. 562) and "rather than destroying them, the challenges, constraints, and barriers these students faced transformed them. [They] believed, for example, that racism only made them 'try harder' and 'study more, do better'; they felt it made them stronger" (p. 562). One student said, "[The challenges] made me work harder, try harder, and solidified my goals" (p. 562), and another pointed out that even though prejudice will always exist, "I believe that if I'm good, then they will hire me. Therefore, I know that I have to study harder and have higher education and training. I would not be discouraged by it" (p. 563).

Lillian Rubin (1996) noticed that resilient people's "ability to hold onto a self, even in the face of the assaults they suffered—made it possible to stand back and observe the fray without getting bogged down in it. They may have been pained, angered, and frightened by the events of their lives, but they retained enough distance not to get caught in endlessly blaming themselves" (pp. 225–226). This is referred to as *adaptive distancing*.

A number of programs have been developed to help students increase their resiliency. Researchers with the Penn Resiliency Program, developed by Martin Seligman and his colleagues at the University of Pennsylvania, found that they could "make kids more resilient by teaching better thinking skills" and by teaching "the basic skills of problem-solving" (Andrews, 2000). The researchers also studied groups of high school students and found that those who were taught using a model they termed *positive education* demonstrated improvement in social skills, an increased desire to learn, and higher grades (Novotney, 2009). This model involved teachers who focused on providing and promoting positive messages in their classrooms, a curriculum that highlighted strengths in the fictional characters and historical figures being studied, and a service element.

### Positive Possible Selves

Another way to cultivate self-efficacy is to create positive possible selves. Possible selves are images of yourself in the future—imaginings of what you believe you are likely to become. As Hazel Markus and Paula Nurius (1986) noted:

> Possible selves are represented in the same way as the here-and-now self (imaginal, semantic) and can be viewed as cognitive bridges between the present and future, specifying how individuals may change from how they are now to what they will become. (p. 961)

People create possible selves based on past representations of themselves and past experiences. Markus and Nurius (1986) stated that possible selves are essentially social in nature. They "are the direct result of previous social comparisons in which the individual's own thoughts, feelings, characteristics, and behaviors have been contrasted to those of salient others. What others are now, I could become" (p. 954).

Clearly, not all possible selves are positive. If people have had negative experiences in the past or negative influences surround them, they may envision their future selves negatively. Both positive and negative possible selves can be motivating. As Markus and Nurius (1986) stated, possible selves "function as incentives for future behavior (i.e., they are selves to be approached or avoided). . . . They provide an evaluative and interpretive context for the current view of self" (p. 955).

If there is a balance of both positive and negative possible selves, people can see both what they do and what they do not want to become. As Susan Harter (1999) noted:

> It is most desirable to have a balance between positive expected selves and negative feared selves, so that positive possible selves (e.g., obtaining a well-paying job, wanting to be loved by family, hoping to be recognized and admired by others) can give direction to desired future states, whereas negative possible selves (e.g., being unemployed, feeling lonely, being socially ignored) can clarify what is to be avoided. (p. 146)

Harter also noted that sometimes these possible selves can be adopted or artificial, based on some notion of what we believe others expect of us. She said:

> Discrepancies between actual and ideal selves in the form of how one *wants* to be produce dejection-related emotions (e.g., sadness, discouragement, depression). For example, adolescent females who want to meet the standards of beauty demanded by the culture, but who fail to do so, will become despondent and depressed. In contrast, discrepancies between one's actual self and the self one should or *ought* to become produce agitation-related emotions such as feeling worried, threatened, or anxiously on edge. (p. 144)

Possible selves can be powerful motivators, and by understanding their nature and potential, students can create possible selves that promote self-efficacy.

### Optimism

The final way of thinking that can lead to self-efficacy is optimism, a mindset that Martin Seligman (2006) popularized. In 1965, Seligman and his colleagues studied the reactions of dogs to a mild shock. Initially, they divided the dogs into three groups: (1) dogs that received a mild electric shock they could avoid by jumping over a barrier, (2) dogs that received a mild electric shock they could not avoid, and (3) dogs that received no shock at all. After the initial treatments, they subjected all three groups to a mild shock that could easily be escaped by jumping over a barrier. They found that the first group, the dogs who had learned to jump the barrier to escape the shock, and the third group, the dogs who had never received a shock at all, quickly figured out how to escape the shock. Most of the dogs in the second group, however, who had previously experienced a shock they could not avoid, simply lay down and endured the shock. Although they now had the opportunity to escape, they did not even try (Seligman, 2006). The dogs in the second group had learned there was nothing they could do to make their situation better, and so they gave up trying. This is called *learned helplessness.* Interestingly, after Seligman worked with the dogs in the second group to teach them how to avoid the shock, they returned to normal. They were able to unlearn helplessness just as easily as they had learned it.

Seligman (2006) reported similar experiments, conducted with people, which used noise instead of shock. These experiments found similar results to Seligman's studies with the dogs. Most subjects who were initially exposed to noise that they could do nothing about became helpless when subsequently faced with noise they could turn off. However, a small number of people behaved unexpectedly, demonstrating levels of optimism or helplessness that did not change with treatment. These examples of optimism and helplessness became the basis for the rest of Seligman's life work.

Seligman (2006) studied four hundred third-grade students for five years. Seligman and his colleagues wanted to try to predict the incidence of depression and low academic performance in these children based on their life events and explanatory styles. An *explanatory style* is the way an individual tends to explain the events in his or her life. They found that students with a pessimistic explanatory style usually suffered from depression, which led to poor academic performance. However, students with an optimistic explanatory style were able to overcome negative life events, performed better academically, and stayed healthy over time. The same results can be seen with adults. Seligman reported a study of adult men that began in the 1930s and followed them throughout their lives. It found that those who displayed optimism in their midtwenties were healthier and happier later in life, sometimes quite dramatically so, than the men who had displayed pessimistic styles early on.

Besides gaining an awareness of the role of interpretations and developing a sense of self-efficacy through optimal ways of thinking, students must be aware of and avoid negative thinking.

## Negative Thinking

Negative thinking can lessen many if not all of the positive benefits gained from cultivating a mindset that promotes self-efficacy. Even if one has tried to cultivate a positive mindset, negative thinking can dramatically interfere with that mindset at any point in time. There are at least two types of negative thinking that can be addressed as an aspect of 21st century skills: (1) emotional thinking and (2) worry.

### Emotional Thinking

When people experience strong emotions, they think very differently from when they are calm. According to Daniel Goleman (1995), when a person experiences a strong emotion, the thalamus (the part of the brain that processes sensory input) sends signals to various areas of the brain in order to prepare the body to respond. One signal is sent to the amygdala, the part of the brain that triggers emotional responses, and another signal is sent to the prefrontal cortex, which helps a person decide on a smart course of action. The signal sent to the amygdala arrives about a fraction of a second before the signal sent to the prefrontal cortex reaches its destination. This results in precognitive emotion, meaning that the body's emotional reaction is triggered before the situation is processed cognitively. The amygdala releases a burst of adrenaline, filling the body with energy and making it difficult to control one's actions.

Commenting on this *amygdala hijack* (a term Goleman coined in 1995), Relly Nadler (2009) stated that "any strong emotion, anxiety, anger, joy, or betrayal trips off the amygdala and impairs the prefrontal cortex's working memory." Essentially, when the amygdala takes over, a person's prefrontal cortex is less active, so he or she cannot make good decisions or judgments: "It is like losing 10 to 15 IQ points temporarily" (Nadler, 2009).

In addition to understanding the pitfalls of strong emotions, it is important to understand the causes of strong emotions. According to Goleman (1995), a feeling of endangerment can trigger strong emotions. A person might feel endangered due to a physical threat, but also in response to a threat to his or her dignity or self-esteem. Rude comments, demeaning remarks, insults, or unjust treatment are all examples of nonphysical threats. When a person feels endangered, the fight-or-flight response is activated, producing an energy surge that lasts for a few minutes. However, endangerment also triggers a more prolonged reaction, designed to put all the body's systems on high alert in preparation for possible subsequent crises. This heightened level of alertness lasts longer than the fight or flight energy surge, even up to a few days. This alertness can cause subsequent emotions to escalate particularly quickly. Paul Ekman (1994) referred to this heightened alertness as a *mood*:

> While there is no agreement about how long an emotion typically lasts, most of those who distinguish emotions from moods recognize that moods last longer. I have maintained (Ekman, 1984) that emotions can be very brief, typically lasting a matter of seconds or at most minutes. When we speak of an emotion lasting for hours, we probably are summating the recurrent emotion episodes within that time period. Moods last for hours, sometimes for days. If the state endures for weeks or months, however, it is not a mood but more properly identified as an affective disorder. (p. 56)

It stands to reason that a person who is already experiencing a state of heightened alertness would have even more trouble fighting the amygdala hijack and controlling his or her behavior.

Mirror neurons may also cause strong emotions. *Mirror neurons* are a specialized class of neurons in the brain that activate both when an animal or person acts *and* when the animal or person observes another performing the same action. The first studies on mirror neurons were conducted with monkeys in Parma, Italy, in the 1990s (Gallese, Fadiga, Fogassi, & Rizzolatti, 1996; Rizzolatti, Fadiga, Gallese, & Fogassi, 1996). The researchers were studying a neuron in a monkey's brain that always activated when the monkey reached for a peanut. The researchers discovered that the same neuron activated in exactly the same way when the monkey observed one of the researchers reaching for a peanut (Rizzolatti & Craighero, 2004). Researchers at UCLA conducted this same type of experiment. They found that pain neurons activated both when a patient was poked with a needle and when the patient observed another patient being poked (Ramachandran, 2006).

This connection means that when a person observes positive or negative emotions and behaviors, the brain is hardwired to imitate them. For students who do not understand this tendency in the brain, this mirroring could make them susceptible to a wide range of thoughts and emotions in the people they encounter each day. Students who understand this tendency, however, can recognize when they are allowing those around them to control their moods and emotions, and they can choose more positive patterns of behavior.

### Worry

*Worry* is a potentially debilitating type of negative thinking. There are many definitions and descriptions of worry. Kevin McCaul and Amy Mullens (2003) explained that "worry has been conventionally defined as a chain of thoughts and images, which are negatively affect-laden and relatively uncontrollable" (p. 143). They also summarized Mathews's (1990) definition of worry: "The constant rehearsal of a threatening outcome or threat scenario that may hinder successful problem solving" (McCaul & Mullens, 2003, p. 143).

Debra Gustafson (2007) noted the prevalence of worry in students:

> Community samples have found that over 70% of elementary-age children from 8- to 12-years old reported that they worry every now and then (Orton, 1982; Muris Merckelbach, Gadet, & Moulaert, 2000; Silverman, La Greca, & Wasserstein, 1995). Bell-Dolan, Last, and Strauss (1990) assessed the prevalence of worry in a community sample of children ages 5–18-years-old and found that over 30% endorsed symptoms of excessive worry. . . . Brown, O'Keefe, Sanders, and Baker (1986) reported that anxious and ruminative thoughts during stress are prevalent from middle childhood through adolescence. (pp. 3–4)

In 2007, a Nemours Foundation/KidsHealth, Department of Health Education and Recreation, and National Association of Health Education Centers survey asked 1,154 kids ages nine to thirteen how much they worry (almost all the time, a lot, a little, or almost never) about a variety of concerns that are common among kids their age. The majority of children (86 percent) said they worry "almost all the time" or "a lot" about the health of someone they love. Many kids said they worry "almost all the time" or "a lot" about other things, including schoolwork, tests, or grades (77 percent), their future (76 percent), and looks or appearance (63 percent). Table 2.3 summarizes the results of the surveys.

## Table 2.3: KidsHealth Survey Results for Worry

| Reason for Worry | Percentage of Kids Who Worry "Almost All of the Time" | Percentage of Kids Who Worry "A Lot" |
|---|---|---|
| Health of loved one | 55 | 31 |
| The future | 43 | 33 |
| Schoolwork, tests, or grades | 37 | 40 |
| Looks or appearance | 37 | 26 |
| Making mistakes or messing up | 26 | 35 |
| Friends and their problems | 24 | 33 |
| War or terrorism | 25 | 25 |
| The environment | 10 | 21 |

Source: Adapted from Nemours Foundation/KidsHealth et al., 2007.

In an earlier study (Nemours Foundation/KidsHealth et al., 2005) that focused on stress, 875 children ages nine to thirteen answered questions about what makes them feel stressed. Top responses included grades, school, or homework (36 percent), family (32 percent), and friends or peers who tease, lie, or gossip (21 percent).

Worry is cause for concern because it negatively affects many different aspects of life. Jeffrey Sanchez-Burks, Caroline Bartel, and Sally Blount (2009) found that "social cognition research has shown that mental energy spent worrying about how others view the self can slow down mental processing and lower performance" (p. 219).

Stéphane Duchesne, Frank Vitaro, Simon Larose, and Richard Tremblay (2008) conducted a study with two thousand children in Quebec, following them from kindergarten through high school. They found that "children whose trajectory of anxiety was high or chronic during elementary school had a higher probability of not completing high school than children whose trajectory of anxiety was moderate" (pp. 1142–1143). These findings are depicted in figure 2.1.

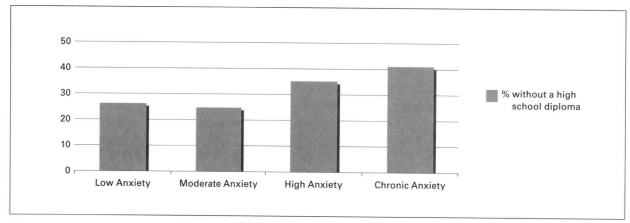

**Figure 2.1: Percentage of high school noncompletion based on anxiety trajectory group.**

Source: Adapted with kind permission from Springer Science+Business Media B.V. *Journal of Youth and Adolescence, 37,* 2008, 1134–1146. "Trajectories of Anxiety During Elementary-School Years and the Prediction of High School Noncompletion." Duchesne et al. Figure 2. © Springer Science+Business Media, LLC 2007.

Duchesne et al. (2008) reported several other studies that have corroborated the relationship between worry and academic achievement.

- Students who exhibit signs of anxiety as kindergartners are more likely to have academic problems at the end of their first year of high school (Duchesne et al., 2005).

- Students with high levels of anxious behaviors in first grade were more likely to have low academic achievement at the end of fifth grade (Ialongo, Edelson, Werthamer-Larsson, Crockett, & Kellam, 1995).

- In a meta-analysis, highly anxious children scored about one-half a standard deviation on achievement measures below children with low levels of anxiety (Seipp, 1991).

Test anxiety is a common form of worry that many students experience. Ray Hembree (1988) conducted a meta-analysis on the causes and effects of test anxiety. He found that "TA [test anxiety] is directly related to fears of negative evaluation, dislike of tests, and less effective study skills" (p. 73). Also, test anxiety lowers focus. In the presence of distractions, "HTA [high test anxiety] subjects seemed significantly more distractible than LTA [low test anxiety] students; their performance was accordingly depressed" (p. 65). Hembree also found that anxiety impairs performance on complex and difficult tasks that demand cognitive resources, because it involves task-irrelevant thinking, which reduces task-related attention. Finally, students with high test anxiety were inclined to an "external locus of control" (p. 56), which means they tended to blame others for failure.

## Conative Skill: Understanding and Interacting With Others

Understanding and interacting with others is the second category of conative skills essential for the 21st century. David Johnson and Roger Johnson (1989) pointed out that people are essentially social creatures with the cooperation imperative, which means that humans naturally desire and seek out opportunities to interact with others and achieve mutual goals. The 21st century will undoubtedly require people to interact with others who have different positions on provocative and volatile issues. There are three skills that are important to one's ability to understand and interact with others: (1) perspective taking, (2) responsible communication, and (3) thoughtful conflict and controversy.

### Perspective Taking

*Perspective taking* involves understanding how a situation appears to another person and the reasons for his or her cognitive and emotional reactions. In contrast, *egocentrism* is the inability to see any point of view other than one's own or to understand how another person reached different conclusions than one's own. Johnson and Johnson (1989) noted that although it is often attributed to selfishness, egocentrism is actually a cognitive limitation.

A number of educational practitioners have created models and strategies designed to enhance students' perspective-taking skills. For example, Edward de Bono (1969) created the term *lateral thinking* to describe his method for training one's brain to look at multiple perspectives. De Bono has developed several programs for such training, including the Cognitive Research Trust (CoRT). According to Nickerson (1999), these programs use questions that "are intended to get one to consider possibilities and to take perspectives about a situation that one otherwise would be unlikely to consider or to take" (p. 403).

Sandra Dingli (2001) reported research on the effectiveness of de Bono's programs, including John Edwards's studies of de Bono's CoRT model (Edwards, 1988; Edwards & Baldauf, 1983; Edwards & Clayton, 1989). Edwards found that students positively received CoRT, and it improved achievement, although there were methodological problems with the studies (Dingli, 2001). Although de Bono has received criticism for his lack of a theory base and the use of questionable experimental designs in research validating his programs (Polson & Jeffries, 1985; Sternberg & Lubart, 1999), his strategies are nevertheless widely used in business, technical fields, and education. Describing the aim of his work, de Bono seemed to be more concerned with pragmatic matters than with research evidence. He stated that his goal was "improving thinking not in academic contexts but in practical everyday life" (Perkins, 1995, p. 193).

Spencer Kagan (Kagan & Kagan, 2009) emphasized the development of a cooperative perspective, rather than an individualistic one, through his use of cooperative structures for learning. He argued that most of the structures that teachers traditionally use in the classroom emphasize competition and encourage students to compete against each other. Much of the research Kagan cited for the efficacy of his strategies comes from the work of Johnson and Johnson.

In 1989, Johnson and Johnson conducted a meta-analysis of 378 studies to investigate the effects of interdependence and cooperation on performance. They found that "cooperation promoted greater productivity and achievement than did interpersonal competition or individualistic efforts" (p. 54). In another meta-analysis (Johnson, Johnson, & Stanne, 2000) of 164 studies, they examined eight different approaches to cooperative learning and found that "all methods have produced higher achievement than competitive and individualistic learning, and the more conceptual approaches to cooperative learning may produce higher achievement than the direct methods" (p. 16).

In their most recent meta-analysis examining the effects of *constructive controversy*, a technique designed to help students discuss conflicting ideas and perspectives in productive ways, Johnson and Johnson (2009) found that "[constructive] controversy tended to result in greater mastery and retention of the material and of the skills being learned than did concurrence seeking (effect size [*ES*] = 0.70 [translating to a 26 percentile point gain]), debate (*ES* = 0.62 [translating to a 23 percentile point gain]), or individualistic efforts (*ES* = 0.76 [translating to a 28 percentile point gain])" (p. 44). They also found that constructive controversy improved students' cognitive reasoning, perspective taking, motivation, attitudes toward their tasks, interpersonal attraction, social support, and self-esteem.

## Responsible Communication

As it relates to understanding and interacting with others, responsible communication involves understanding how one's actions and words either positively or negatively affect another person's reactions. The research and theory on active listening are particularly relevant to responsible communication.

According to Carl Rogers and Richard Farson (1957/2007), *active listening* is listening that will help people "gain a clearer understanding of their situations, take responsibility, and cooperate with each other" (p. 279). In active listening, the listener has a responsibility both to listen *and* to help the speaker articulate his or her thoughts more clearly in order to find solutions for his or her problems. Active listening is grounded in the idea that a listener "respects the potential worth of the individual" and "considers his rights and trusts his capacity for self-direction" (p. 280). The basic goal of active listening is to understand someone else's point of view.

Rogers and Farson (1957/2007) summarized the message that a listener conveys through actively listening:

> I'm interested in you as a person, and I think that what you feel is important. I respect your thoughts, and even if I don't agree with them, I know that they are valid for you. I feel sure that you have a contribution to make. I'm not trying to change you or evaluate you. I just want to understand you. I think you're worth listening to, and I want you to know that I'm the kind of person you can talk to. (p. 284)

The mirror image of active listening is active speaking. *Active speaking* involves using one's words to encourage another person toward possible solutions. This might involve using a certain tone of voice, actively summarizing the conversation, or conveying empathy through gestures and facial expressions. An active speaker asks questions that allow others to feel that they are actively participating in a decision-making process. Asking questions such as "What can I do to help you succeed?" and "How can we make this work for everyone?" helps create an environment of cooperation.

Daniel Yankelovich (2000) approached responsible communication from the perspective of dialogue. Yankelovich characterized authentic dialogue in the following way:

> In such dialogue, "I" do not, while talking with you, selectively tune out views I disagree with, nor do I busy myself marshaling arguments to rebut you while only half attending to what you have to say. Nor do I seek to reinforce my own prejudices. Instead, I fully take in your viewpoint, engaging with it in the deepest sense of the term. You do likewise. Each of us internalizes the view of the other to enhance our mutual understanding. (p. 13)

## Thoughtful Conflict and Controversy

Johnson and Johnson (2005) provided some important distinctions between conflict and controversy. Specifically, *controversy* is "when one person's ideas, information, conclusions, theories, and opinions are incompatible with those of another and the two seek to reach an agreement" (p. G:2). A *conflict* exists when two people are trying to accomplish incompatible goals or complete incompatible activities at the same time. An activity is incompatible with another activity if it "prevents, blocks, or interferes with the occurrence or effectiveness of the second activity" (p. G:2). Essentially, a conflict occurs when one person is getting in another person's way.

For example, if two students are working on separate reports, but they both need to check the same book out of the library to use at home that night, there is potential for conflict, since one student's goals are blocking the other student from accomplishing his or her goals. However, if those same students, in the course of working on their reports, find themselves in a conversation wherein they are discussing their different views on how to best help victims of natural disasters, they are experiencing controversy, not conflict. Controversy is the meeting of incompatible ideas; conflict is the meeting of incompatible actions.

Many teachers avoid using controversy in the classroom for fear of losing control. Instead, these teachers predominantly use a recitation format. In a recitation format, the teacher calls on a student who then provides an answer that the teacher evaluates as being right or wrong. As a result, many classrooms become focused on concurrence seeking. *Concurrence seeking* is an inhibition of discussion to avoid disagreement or argument. In this atmosphere, individuals feel they must set aside their own opinions, doubts, or misgivings in order to preserve an overall harmonious atmosphere (Johnson & Johnson, 2007). Johnson and Johnson (2007) pointed out that students' self-esteem can become dependent on maintaining the harmonious atmosphere, making them increasingly reluctant to offer opinions or ideas. The recitation format also places an emphasis on *static knowledge*—knowledge gained through the lower-order cognitive processes of recognition or recall.

Although it might seem counterintuitive, there are a number of benefits related to conflict and controversy. For example, Johnson and Johnson (1979) noted that "controversies among students can promote transitions to higher stages of cognitive and moral reasoning" (p. 55). Further:

> Interpersonal controversies, which lead to conceptual conflict and feelings of uncertainty; which lead to a search for additional information and experiences, greater accuracy of cognitive perspective-taking, and the transition to more mature cognitive and moral reasoning process, seem to promote high quality problem-solving and decision-making. . . . Students who experience conceptual conflict resulting from controversy are better able to generalize the principles they learn to a wider variety of situations than are students who do not experience such conceptual conflict (Inagaki & Hatano, 1968, 1977). (p. 56)

Conflict and controversy should be handled thoughtfully. Negotiation is a common tool to address conflict and controversy. Johnson and Johnson (2005) defined negotiation as "a process by which persons who have shared and opposed interests and want to come to an agreement try to work out a settlement" (p. 5:1). They distinguished between win-lose and problem-solving negotiations. Consider two students arguing over who gets to use a ball at recess. In a *win-lose* negotiation, one student would refuse to consider any solution except one in which that student gets exactly what he or she wants (the ball all to himself or herself). *Problem-solving* negotiation would prioritize the relationship between the two students and seek to find a solution that makes both parties happy (such as playing a game together in which they can share the ball). Johnson and Johnson said that going for the win is "appropriate under certain circumstances, but in ongoing relationships, it is problem-solving negotiations that is [*sic*] most appropriate" (p. 5:1).

## Assessing 21st Century Skills

Instruction in 21st century skills without commensurate assessment can be vacuous. One reason for this is that without assessments to accompany instruction, students receive little if any concrete feedback regarding their progress. This is a severe impediment to learning as feedback appears to be a vital component of the learning process.

John Hattie and Helen Timperley (2007) synthesized the findings from twelve meta-analyses of studies on feedback, which incorporated 196 studies and 6,972 effect sizes. They calculated an overall average effect size of 0.79 for feedback, which translates into a 29 percentile point gain. As shown by Hattie (2009), this is twice the average effect size of typical educational interventions.

Assessment designed to provide feedback that enhances learning is typically referred to as formative assessment. While there is no universally accepted definition of formative assessment, there are some characteristics on which many researchers and theorists agree. One area of agreement is that formative assessment is a process as opposed to a specific type of test. How data from an assessment are used constitutes whether or not the assessment is formative or summative. If the information from an assessment is used to track students' progress over time, then it is considered formative. If the assessment is used to provide a final score for a student (such as at the end of a grading period), then it is considered a summative assessment.

In the book *Formative Assessment and Standards-Based Grading*, Marzano (2010) synthesized much of that research. Of particular interest to the assessment of 21st century skills is the research supporting the utility of tracking student progress over time. Specifically, in a synthesis of fourteen studies conducted at Marzano Research Laboratory (Haystead & Marzano, 2009), tracking student progress was associated with a 31 percentile point gain in achievement. Figure 2.2 illustrates a useful method of tracking student progress.

Figure 2.2 depicts an individual student's scores over time on a specific 21st century skill. On the student's side, this chart helps him or her see progress over time and stimulates motivation. Even if a particular student has not yet achieved high scores, he or she can see progress. On the teacher's side, this chart helps to identify the appropriate pace of instruction. If students in class are not progressing (that is, if their scores are not increasing), it indicates that content must be revisited or retaught. In this book, we present a system of assessment of 21st century skills that focuses on tracking student progress as outlined here.

## Translating Research and Theory Into Practice

In subsequent chapters, we draw from the research and theory in this chapter and from sources such as *The Art and Science of Teaching* (Marzano, 2007) and *Classroom Management That Works* (Marzano, 2003) to translate our model of cognitive and conative 21st century skills into both short-term and long-term strategies.

As mentioned in the introduction, as you progress through the remaining chapters, you will encounter comprehension questions that ask you to examine the content presented. After completing each question, you can check your answer with those in appendix A, page 193. Some of the questions are more open ended and ask you to generate applications for what you have read.

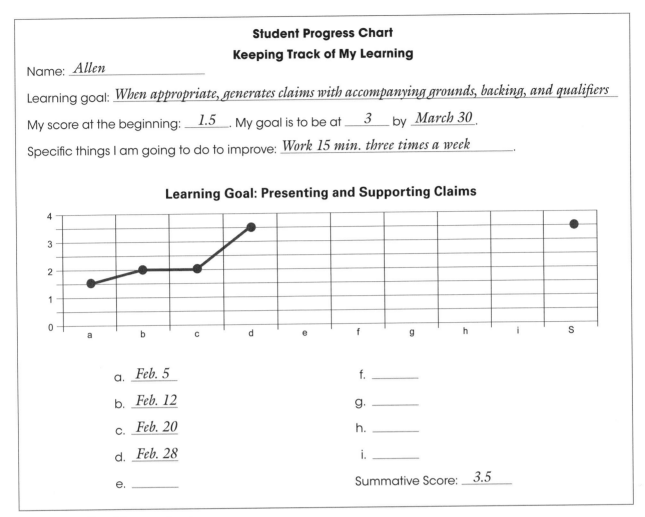

**Student Progress Chart**
**Keeping Track of My Learning**

Name: _Allen_

Learning goal: _When appropriate, generates claims with accompanying grounds, backing, and qualifiers_

My score at the beginning: _1.5_. My goal is to be at _3_ by _March 30_.

Specific things I am going to do to improve: _Work 15 min. three times a week_____.

**Learning Goal: Presenting and Supporting Claims**

a. _Feb. 5_                          f. _____
b. _Feb. 12_                         g. _____
c. _Feb. 20_                         h. _____
d. _Feb. 28_                         i. _____
e. _____                          Summative Score: _3.5_

**Figure 2.2: Tracking student progress.**

Source: Adapted from Marzano, 2010.

# Part I: Cognitive Skills

Chapter 3

# ANALYZING AND UTILIZING INFORMATION

Chapter 2 painted a sobering picture of information expanding at exponential rates in the 21st century with virtually no controls on that information. Therefore, analyzing and utilizing information will be a signature 21st century skill.

In this chapter, we address four general categories of strategies and skills that help students effectively analyze and utilize information: (1) navigating digital sources, (2) identifying common logical errors, (3) generating conclusions, and (4) presenting and supporting claims. (Visit **marzanoresearch .com/classroomstrategies** for a reproducible appendix with additional exercises for analyzing and utilizing information.)

## Navigating Digital Sources

Contrary to popular belief, research suggests that students are not experts at finding information. In a review of forty-nine research studies on the information behavior of young people, Peter Williams and Ian Rowlands (2007) stated that "there is little evidence that young people are expert searchers, or even that their search prowess has improved with time" (p. 9). They reported on research findings that suggest students have difficulty with selecting and modifying search terms, using keywords instead of natural language (sentences) when searching, narrowing their topics, using command language in databases, and planning their searches beforehand. They also noted that students have trouble evaluating their sources for relevance and credibility.

In 2005, Els Kuiper, Monique Volman, and Jan Terwel reviewed twenty-three research studies addressing student search and exploration techniques in electronic environments. They found the following characteristics to be true of student searching and processing strategies.

- **Students have a preference for browsing rather than keyword searching:** For example, a student gathering information on the topic of food chains might simply browse information on specific animals within a given food chain rather than use keywords to search for information specifically related to how animals in a food chain affect one another.

- **Students have difficulty formulating keywords:** For example, when gathering information on black holes, the student might only think to use the keyword *black hole* instead of broadening his or her search with terms such as *stellar mass* and *supermassive* (types of black holes) or including terms such as *Chandra* or *Hubble* (telescopes that have captured images of black holes).

- **Students limit their exploration, often defaulting to well-known websites:** For example, students might limit themselves to search engines like Google or Yahoo!, information collections like Wikipedia, and sites for nationally recognized newspapers like *The New York Times* to gather information rather than using more specialized search engines like Google Scholar, or searching library or academic-research databases.

- **Students have little patience:** For example, when researching a complex topic such as the strained relationship between the Sri Lankan government and the Tamil Tigers, students might read only one article and a portion of another article referenced in the first before coming to a conclusion about who in the conflict is right or wrong. Students do not want to take the time to read a wide variety of articles or reports from different sources that will help them gain a complete picture of their topic.

- **Students stop short when reading large amounts of text:** For example, a student might read only the abstract of a lengthy research article, therefore missing whether or not the experimental methods used were appropriate or sound and what errors or qualifiers the researchers noted.

- **Students focus on collecting factual knowledge:** For example, a student might simply collect a list of battles and the winners and losers of a war rather than finding information about the conflicting points of view leading up to a war; he or she may refrain from collecting varied postwar viewpoints and beliefs of important parties. In other words, he or she might gather information on what happened and neglect completely the more complex question of why it happened.

- **Students have a tendency to search for one correct answer:** For example, a teacher might recommend specific sites to students prior to allowing them to freely research a topic, but students who expect to find one specific answer on those websites may not go beyond them to look for more or different information.

- **Students have a tendency to change the search question when a literal answer is not easily found:** For example, when conducting research on one of the specific kinds of cells in the body, a student who does not immediately find information on the kind of cell he or she has chosen may simply shift his or her search question and begin looking for information about another kind of cell.

- **Students pay little attention when reading and processing information:** For example, students might simply gather a variety of statistics on a topic without reading through them to find that some statistics are in conflict with one another.

- **Students have difficulty assessing the relevance of information found on the Internet:** For example, while gathering information on a recent civil war in an African nation, a student might collect articles that refer to past wars in the same country or information on conflicts in different African countries.

- **Students have difficulty assessing the reliability of information found on the Internet:** For example, a student might not see that information that a tourist reports on a blog cannot be relied upon as fact.

To counteract some of these common problems students face, the following guidelines (figure 3.1) can be presented to students or developed with students' input.

1. **When searching for information, look for specifics, don't just browse:** You know you are browsing when you jump quickly from one site to another. If you need to, make a list of the information you are searching for, and make sure what you are looking at is relevant to that list.

2. **When searching for information, use multiple websites:** This means using library (school, local, and otherwise) resources, specialized search engines such as Google Scholar, research databases such as the Education Resources Information Center (ERIC), and sites that content experts operate. For example, NASA's site might be relevant to you if you are looking for information about the moon.

3. **Create a wide range of possible keywords to use when gathering information:** This might mean including synonyms (such as including *arachnids* when looking for information on spiders), words for causes or effects (such as including *spay* or *neuter* when looking for information on controlling the local animal population), or words for parts of a whole (such as including *ultraviolet* or *infrared* when looking for information on the light spectrum). You might also use specific terms or examples of a general phenomenon; for example, you might search for *Chernobyl nuclear accident* when looking for the general effects of nuclear radiation.

4. **Make sure that the information you find is relevant to the topic being researched:** You can do this by referring often to your search question. If you cannot explain the connection between your search question and what you are looking at in two sentences or less, then you might not be looking at relevant information.

5. **Make sure the information you find comes from a valid, reliable source:** You can do this by making sure you know who is providing the information. If the source has no credentials, then you should not use that information. Look for bias and for agenda: does this source benefit from the information being reported? For example, if you find information that appears to prove that a particular prescription drug is beneficial, but the information comes from a source that profits from the sale of that or other prescription drugs, the information may not be reliable. In general, blogs and wikis are not reliable sources of information. Use common sense, and think about the information being reported: is it more similar to something you would find in a newspaper or in a tabloid? It never hurts to double-check the information you find. If you cannot find another valid source that confirms the truth of the information you initially found, it might not be reliable.

6. **Make sure you read and think about the information you gather:** Remember that getting the information is not enough. Make sure that there are no contradictions, and that the information you found really supports your thesis or answers your question. You can do this by regularly comparing your thesis or question to the information you have found.

7. **When gathering information, sometimes there will be a lot of material to read:** Break it down into chunks you can manage. Remember that if you give yourself enough time, you can read everything, but you do not have to read everything at once.

8. **When searching for information, keep in mind the complexity of your topic:** Are there different points of view to consider? Are there different ways of looking at the topic? Remember that one clear and easy answer is not always available.

9. **When searching for information, remember that depth is not found strictly in facts:** In order to really understand a complex topic you may need to go beyond facts and look at points of view, future speculations, and so on. For example, think of the facts of your life. Your height, age, gender, address, and grade point average are facts about you; however, knowing those things might not help someone know you as a person.

Visit **marzanoresearch.com/classroomstrategies** to download a reproducible of this figure.

**Figure 3.1: Student guidelines for successful Internet searching.**

To help students understand the importance of these suggestions, it is useful to link specific suggestions to common errors that are made when searching for information. To reinforce the importance of suggestion six in the preceding list (make sure you read and think about the information you gather), a teacher might dramatize the drawbacks of not doing this. For example, the teacher might display a rather lengthy article from one site, the initial part of which presents information on a topic that is revisited in a later section of the report. If students are impatient and read only the first section, they will receive an incomplete view of the topic. The following vignette depicts how a teacher might introduce two of the searching suggestions.

> *Mr. Tosh's class has been studying the Ice Age, and he wants to encourage his students to use a wide range of possible keywords as they search the Internet for information, and to remember that depth is not found strictly in facts. Jess uses an online thesaurus to make a list of keywords including* Cro-Magnon man, the Dreamtime, Homo erectus, Jurassic, *and* Neanderthal. *Marcus browses a number of websites and decides to use keywords such as* troglodyte *and* Black Sea flood theory.*
>
> *As his students begin to collect information, Mr. Tosh notices that they are tending to simply find and report facts on the topic.*
>
> *"I think you may need to look beyond the facts you're collecting," he says to Marcus. "We know that according to the theory, the Mediterranean Sea became swollen and flooded into the Black Sea. We know that the flow was over two hundred times the flow of Niagara Falls, and we know that the lake rose six inches each day. But remember that depth is not found strictly in facts. Let's think about what these facts meant for the people and the animals of that time. That kind of flood would have killed animals, plants, and people literally by the tons. Torrential storms, lightning, and earthquakes would have accompanied it. Imagine if this happened today and continued for over two years. Imagine how life would change!"*
>
> *He also asks students to consider the long-term effects of the migrations such a flood would have caused.*
>
> *After looking at the facts more carefully and reflecting on them, Marcus notices that, according to the theory, the flood caused massive migrations to Central Europe, Asia, and Egypt. He begins to see that this one apocalyptic historical event could have shaped much of human history.*

In addition to the challenges already mentioned, there are some technical aspects of Internet searches that can also prove problematic for students. Nancy Frey, Douglas Fisher, and Alex Gonzalez (2010) reported that many students do not effectively use Boolean operators. The following are common operators.

- **Quotation marks:** This set of operators limits a search to the exact search string as written (for example, entering **"World War I"** in the search engine tells it to look for the whole phrase in the order entered, and not just the individual words).

- **OR:** This operator broadens a search to include all pages with any of the search terms (for example, entering **cats OR dogs** tells the search engine to look for any page with the words *cats*, *dogs*, or both words).

- **AND:** This operator narrows a search to pages that have all of the words listed (for example, entering **cats AND dogs** tells the search engine to look for pages that have both *cats* and *dogs*, but rejects pages that only have one of the words). Some search engines and databases use a plus sign (+) instead of AND.

- **NOT:** This operator removes pages from a search that have contents related to the term specified as NOT (for example, entering **cats NOT musical** tells the search engine to look for pages with the word *cats*, but to exclude any pages that contain content with the word *musical*). Some search engines, like Google, use a minus sign (–) instead of NOT (**cats –musical**) to completely exclude the word from the results.

Teachers should clearly illustrate the effects of each of these operators to students by comparing and contrasting the information obtained using the various operators. Once students have been exposed to these operators, their understanding can be reinforced by providing exercises like those in figure 3.2.

---

**Directions:** Select the correct answer from the choices given.

1. You have entered the following into a search engine: "World War I" AND women. Which of the following would you obtain from the search?

    A. Stories about World War I

    B. Roles women played in World War I

    C. World War I heroes

    D. How World War II began

2. If you want information on the relationship between violence, poverty, and education and how each one affects the other, which operator might you use?

    A. Quotation marks

    B. OR

    C. AND

    D. NOT

3. If you want to find information about whales and porpoises, and you'd like to see any website that mentions whales, porpoises, or both, which operator would you use?

    A. Quotation marks

    B. OR

    C. AND

    D. NOT

---

**Figure 3.2: Sample exercise on Boolean operators.**                    Continued on next page →

4. If you want information on Martin Luther, but you know that a search engine is likely to bring up more information on Martin Luther King Jr., what operator might you use?

   A. Quotation marks

   B. OR

   C. AND

   D. NOT

5. If you want information on a book titled *Out and About in the City*, but you know that the search engine will cut out many of the words, what operator might you use?

   A. Quotation marks

   B. OR

   C. AND

   D. NOT

**Answers:** 1—B; 2—C; 3—B; 4—D; 5—A

The following vignette depicts how a teacher might introduce Boolean operators to students.

> Ms. Vick's class has been practicing using the AND, OR, and NOT operators. She draws a Venn diagram on the board to illustrate the effects of each operator. She labels one circle Israel and the other Palestine—two countries students have recently been studying. "If I were to use AND in my search, what area of the diagram would the search engine likely pick up?" she asks.
>
> "Anything that falls in the center area, between both circles," Audra answers.
>
> "Right," Ms. Vick says. "So, what does that do to the overall search? Would you say that it limits or expands it?"
>
> "It limits it," Audra says. "Because you only get what pops up in that center area. You only get the sources that talk about both Israel and Palestine."
>
> Ms. Vick goes over the NOT and OR operators as well, and the students discuss how each operator would alter the search and how each different set of results could affect the information they gather.

Alan November (2010a) uses the acronym MAP to present the elements that students should understand if they are to have a comprehensive understanding of the Internet.

- *M* stands for *metaweb information*: This refers to how information on the Internet is structured using web addresses and URLs, links, and search engines.

  - **Web address and URLs**—These contain clues that tell whether the website is official or personal; if students are taught to read the structures of URLs, they will have clues about the credibility of the information. For example, if they know that *.gov* means the site is an official government site, then they might look for those sites when looking for information about the U.S. Mint.

- **Links**—Links on a website do not necessarily indicate that there is a legitimate relationship or official endorsement between that site and the linked site, since anyone can link to any other site; just because a site contains links to credible sites does not mean the site is credible. For example, a person's blog might have links to Harvard University's website, but that does not mean that person is affiliated with Harvard.

- **Search engines**—These use many different criteria to rank results. Some use popularity to rank results, some only search reference materials, and some use expert opinion to rank results. The first site listed is not necessarily accurate or credible. For example, sites that come up first in Google searches may have paid money for that position or might simply be the most popular sites.

- *A stands for authors*: This refers to the fact that anyone can claim to have credentials like those of a doctor. The truth of such claims should not be assumed. For example, a site might claim to offer expert health advice, but the author of the site might never have received medical training.

- *P stands for purpose*: This refers to the idea that sites are usually created for a specific purpose—to sell products or services, to advocate ideas, to entertain, or to present information. For example, information found on a nonprofit agency's site might be reliable, but the purpose of the site is not only to inform but to convince people to donate money.

The best way to provide students with an awareness of the elements in November's framework is to provide them with clear examples of how these elements can lead to more or less successful searches. The following vignette depicts this.

> *Mr. Pandor's class has been working on a community service project. He wants students to raise fish in class, monitor them, and then release them into a local river. They need supplies for this, however, and he asks them to focus on using the Internet to figure out where they will get the fish eggs and how much they will cost. Jason says he has found a hatchery a few hours away that has given him a price on a certain number of eggs. Gordon says he has contacted the Division of Wildlife, and it would be willing to donate the eggs, bring them to the school, and donate supplies such as fish tanks. Mr. Pandor asks Jason how he found his source. "I did a Google search, and the hatchery popped up first. I figured it was the most popular site for what I wanted, so I clicked on that," he says.*
>
> *Gordon searched differently: "I looked down the list when I did my Google search, and I saw the Division of Wildlife had a .gov URL. I figured it would be more legitimate than a regular .com site that probably just paid to be at the top of the list, so I clicked on that one."*
>
> *Mr. Pandor discusses with his class the role of priority listing on search engines like Google, and the students learn that it is important to know what criteria a search engine uses to rank search results.*

## Identifying Common Logical Errors

During the 20th century, certain philosophers (for example, Johnson-Laird, 1983; Johnson-Laird & Byrne, 1991; Toulmin, Rieke, & Janik, 1981) identified, codified, and described many common logical errors to which people are prone including faulty logic, attack, weak reference, and misinformation. These efforts were intended to help people analyze the veracity of information, which is as important in the 21st century as it has been in the past.

Common logical errors appear frequently in the media. For example, a politician makes a common logical error when he or she ascribes characteristics to all members of an opposing party (for example, "All Democrats like to tax and spend" or "All Republicans support capital punishment"). A newscaster makes a common logical error when he or she uses sources that lack credibility (for example, "A friend of the victim indicated that the victim's ex-husband was to blame"). As discussed previously, understanding and being able to identify these errors is one of the most critical skills for the 21st century student, because so much information is available from so many different sources.

In this section, we have organized these common logical errors into four categories: (1) faulty logic, (2) attack, (3) weak reference, and (4) misinformation. Twenty-first century students should be well versed in all of these types of errors. We also discuss common logical errors in modern-day media.

### Faulty Logic

Errors that occur due to faulty logic happen when the person committing the error is not using sound reasons to form conclusions. Marzano (2007) identified the following seven ways that faulty logic can occur: contradiction, accident, false cause, begging the question, evading the issue, arguing from ignorance, and composition and division. (See table 3.1.)

After providing examples for the various errors of faulty logic, a teacher can reinforce students' understanding of these errors by providing exercises like the one in figure 3.3 (page 46).

After students have an understanding of these types of errors, a teacher can ask them to find examples in the media. The following vignette depicts this.

> *Mr. Dale's class has been studying faulty logic. He asked his students to find real-world examples of faulty logic and bring them to class. Paula has found a sales brochure advertising a new hotel downtown. It states that it is the best hotel in town because it is superior to all other hotels, and she has recognized this as an example of begging the question. Gareth has found a scene in a science fiction book he has been reading. He has noticed that at one point the author has written a scene in which the main character must fly his ship in very dangerous conditions because he cannot risk stopping at the only nearby planet because of a bitter feud, but in the next book he stops at that same planet without any trouble at all. Gareth sees this as an example of contradiction.*

## Table 3.1: Types of Faulty Logic

| Contradiction | Accident | False Cause | Begging the Question | Evading the Issue | Arguing From Ignorance | Composition and Division |
|---|---|---|---|---|---|---|
| *Contradiction occurs when someone presents conflicting information.*<br><br>An athlete who says that the use of performance-enhancing drugs creates an unfair situation but then speaks out against drug-testing procedures has committed an error of contradiction. | *Accident occurs when there is a failure to recognize that an argument is based on an exception to a rule.*<br><br>Someone who concludes that parakeets cannot fly because his pet parakeet has a damaged wing and cannot fly has committed an error of accident. | *False cause occurs when there is an assumption that something that happened first caused something that happened later.*<br><br>A student who thinks his hockey team lost the game because he was not wearing his lucky socks has committed an error of false cause. | *Begging the question occurs when someone defends a claim by only restating it.*<br><br>If a student claims that speed limits should be eliminated because they do not make the roads any safer and backs up this claim by saying that the limits do not contribute to the safety of drivers or passengers, he is begging the question. | *Evading the issue occurs when someone changes the topic to avoid an issue.*<br><br>If a student is asked whether or not she recently broke a specific school rule, and she talks about all the other rules she has followed in the past, she is evading the issue. | *Arguing from ignorance occurs when someone makes a claim that something is true because it has not been proven untrue.*<br><br>If a student argues that a defendant in a specific court case is guilty because there is no proof he is not, she is arguing from ignorance. | *Composition and division are errors of the parts and whole. Composition occurs when someone asserts something about a whole that is only true of its parts, and division occurs when someone asserts something about all of the parts that is only generally true of the whole.*<br><br>• **Composition:** A student who asserts that all Muslims want to harm Americans because a small group of them attacked the United States has committed an error of composition.<br><br>• **Division:** A student who asserts that she does not like any ingredients in her mother's chili because she does not like the chili has committed an error of division. |

**Directions:** Match the type of error with the example.

A. Contradiction

B. Accident

C. False cause

D. Begging the question

E. Evading the issue

F. Arguing from ignorance

G. Composition

H. Division

1. Tali and Ben are discussing an assignment they have partnered on. Tali asks Ben if he has completed his part of it, and Ben says, "Are you going to the pep rally this afternoon? It should be fun."

2. Monica and Lewis are discussing the AIDS epidemic. "Maybe someday they'll find a cure," Monica says. "There is no cure for AIDS," Lewis says. "They haven't found one yet, have they? And they've tried for a long time. That means there is no cure."

3. Connor's family has a dog that is almost twenty years old. When one of his friend's dogs dies, he asks his mom how it could have happened. "His dog was only twelve," Connor says. "He should have lived a lot longer."

4. James is working on an essay for class, and Jamal asks him why he is writing it out by hand instead of using the computer. James says that the last time he used the computer only he got a bad grade; he now writes everything by hand first and then copies it on the computer later.

5. Daniel and Saladin are discussing the topic of war. Saladin says that sometimes war is necessary, even though no one likes that. "No, war is always bad," Daniel says. "Why is it always bad?" Saladin says. "Because it's horrible," Daniel says.

6. Farukah tells Li he should be nice to her little sister, Tasha, instead of picking on her like other people do. Later that afternoon, when they are at home, Farukah makes fun of Tasha's outfit and refuses to play with her.

7. Kelly is trying to teach her little sister, Nora, about odd and even numbers. "I don't understand," says Nora. "You said that 1 is an odd number and that 3 is an odd number, and I know 1 + 3 = 4, so shouldn't 4 be an odd number, too?"

8. Jessup is studying for a science test with friends. He refers to the $H_2O$ molecule as being liquid, and a friend tells him that the molecule itself is not liquid, only the water is.

9. Kellis and Sloane are discussing a local restaurant that has recently gone out of business. "They had really great fries," Kellis says. "It's too bad." "It happened because of that new place out by the mall," Sloane says. "Why do you say that?" Kellis says. "Well, that place opened up, and just three months later Rudy's shut down. It's obvious," Sloane says.

10. Hannah asks Richard if he would like to go ice-skating with her and some friends on Saturday. He tells her he doesn't like ice-skating, but that winter he joins a hockey team.

**Answers:** 1—E; 2—F; 3—B; 4—C; 5—D; 6—A; 7—G; 8—H; 9—C; 10—A

**Figure 3.3: Sample exercise on errors of faulty logic.**

## Attack

Errors related to attack happen when the person committing the error defends his or her thinking by focusing on related but irrelevant aspects of the issue. According to Marzano (2007), the three ways that attack occurs are: poisoning the well, arguing against the person, and appealing to force. (See table 3.2.)

## Table 3.2: Types of Attack

| Poisoning the Well | Arguing Against the Person | Appealing to Force |
|---|---|---|
| *Poisoning the well* occurs when a person is so committed to a position that he or she explains away any evidence to the contrary.<br><br>If a student believes that cutting down trees is so wrong that she explains away the results of a study showing that overgrowth in forests can actually lead to more severe wildfires, she is poisoning the well. | *Arguing against the person* occurs when a person says derogatory things about someone making a claim in order to invalidate that claim.<br><br>If a student who is concerned about the effects of global warming tells a peer who does not believe the global change is man-made that he is selfish, she is arguing against the person. | *Appealing to force* occurs when someone uses threats to establish the validity of a claim.<br><br>If a student threatens his peer with telling the principal that she cheated on a recent test if she decides to run for the same position in a student-council election, he is appealing to force. |

After presenting examples for the types of attack, teachers can reinforce students' understanding of these errors by presenting exercises like the one in figure 3.4.

**Directions:** Match the type of error with the example.

A. Poisoning the well

B. Arguing against the person

C. Appealing to force

1. Morris and Carl are talking about the United States' response to North Korea's nuclear program. "We should just invade the country," Morris says. "We should take them down and just take the whole country over. That would stop them."

2. Latika and Jeanette are discussing a recent local trial. Latika says she knows the defendant is guilty because her brother used to be friends with him and said he was always selfish and out of control.

3. Drew really wants to get tickets to an upcoming concert, but when they go on sale, Drew is late getting to the ticket office, and a long line has already formed. He sees a student from his school standing near the front of the line and goes up to him and pretends to be with him. "Act like you were saving a place for me," Drew whispers in the student's ear. "Otherwise, I'll tell your parents that you skipped school last week."

4. Jada and her friends are talking about what they are going to do after they graduate from high school. Jada says, "I'm going to college. If you don't go right after high school, you never go." "But my mom didn't do that," says Annie. "She worked a few jobs to see what she liked doing and then went to college and got a degree doing what she enjoyed." "Yeah," says Jada, "but your mom is different from most people, so she's not a good example. I'm sure that I'm right."

5. Annabelle and Zelda are assigned to debate whether or not Woodrow Wilson was a good choice for president of the United States. Zelda goes first and presents her arguments for why Wilson was a good choice for president. When it is Annabelle's turn to speak, she begins by saying, "Since you all know Zelda, you'll understand that she is wrong, because she is always so rude."

6. Nicholas is trying out for the softball team. He knows that Frank is the only other first baseman trying out, and that Frank is a better player than he is, but he explains this away by telling himself that it doesn't matter because he is more excited than Frank is and because Frank is already on the swim team.

**Answers:** 1—C; 2—B; 3—C; 4—A; 5—B; 6—A

**Figure 3.4: Sample exercise on errors of attack.**

After students have an understanding of these errors, the teacher might ask them to find examples. The following vignette illustrates this.

> Ms. Sinclair's students have been looking for real-world examples of attack. Margot has found an example of appealing to force in a movie she really likes called Avatar. In the movie, a group of men try to take over a planet by destroying sacred sites and killing or enslaving the native people. Roger has found many examples of arguing against the person on a website dedicated to gossip about celebrities. He pulls up the site to show Ms. Sinclair how the person who runs the blog writes that an actor is lousy at his job because he dresses poorly when he shows up for red-carpet events.

### Weak Reference

Errors of weak reference occur when untrustworthy or unreliable sources are used. Marzano (2007) identified five ways that weak reference can occur: using sources that reflect bias, using sources that lack credibility, appealing to authority, appealing to the people, and appealing to emotion. (See table 3.3.)

## Table 3.3: Types of Weak Reference

| Using Sources That Reflect Bias | Using Sources That Lack Credibility | Appealing to Authority | Appealing to the People | Appealing to Emotion |
|---|---|---|---|---|
| *Using sources that reflect bias* occurs when a person uses information from sources who have something to gain or lose from the ideas presented.<br><br>A student who references a study by a taxi drivers' advocacy group that says taxi drivers are safer than other drivers is using a source that reflects bias. | *Using sources that lack credibility* occurs when a person uses a source that is not trustworthy (for example, the source is not an expert, has been proven to be biased, or has a track record of being unreliable).<br><br>A student who says that a certain musician is the greatest guitar player who ever lived because his favorite sports star (who is not a musician nor interested in the history of music) said so is using a source that lacks credibility. | *Appealing to authority* involves invoking an authority figure as the last word.<br><br>If a student tells his friend that NFL teams should release more information about hiring and trade decisions because John Elway said so, he is appealing to authority. | *Appealing to the people* involves saying something is right because everyone is doing it.<br><br>A student who tells her friend that she should attend a certain college because all their mutual friends have already enrolled is appealing to the people. | *Appealing to emotion* involves playing on emotions or using a sob story as proof for a claim.<br><br>A student who urges her friend not to go to a party because she herself is grounded, and it would make her sad to be the only one to miss out, is appealing to emotion. |

After providing examples for the various errors involving weak reference, a teacher can reinforce students' understanding of these errors by providing an exercise like the one in figure 3.5.

**Directions:** Match the type of error with the example.

A. Using sources that reflect bias

B. Using sources that lack credibility

C. Appealing to authority

D. Appealing to the people

E. Appealing to emotion

1. Bess crosses the street before getting to the crosswalk, but George does not. After he crosses the street, she tells him that the crosswalk doesn't really matter. She says, "My uncle is a police officer, and he says no one cares where you cross the street."

2. Violet believes that violent crime in her city has decreased because her cousin lives in a bad part of town, and he told her that there have not been as many muggings as there used to be.

3. Karen tells her mother that she is very sorry she did not complete her chores. "I've had a really bad week. A friend of mine really hurt my feelings, and I've had to study for a really big test, and I'm scared I'll get a bad grade, because I don't understand what's going on in class."

4. Taylor asks Gale why she is wearing a jacket with a hole in the elbow. Gale tells him it is the new style. "Look around," she says. "Everyone is doing it."

5. Brock says that a friend of his who lives near the site of a recent tornado told him that another one will hit the same area really soon.

6. Wren tells Pat that he should recycle because he heard the mayor talking about how important it is.

7. Sasha has written a paper about the presidency of Ronald Reagan. Her teacher notices that most of the people Sasha quotes said that he was an excellent president. Almost all of them were people who worked very closely with him in office as well, and the quotes were taken from a time when they still worked for him.

8. Svetlana tells Cori that she knows Michael Phelps was cheating in the Olympics. Cori says she doesn't believe that, and Svetlana says, "My cousin was a swimmer in college, and he said that Michael Phelps couldn't be as fast as he was without cheating."

9. Dina tells her dad that he has to let her go to the away game with her friends because everyone in the school is going. She says that she will miss out if she doesn't go.

10. Laura gives a speech to the school, telling her peers that she should be elected president of the student body because she has had a really tough year, and it would be nice to have something good happen.

**Answers:** 1—C; 2—B; 3—E; 4—D; 5—B; 6—C; 7—A; 8—B; 9—D; 10—E

**Figure 3.5: Sample exercise on errors of weak reference.**

Once students have an understanding of these errors, they can be asked to find examples. The following vignette provides an example of such an activity.

*Mr. Cast's students have been bringing in examples of errors of weak reference from their favorite books and movies. Daisy brings in a clip of the television show* The Simpsons *with a character called Dr. Nick, who is a funny example of lacking credibility. Dr. Nick didn't actually go to medical school, and in the clip he diagnoses a medical problem by saying, "This is easy; his body has too many bones!" Joshua brings in a clip of a commercial that depicts a famous basketball star eating a certain kind of cereal. "I only ate that cereal for years because of that commercial," he says. "I was convinced that if he ate it, it was the best cereal in the world.*

> *I was appealing to authority." Diane has found an error regarding weak reference in her favorite movie—Dreamgirls. She says, "When C.C. comes back to Effie after eight years, he knows she does not have to forgive him for what he did, but he reminds her that he is her brother. He appeals to her emotions about family to get back in her good graces."*

### Misinformation

Misinformation is the use of incorrect information to defend a claim or the misapplication of information. Marzano (2007) noted that misinformation occurs in two ways: confusing the facts and misapplying a concept or generalization. (See table 3.4.)

## Table 3.4: Types of Misinformation

| Confusing the Facts | Misapplying a Concept or Generalization |
|---|---|
| *Confusing the facts* occurs when someone uses information that seems to be factual, but an element has been changed so the information is no longer accurate.<br><br>A student who believes that she can consume as much ice cream as she wants because the label on the ice cream carton says it only contains three grams of fat is neglecting to consider the serving size and therefore confusing the facts. | *Misapplying a concept or generalization* occurs when someone uses a generalization in an instance for which it cannot be properly applied.<br><br>A student who thinks that there should be no bosses in the world because bosses violate the Golden Rule is misapplying a concept. |

After providing examples for errors of misinformation, a teacher can reinforce students' understanding of these errors by providing exercises like the one in figure 3.6.

---

**Directions:** Match the type of error with the example.

A. Confusing the facts

B. Misapplying a concept or generalization

1. Christian wants Harrison to loan him some money. Harrison says no, and Christian says, "But you're a Democrat. Democrats are fiscally liberal!"

2. Ina's mother's handwriting is a little messy. While reading a note from her mother, Ina mistakenly reads the word *before* as *after*. When her mother gets home and discovers that Ina hasn't done the chores that she asked her to do before dinner, Ina replies, "Your note said that you wanted me to do them after dinner."

3. Lawrence says he wants to get a master's degree after going to college, and Charlotte says she thinks that's great. "What kind of business do you want to go into?" she asks. Lawrence replies, "I don't want to go into business. I just want to make more money. People with MBAs make more money."

4. Phillip is looking at a bus schedule to find out when he needs to be at the bus stop in the morning. He sees that the B route picks passengers up at his stop at 8:05. The next morning, he gets to the bus stop at 8:00, but a bus doesn't arrive until 8:45. He asks the driver why he is late, and the driver replies that he is right on time. Phillip shows him the bus schedule, and the driver points to the date on it. "That bus schedule is two years old," he says.

**Answers:** 1—B; 2—A; 3—B; 4—A

---

**Figure 3.6: Sample exercise on errors of misinformation.**

After students understand these errors, they can be asked to find examples, as the following vignette illustrates.

> *Mr. Ratcliff's class has been bringing in examples of misinformation. Nate brings a home video of his brother Caleb, who is claiming that when Google has a drawing accompanying its homepage, it means everyone who works for Google got the day off. Nate asks why he thinks this, and Caleb says, "That's what it means. When they first started the company, they were going to go to the Burning Man festival in Nevada, and they put up a drawing of a burning man to let people know they wouldn't be there to fix any problems."*
>
> *Nate laughs on the video. He says, "They did that once, Caleb. After that, they kept the drawings around because they liked them, but it doesn't mean everyone got the day off. Google is a huge company now; they'd never do that!" Nate explains that this is an example of confusing the facts.*

## Modern-Day Media

With a basic understanding of common logical errors, students can be asked to identify these errors in the information to which they are exposed through mass media. The following are examples of activities teachers can design to this end.

- Teachers can use videos of public service announcements (PSAs) to discuss appealing to the people and appealing to emotion. For example, a PSA for fighting childhood obesity might appeal to the people by showing many kids outside playing a game and having fun while a PSA for prevention of bullying might appeal to emotion by showing someone upset by the actions of a bully. PSAs can be found through Google Videos, YouTube, and the Ad Council (www.adcouncil.tv). Teachers can show both old ads, such as the first ones designed to discourage drunk driving, and newer ads, such as ones designed to discourage young people from using meth. A teacher might ask students to compare them. The old PSAs tend to be humorous from a contemporary perspective, and students might be asked to discuss why ads that were effective in the 1980s would no longer be effective today. Students can be asked to explain their reasoning in terms of appealing to the people and appealing to emotion.

- Teachers can use YouTube and Hulu to find clips from sitcoms that display errors in reasoning. After playing the clip or a series of clips, the teacher could ask students to identify which errors in thinking were present. For an extra challenge, a montage of clips could be played quickly, and students could be asked to identify the correct error in thinking as quickly as possible.

  Clips from a show like *The Simpsons* could be used.

  - In "Stark Raving Dad" (Jean, Reiss, & Moore, 1991), Homer is sent to an insane asylum, where he asks how they know who is insane and who isn't. The doctor stamps his hand with the word *Insane* and explains that everyone with the stamp is insane. This is an example of begging the question.

Jon Stewart conducts interviews and provides commentary on *The Daily Show with Jon Stewart* that can provide excellent examples of errors in reasoning.

- In "Rod Blagojevich" (Bodow & O'Neil, 2010b), Stewart interviews former Illinois Governor Rod Blagojevich, who was convicted of lying to the FBI. Throughout the interview, Blagojevich commits errors of begging the question and contradiction. For example, Stewart points out that Blagojevich said before his trial that he was anxious for his chance to defend himself, but when the opportunity came to defend himself, he declined to defend himself. This is contradiction. Stewart also confronts Blagojevich about lying during a previous episode of the show, and Blagojevich defends himself by simply repeating his lie. This is begging the question.

- In "Rick Perry Pt. 2" (Bodow & O'Neil, 2010a), Stewart interviews Governor Rick Perry from Texas. Perry states that many companies are moving out of California and into Texas. He attributes this to Texas's low taxes and low levels of regulation. Stewart asks if those arguments could also support the movement of companies to India or China. Rick Perry responds with the unrelated question, "Would you rather live in Texas or in India?" This is an example of evading the issue.

- Teachers can also show students political attack ads and ask them to find out whether the claims the politicians make against their opponents are true. Many political attack ads are guilty of confusing the facts, misapplying generalizations, and appealing to emotion.

These activities can help teachers provide students with a grasp of the different types of errors in reasoning and how they are often seen in the mass media.

## Generating Conclusions

Twenty-first century students must be facile at gathering, organizing, and scrutinizing information, but they must also be skilled at generating valid conclusions based on that information as well. Ultimately, the purpose of gathering information is to generate new conclusions.

Generating conclusions is a natural human phenomenon. For example, assume a child sees a kitten and reaches out to pet it but gets scratched. The child forms the conclusion that kittens can be dangerous and avoids them from then on. So, from this perspective, students do not have to be taught how to generate conclusions. One might say they are hardwired to do so. However, generating sound conclusions that have a tight internal logic is quite another issue. Teachers can and should teach students to analyze and revise their conclusions for the purpose of making them as powerful and useful as possible. Here we consider two types of conclusions: probabilistic and deductive, each of which has specific characteristics.

### Probabilistic Conclusions

Probabilistic conclusions are drawn when someone says something like: "It is probably going to rain today" or "It doesn't seem like I am going to be able to get my homework done." Both statements represent a conclusion that has a tacit probability attached to it. In the first statement, the person is asserting that it is going to rain, but he or she is not absolutely sure of the assertion. The next statement communicates a little less certainty regarding the possibility of the person getting his or her homework done. When we have formed conclusions about which we are unsure, we tend to use words such as *probably, maybe, likely, unlikely, possible,* and *not sure.*

While knowing whether or not it is going to rain does not usually involve much risk, students should be aware that uncertainty can lead to negative consequences. Questions like the following can help students assess the level of risk involved in their probabilistic conclusions:

- Is it important that I am right about this?

- If so, how sure am I about my prediction?

- If I'm not very sure, what should I do about it?

To illustrate, assume that a student has generated the following conclusion: "I think I can study for the examination on Friday and still go to the football game tonight." Basically, this statement is a prediction that the student can accomplish two things in a specific interval of time—go to the football game and study. Using the first question, the student asks himself how important it is that he is right. Let's assume that the student believes it is important because the test will count a great deal toward his final grade. Now the student progresses to the second question, which requires him to consider how sure he is about his prediction. When he considers this, he realizes that he has not thought through how much time it will take to go to the game and how much time it will take to study adequately for the test. After considering the third question, the student decides that he is going to develop a more detailed plan about how many hours are needed to adequately study for the test. After he lays out his study plan, he will reconsider how likely it is that he can do both activities.

Consider a more serious situation: while on a camping trip in the mountains, a student is hiking from one sheltered campsite to another when snow begins to fall. The student makes the following conclusion: "I probably can make it to the next sheltered campsite before the snow gets too deep." Again, this is a conclusion that is grounded in a statement of probability. However, there is significant risk if her conclusion is inaccurate. In this case, she believes that she has a chance of making it to the next covered campsite before the snow gets too deep. If she is incorrect, she might be literally risking her life by being trapped overnight in a snowstorm. This is a probabilistic conclusion that requires as much accuracy as possible.

In short, relative to probabilistic conclusions, students should be able to discern which conclusions bear some risk if they are inaccurate. They must then strive to be as certain as possible regarding the conclusions that bear risk. If their level of certainty drops too far, then they must reconsider their conclusions and the resulting actions they will take. The following scale can be useful to this end:

- 4—I am sure this will happen.

- 3—There is a very good chance this will happen.

- 2—There is about an equal chance of this happening or not happening.

- 1—This might happen, but it isn't very likely.

- 0—I am sure this will not happen.

To illustrate, reconsider the student who is thinking about going to the football game even though he has to study for his test on Friday. The student might assign a probability score of two (there is an equal chance he will and will not have enough time to study for the test) to the conclusion that he will be able to go to the football game and prepare adequately for the test. This realization should spur him to develop a detailed plan regarding when he will find time to study.

Older students might be asked to assign percentages to their level of certainty. For example, the girl on the camping trip might reason that she has a 60 percent chance of making it to the next sheltered campsite. Looking at things from this perspective might stimulate her to reconsider her decision or develop a better plan should she still want to try to make it to the next campsite. She might ask herself: "Is it really worth risking my life if there is a 40 percent chance I am wrong?" The following vignette depicts how a teacher might provide students with the concept of assigning a probability estimate to events.

> *Ms. Valentina's students have been studying an upcoming election. After presenting and discussing the zero-to-four probability scale, Ms. Valentina asks her students to choose one of the candidates and assign a probability score regarding how likely he or she is to win the election. "This is just an estimate," she says. "But you need to justify the probability you assign. Are you basing the score on this candidate's platform popularity with a predominant class of constituents, such as a religious or ethnic group? Do you think recent commercials, debates, or appearances have particularly helped or hurt his or her candidacy?" She tells students they will assign probability scores and then have a class discussion, during which they will attempt to come to a consensus on which candidates are most and least likely to win the election.*

With middle and high school students, a teacher might introduce some common errors to consider when engaging in probabilistic thinking. These errors include regression toward the mean, conjunction, base rates, and the cumulative nature of risk. (See table 3.5.)

## Table 3.5: Types of Errors in Probabilistic Thinking

| Regression Toward the Mean | Conjunction | Base Rates | Cumulative Nature of Risk |
|---|---|---|---|
| *Regression toward the mean* errors neglect the fact that an extreme score on a measure is most commonly followed by a more moderate score that is closer to the mean.<br><br>A student who thinks that a recent spike in worldwide conflict is sure to lead to another world war is failing to recognize regression toward the mean. | *Conjunction* errors neglect the fact that it is less likely that two or more independent events will occur simultaneously than that they will occur in isolation.<br><br>If a student fails to recognize that it is more likely that his city's professional baseball or his city's professional football team will win a national championship than it is that both teams will win national championships, he has committed an error of conjunction. | *Base rates* errors neglect to use general or typical patterns of occurrences in a category of events as the basis on which to predict what will happen in a given situation.<br><br>If a student believes that investing in a company is a good idea because he likes its product, while ignoring the fact that the company has lost money for the last three consecutive years, he is committing a base rate error. | *Cumulative nature of risk* errors neglect the fact that even though the probability of a risky event might be low, the probability of the event occurring increases with time and the number of events.<br><br>A student who believes he will not get caught speeding because he has never been caught speeding is ignoring the cumulative nature of risk. |

These errors are not self-evident and must be illustrated to students using examples. To provide students with some practice identifying these types of probabilistic errors, exercises like the one in figure 3.7 might be used.

---

**Directions:** Match the type of error with the example.

A.  Regression toward the mean

B.  Conjunction

C.  Base rates

D.  Cumulative nature of risk

1.  Kevin and Lauren are talking about a new teacher at the school, Ms. Garcia. "She grew up in the slums of Mexico, but she immigrated to the United States and now has a doctorate!" Kevin says to Lauren. "I'll bet she had to work her way through college," Lauren says. Kevin replies, "It's more likely that she had to work her way through college and that she still sends money back to her family in Mexico."

2.  "I'm probably going to have a horrible year this year," says Marty to Angela. "What makes you say that?" asks Angela. Marty replies, "Well, last year my dog died, my parents got divorced, and I wrecked my car. This year is obviously going to be worse."

3.  Charity often wears flip-flops to school. "No one's ever stepped on my foot, so I'm sure no one ever will," she says.

4.  Jen is late to a party, and her friends aren't able to contact her on her cell phone. "Oh, she probably just forgot to charge it," says Charlie. "No, it's even more likely that she forgot to charge it and left it at home," responds her friend Jordan.

5.  Pete often parks his car in the handicapped spots at stores and restaurants. "I've never gotten caught, and I probably never will," he says. "Besides, it's so much more convenient."

6.  Eva is figuring out how long it will take her to write her research report. "Well, it should take me a week to do the research, a week to write my rough draft, and a week to revise it," she plans. However, Eva fails to remember that she has never before completed a research paper in three weeks, normally taking closer to six weeks.

7.  Sara and Steven are participating in a stock-market simulation for their economics class. Each student is given imaginary capital and must manage a fictitious stock portfolio for six weeks. Steven tells Sara after class one day that he's going to buy stock in Company X. He says, "Company X is really on a tear right now; the stock is as high as it's ever been in five years. It's sure to keep going up and up!"

8.  Halle and Jessica are trying to figure out the odds of their soccer team winning the next game. "I know we lost the first ten games of the season," says Halle, "but we've won the last two. We'll probably win the next ten."

**Answers:** 1—B; 2—A; 3—D; 4—B; 5—D; 6—C; 7—A; 8—C

---

**Figure 3.7: Sample exercise on probabilistic errors.**

With a basic understanding of the nature of probabilistic thinking, and the errors that can be made when engaging in such thinking, students might be presented with a general strategy like the following.

1.  If you are predicting that something will or will not occur, determine if there are any negative consequences or any risk associated with being wrong.

2.  If there are risks, carefully determine how accurate your prediction is by being more precise about your probability statements and making sure you are not making errors.

3.  If the chances of a negative outcome appear too great, come up with a new plan regarding your actions.

The following vignette depicts how a student might use the general strategy.

> *Lacy has been applying for summer jobs. However, despite the fact that she has been applying to many places over a period of months, the economy is very bad, and she has had no luck. She is wondering if she should even bother to keep trying to find a summer job or if she should give up and go to camp like she has every other summer for five years. She feels that, based on the pattern of being rejected so far, she is not very likely to get a job. If she is going to go to camp, she must tell her mother soon or all the spots will be taken. She would rather get a job and stay home for the summer, but going to camp would be better than being stuck at home without anything at all to do. She looks at the issue carefully, and she sees that, although there is a pattern of rejection, there is also an element of the cumulative nature of risk. That is, even though the probability of getting a job is low, the more applications she fills out, the more likely it is she will get a job. She decides that the negative consequence of being stuck at home without a job is not serious enough to give up trying and go to camp—she would rather keep trying to find a job than give up and tell her mother she wants to go to camp.*

## Deductive Conclusions

Deductive conclusions focus on premises. For example, a person is making a deductive conclusion when he concludes that his automobile, which has recently been in the repair shop for maintenance, has been checked for oil. He bases his conclusion on the premise that repair shops always check the oil in cars when they perform maintenance. His reasoning might be stated in the following way:

1. The repair shop always checks for oil.

2. My car has been in the repair shop.

3. Therefore, it has oil.

The foundational premise here is that repair shops always check for oil. Based on this premise and the fact that his car has been to a repair shop, it is reasonable to conclude that the car has oil.

Another deductive conclusion might be stated as follows: "He is going to vote Republican because he was raised a Lutheran." The logic of this conclusion is as follows:

1. All Lutherans vote Republican.

2. He is a Lutheran.

3. Therefore, he will vote Republican.

The foundational premise here is that all Lutherans vote Republican. Once this is established, anyone who is a Lutheran is automatically assumed to vote Republican.

The basis for a deductive conclusion is always a foundational premise, such as "All cars that have been to the repair shop have been checked for oil" or "All Lutherans vote Republican." With these foundational premises established, deductive conclusions are easily generated. For example, once you know that a car has been to the repair shop or that a person is a Lutheran, you then can conclude with certainty that a given car has been checked for oil (if it has been to the repair shop) or a specific person will vote Republican (if he or she is a Lutheran).

The information that a specific car has been to a repair shop and that a specific person is a Lutheran are sometimes called minor premises. The statements that a specific car has oil and a specific person will vote Republican are the deductive conclusions. A deductive conclusion, then, can be said to have the following form:

Foundational premise ⟶ minor premise ⟶ deductive conclusion

The most challenging and even disturbing aspect of deductive conclusions is that they can be valid but untrue. The validity of a conclusion is a function of whether it logically follows from the premises. Both of the previous conclusions are valid. Given that the repair shop always checks for oil (foundational premise) and a given car has been to the repair shop (minor premise), it is valid to conclude that the car had oil (deductive conclusion). Given that all Lutherans vote Republican (foundational premise) and a specific person is Lutheran (minor premise), it is valid to conclude that the person will vote Republican (deductive conclusion).

Conversely, the truth of a conclusion is a function of the truth of the premises. If the premises are true, then a valid conclusion is also true. If the foundational or minor premise is false, then even a valid conclusion is untrue. The conclusion about the car having oil is both valid and true only if both premises are true. If it is not true that all repair shops check for oil, or the particular car has not been to a repair shop, then the conclusion is valid but untrue. The conclusion about the person voting Republican is valid and true only if the foundational premise and the minor premise are both true. If either is not, the conclusion is valid but not true.

Clear examples can provide students with an awareness of the fact that deductive conclusions can be valid but untrue. For example, the preceding example about the person voting Republican is valid but most certainly untrue. This is because the foundational premise is untrue. That is, it is not true that all Lutherans vote Republican; therefore, any conclusion based on this foundational premise would be false.

As practice in this type of analysis, it is useful to provide students with structurally valid deductive conclusions, some of which are true and some of which are not. For example, students might be provided with the following deductive conclusions.

1. **Foundational premise:** Men are not very sensitive.

   **Minor premise:** Bob is a man.

   **Deductive conclusion:** Therefore, Bob is not very sensitive.

2. **Foundational premise:** Puppies tend to chew on anything they can find.

   **Minor premise:** I'm getting a puppy.

   **Deductive conclusion:** My puppy will tend to chew on anything it can find.

Students would be asked to discuss which of these valid deductive conclusions is probably true and which is probably untrue. To this end, exercises like the one in figure 3.8 (page 58) are very useful.

Once students have an understanding of the nature of deductive conclusions, they can examine the validity and truth of conclusions they read or hear about. In general, statements that use the word *because* or similar terms are grounded in deductive conclusions. For example, consider the following statement: we need to stop Country X because it is developing weapons of mass destruction. The logic of this conclusion might be as follows:

**Directions:** Decide whether each deductive conclusion is more likely to be true or not true.

A.  Probably true

B.  Probably not true

1.  **Foundational premise:** Golden retrievers are friendly.

    **Minor premise:** My friend's dog is a golden retriever.

    **Deductive conclusion:** My friend's dog is friendly.

2.  **Foundational premise:** All military personnel have uniforms.

    **Minor premise:** I am a member of the military.

    **Deductive conclusion:** I have a uniform.

3.  **Foundational premise:** All girls like pink.

    **Minor premise:** Natalie is a girl.

    **Deductive conclusion:** Natalie likes pink.

4.  **Foundational premise:** Only rich people can afford Ferraris.

    **Minor premise:** Steve has a Ferrari.

    **Deductive conclusion:** Steve is rich.

5.  **Foundational premise:** Typical adult humans have 206 bones.

    **Minor premise:** Sally is a typical adult human.

    **Deductive conclusion:** Sally has 206 bones.

6.  **Foundational premise:** Elephants are the only mammals that cannot jump.

    **Minor premise:** Sam is a sloth.

    **Deductive conclusion:** Sam can jump.

7.  **Foundational premise:** Purchasing goods in Mexico requires the purchaser to bargain.

    **Minor premise:** I am in Mexico, and I want to buy something.

    **Deductive conclusion:** I will have to bargain.

8.  **Foundational premise:** The Japanese Bullet Train moves at three hundred kilometers per hour.

    **Minor premise:** I am riding the Bullet Train.

    **Deductive conclusion:** I am moving at three hundred kilometers per hour.

**Answers:** 1—A; 2—A; 3—B; 4—A; 5—A; 6—B; 7—B; 8—A

**Figure 3.8: Sample exercise on deductive conclusions.**

1.  All countries developing weapons of mass destruction must be stopped.

2.  Country X is developing weapons of mass destruction.

3.  Therefore, we need to stop Country X.

This conclusion is valid, but it might be argued that the foundational premise is untrue. Specifically, it is arguable whether all countries developing weapons of mass destruction must be stopped. It is this type of premise that will need to be articulated and debated in the 21st century.

Teachers can provide activities like the one in figure 3.9 to help students deconstruct *because* statements into their deductive structure.

It is very important to note that the foundational premises underlying a conclusion can be quite complex in nature. For example, consider again the following premises and resultant conclusion.

**Directions:** First, read the deductive conclusion. Then, identify the foundational and minor premises for each statement. Finally, determine if the conclusion is more likely to be true or not true, and explain why.

1. **Deductive conclusion:** Aja must know a lot about all of the candidates because she voted.

   **Foundational premise:** _____

   **Minor premise:** _____

   This conclusion is probably true/not true (circle one) because _____

2. **Deductive conclusion:** Molly's new boyfriend must be Derek because I saw them walking in the hall together.

   **Foundational premise:** _____

   **Minor premise:** _____

   This conclusion is probably true/not true (circle one) because _____

3. **Deductive conclusion:** Danny doesn't know anything about math because he was quiet the whole class.

   **Foundational premise:** _____

   **Minor premise:** _____

   This conclusion is probably true/not true (circle one) because _____

4. **Deductive conclusion:** Brendan is bound by the legal contract because he signed it.

   **Foundational premise:** _____

   **Minor premise:** _____

   This conclusion is probably true/not true (circle one) because _____

5. **Deductive conclusion:** This figure is an octagon because it has eight sides.

   **Foundational premise:** _____

   **Minor premise:** _____

   This conclusion is probably true/not true (circle one) because _____

6. **Deductive conclusion:** Maurice will be a veterinarian because his father is a veterinarian.

   **Foundational premise:** _____

   **Minor premise:** _____

   This conclusion is probably true/not true (circle one) because _____

### Answers

1. **Foundational premise:** People who vote know a lot about all the candidates.

   **Minor premise:** Aja voted.

   This conclusion is probably not true because the foundational premise is not true.

2. **Foundational premise:** People who walk together are boyfriend and girlfriend.

   **Minor premise:** Molly and Derek were walking together.

   This conclusion is probably not true because the foundational premise is not true.

3. **Foundational premise:** If you are quiet, it means you don't know anything about the subject being discussed.

   **Minor premise:** Danny was quiet during math class.

   This conclusion is probably not true because the foundational premise is not true.

**Figure 3.9: Sample exercise on analyzing deductive conclusions.** Continued on next page →

4. **Foundational premise:** Legal contracts become binding when signed.

   **Minor premise:** Brendan signed the legal contract.

   This conclusion is probably true because both the foundational and minor premises are true.

5. **Foundational premise:** Octagons are eight-sided figures.

   **Minor premise:** This figure has eight sides.

   This conclusion is probably true because both the foundational and minor premises are true.

6. **Foundational premise:** People always pursue the same profession as their fathers.

   **Minor premise:** Maurice's father is a veterinarian.

   This conclusion is probably not true because the foundational premise is not true.

1. All countries developing weapons of mass destruction must be stopped.

2. Country X is developing weapons of mass destruction.

3. Country X must be stopped.

Recall that these premises were derived from the statement "We need to stop Country X because it is developing weapons of mass destruction." If the preceding foundational and minor premises were in fact the basis for this statement, it would be fairly easy to challenge the truth of the foundational premise—why must all countries developing weapons of mass destruction be stopped? Will all of them inevitably attack the United States? However, quite frequently foundational principles are not as simple as "All countries that are developing weapons of mass destruction must be stopped." Rather, a person who concludes that Country X must be stopped might be operating from a complex foundational premise like the following: "All countries based on dictatorships that are antithetical to democratic forms of government and have weapons of mass destruction will eventually use those weapons against the United States."

It is probably safe to say that many people who make statements such as "Country X must be stopped because it is developing weapons of mass destruction" are operating from complex foundational premises like this one. It is through thoughtful, in-depth discussion that a teacher can help students identify the complex foundational premises that might render a controversial conclusion both valid and true. The following vignette depicts how a teacher might facilitate such a discussion.

Mr. Langdoc's class has been looking at deductive conclusions in literature. He asks his students to trace one important conclusion of any character in a book they are reading about censorship. Marcy discusses the conclusion of the main character's mother to punish her for stealing boxes of books from a library before they were set to be burned the next day.

Marcy says, "Her mother thought that everything the authority figures did was right, and since they were planning on burning those books, she thought burning them was the right thing to do. She punished Clara because Clara went against the authority."

> Mr. Langdoc says that he thinks Marcy has a point, but he would like to consider the matter further. "It might be a bit more complex than that. We know that her mother only left the small town she grew up in one time, and that trip resulted in the death of her brother. We know that she is very fearful of anything outside the town. The books contained many stories of many people from all around the world. Is it possible she was frightened of the ideas in the books?" he asks.
>
> Marcy says it is possible, and she adds, "She might have been generating conclusions from the premises that reading provides people with a wide array of experiences, and experiences make people change. She might have concluded that once people start changing, they end up leaving forever."

Visit **marzanoresearch.com/classroomstrategies** for a reproducible appendix with additional information about deductive conclusions.

## Presenting and Supporting Claims

Making and defending claims is at the heart of a well-functioning society, particularly one that is founded on democratic principles. Indeed, political dialogue is frequently based on asserting and defending claims.

### Claims

*Claims* are new ideas or assertions. A claim may simply present information, or it may suggest that a certain action is needed. For example, a student might claim that school lunches are unhealthy (informational claim) or that passing periods or recess breaks should be longer (a claim suggesting action is needed). To illustrate, consider the following claims.

- The Unites States should offer medical care for all its citizens.

- U.S. representatives should not be allowed to accept gifts or payment in exchange for voting a certain way on a particular issue.

- The U.S. government has a right to tax its citizens, but it must do so in a fair way.

The extent to which any of these claims are actually acted upon is commonly a function of how well they are explained and supported. Indeed, Oliver Wendell Holmes Jr. stated that "the ultimate good desired is better reached by free trade in ideas . . . the best test of truth is the power of the thought to get itself accepted in the competition of the market" (*Abrams v. United States*, 1919). Stated differently, a free marketplace of ideas is an environment where claims are put forth and supported. Therefore, instead of automatically accepting claims that they encounter (from friends, websites, adults, or themselves), students should be taught that it is legitimate to question claims. Questioning claims is often as simple as asking, "Why do you think that?"

Teachers should provide students with practice in identifying claims that are made in the media. The following vignette depicts how this might manifest.

> *Ms. Flowers's students have been bringing real-world examples of claims made in the media to class. Franco brings one he found in a men's health magazine: men who are weight lifters need more sleep than men who aren't. Sasha brings one she found in a research article published in a peer-reviewed journal—a very different source. The class discusses the prevalence of claims in society. They are everywhere, and though they sound like simple facts, they are not.*

Students should also understand that having their claims challenged is not insulting. Instead, they should be able to calmly and clearly defend their claims. To defend their claims and evaluate the claims of others, students will need to understand the structure of an argument, including grounds, backing, and qualifiers.

## Grounds

To be valid, a claim must have grounds. *Grounds* are the initial evidence for a claim. They are answers to the question, Why do you think your claim is true? Grounds typically identify where the evidence was found and what the evidence is. There are four types of grounds: (1) common knowledge, (2) expert opinion, (3) experimental evidence, and (4) factual information.

### Common Knowledge

*Common knowledge* is information that is generally acknowledged to be true and accurate. Common knowledge is information that can be looked up and verified in a number of sources; however, it does not have to be information that any ordinary person can immediately recall. In the following example, anyone can look up a state's flower in an almanac or online. Common knowledge is information for which a citation is not required. Examples include:

- The state flower of Montana is the bitterroot.

- The American Civil War began in 1861 and ended in 1865.

- China is a country in Asia.

### Expert Opinion

An *expert opinion* is a statement that an individual who is recognized as an expert in his or her field makes. In referring to expert opinions, one can use direct quotes or paraphrase the expert's statement.

When expert opinion is used, the expert should be a well-respected specialist in the particular field that the student is making a claim about. The following are examples of expert opinions.

- An opinion on the reality and severity of global warming that someone with a doctorate in climatology and years of field-research experience offers

- An opinion on the state of the economy that an official at the U.S. Federal Reserve offers

- An opinion on the quality of an acting performance that an experienced and successful director of plays on Broadway offers

### Experimental Evidence

*Experimental evidence* is information generated through professional scientific or student-conducted experiments that are designed to test a hypothesis. The following are examples of experimental evidence.

- A survey that reveals that 80 percent of students in a particular school are planning on going to college

- A report on the migration habits of whales from researchers who used GPS technology to track them for a full year

- An article that uses five years' worth of statistics from the Mayo Clinic and Johns Hopkins University to claim that rates of lung cancer are increasing

### Factual Information

*Factual information* is material with evidential support. The following are examples of factual information.

- Ladybugs help save plants by eating commonly found pests such as aphids (National Geographic, 2011).

- Forks were initially used as dining utensils in roughly the 7th century by courtiers in the Middle Eastern Muslim world (Facts About Forks, n.d.).

- Inside a sandstone mountain on Spitsbergen Island in Norway is a seed vault that can store 4.5 million different samples of seeds. It was created to safeguard against a national emergency and was ranked number six on *Time* magazine's list of best inventions of 2008 (The Global Seed Vault, n.d.).

Providing students with activities like the one in figure 3.10 will help them understand the various types of grounds.

---

**Directions:** For each of the following items, determine the type of grounds.

A. Common knowledge
B. Expert opinion
C. Experimental evidence
D. Factual information

1. An Environmental Protection Agency study that collected information on how much fuel is used in cities around the United States found that Los Angeles is the dirtiest city in the country.
2. The wrestling match between the middleweight class wrestlers in the 1912 Olympics lasted eleven hours.
3. Many doctors believe that smoking is one of the main causes of lung cancer.
4. The United States entered World War II after Japan bombed Pearl Harbor.
5. A survey taken of all a school's athletes indicated that over 90 percent of them worry about balancing sports with school.
6. A genetic mutation called delta 32 can delay the progression of HIV into AIDS or, when inherited from both parents, can render a person immune to the disease.
7. Dr. Seuss is the author of *The Cat in the Hat*.
8. An Apple executive speaking at an industry conference says that he thinks that desktop computers will soon be obsolete because of recent breakthroughs in mobile computing.

**Answers:** 1—C; 2—D; 3—B; 4—A; 5—C; 6—D; 7—A; 8—B

---

**Figure 3.10: Sample exercise on grounds.**

Students should be provided with practice identifying the different types of grounds. The following vignette illustrates how this might be done.

> *Mr. Usher's students have been studying the different kinds of grounds. He fills a hat with slips of paper. On each slip is an example of one of the various types of grounds. He asks his students to each draw a slip and then work together to categorize each example as* common knowledge, expert opinion, experimental evidence, *or* factual information. *Iris selects a slip and reads the following: "In studies by researchers at the University of Washington, children who ate breakfast performed better on academic testing than those who did not." She categorizes this as experimental evidence, noting that studies were conducted, and a conclusion was reached based on the outcome of those studies.*

## Backing

*Backing* is additional information about grounds that helps establish their validity. In some cases, it is simply a more in-depth discussion of the grounds. Students should understand that simply providing grounds may sometimes be insufficient to support a claim, and that additional information, explanation, or discussion may be necessary to support the validity of the grounds. This additional information is called backing.

The Internet contains a number of fake or spoof websites that make outrageous or ridiculous claims and then provide invalid grounds to defend them. Such sites may easily fool students who lack an understanding of backing. Phil Bradley (2006, 2010), an information specialist and author of several books about searching on the Internet, has compiled lists of many of these fake and spoof websites at www .philb.com/fakesites.htm (fake scientific and commercial sites) and www.philb.com/fakesites2.htm (fake social, historical, religious, political, travel and tourism, literary, academic and educational, and news sites). In his lists, Bradley provides information about the type, credibility, and child safeness of each website. Here are a few examples of these spoof websites.

- **Clones-R-Us (www.d-b.net/dti):** This website purports to be the world's "first and largest reproductive cloning provider." The site appears legitimate with frequently asked questions, price lists, order forms, testimonials, and a links page listing legitimate sites concerning cloning; however, a closer look (especially at the price list) reveals that it is a spoof.

- **Dog Island (www.thedogisland.com):** This website encourages dog owners to send their dogs to Dog Island, off the coast of Florida, where the dogs will enjoy a better life roaming free. The site claims that tax dollars support Dog Island, and it includes research about why the island is a better environment for dogs. They also feature Dog Island products (like T-shirts and leashes), information about visiting your dog on Dog Island, and fake press releases.

- **World Trade Organization (www.gatt.org):** This website looks similar to the World Trade Organization's real website (located at www.wto.org), but the content gives away that it is a spoof. Links lead to legitimate sites about the topics featured, so site visitors must think critically about the information being presented in order to identify the site as illegitimate.

To illustrate ways in which backing establishes the validity of grounds, consider the following examples.

- **Claim:** Federal laws are more effective at changing behavior than state laws.

  - **Grounds:** When states each make their own laws about an issue, individuals and businesses will simply move to the state where it is easiest for them to continue their current behavior and practices.

  - **Backing:** Historically, when state governments have different laws about the same issue, businesses tend to move to the states where the laws are most conducive to their practices. For example, before the federal government created legislation to regulate the credit-card industry nationwide, some states' credit-card laws were stricter than others. During this time, the majority of credit-card companies were located either in South Dakota or Delaware, both of which had more lenient usury laws (AuWerter, 2006).

- **Claim:** There has been a recent crime spree in our city.
  - **Grounds:** Police are receiving an average of seven to ten reports a week of burglaries.
  - **Backing:** One year ago, police received an average of three burglary reports a week.
  - **Backing:** Research indicates that an average of seven to ten reports a week is above average for a city of our size.

One useful strategy is to have students examine common claims made in the media and determine if both grounds and backing are provided for these claims. The following vignette depicts how this might be addressed in the classroom.

*Students in Ms. Ellerbrock's science class have each been given a claim and one or two grounds to support it. They have been tasked with providing valid backing for those grounds or proving the claim to be wrong based on backing that proves it invalid. Jesse was assigned the following claim: animals that find alternative ways to solve problems have an advantage over other animals. Research done in the Virgin Islands that showed that leatherback turtles use unique breathing patterns to dive deeper than other reptiles was provided as grounds for this claim. Jesse examined the grounds and provided the following as backing: most animals exhale air from their lungs before diving in order to avoid decompression sickness (known in humans as the bends) when they return to the surface. The leatherback, however, inhales deep breaths before diving and then ascends slowly to avoid decompression sickness. This allows it to dive more deeply than any other reptile, and it can stay submerged up to eighty-five minutes, thanks to its deep breaths. These alternative ways to avoid decompression sickness give the leatherback advantages over other animals; for example, it can access food resources that shallower-diving animals might not be able to reach.*

## Qualifiers

Exceptions to claims should be identified through *qualifiers*, which state the degree of certainty for the claim and exceptions. Qualifiers are important because not all arguments can be made with the same degree of certainty. An example of a claim with qualifiers is as follows.

- **Claim:** People should not smoke.

  - **Grounds:** Many medical organizations recommend that people not smoke in order to avoid getting lung cancer.

  - **Backing:** The American Association for Cancer Research, the American Lung Association, and the National Cancer Institute all advocate that people stop smoking to avoid getting cancer. In 1982, the Department of Health and Human Services identified cigarette smoking as the "major single cause of cancer mortality in the United States" (Centers for Disease Control and Prevention, 1982).

  - **Qualifier:** Just because you quit smoking doesn't mean you are guaranteed not to get lung cancer; it just means it is less likely.

  - **Qualifier:** There are cases of lung cancer that are not caused by smoking.

Again, a useful activity is to have students examine claims found in the media for qualifiers. The following vignette depicts how this might manifest itself in the classroom.

> *Mr. Lamphere's engineering class has been looking at the details of an internal investigation being conducted by a company responsible for a recent oil spill that caused a lot of environmental damage. The report claims eight specific causes for the initial explosion and subsequent failures to block off the well. The students look at the grounds for each specific claim to determine whether or not they believe it to be reasonable. They then look at the backing to determine more exactly how significant the consequences of each claim turned out to be. Finally, they look at the qualifiers in each claim. They notice that in each circumstance there exists a qualifier that this one failure alone could not have caused a spill of this magnitude—that it was the combination of all the mistakes and failures that led to the spill. "I'd like to discuss the overall effect of these qualifiers," Mr. Lamphere says.*
>
> *Shawn says he thinks that the qualifiers add up to the company essentially evading responsibility for the entire incident. "If no one thing or one person or even one branch of the company can be held responsible, then no one can really be held responsible," he says.*
>
> *Mr. Lamphere asks what possible consequences that evasion might have. "Well," Shawn answers, "it means that nothing has to change. No one will change if no one is at fault. It means that this kind of thing could easily happen again." Before moving on, they discuss how important qualifiers can be in an argument.*

## Students Generating and Defending Their Own Claims

Ultimately, students should be able to generate and defend their own claims, a skill that can easily be taught using groups. A teacher might give her students the assignment of working in groups to come up with a claim regarding the single best thing that would improve the academic achievement of the students attending the school. They must have at least two grounds and backing to support those grounds, and if any qualifiers apply they must state those as well.

One group might make the claim that hiring more teachers so that classes are smaller would improve the academic achievement of students more than any other single thing. To support their claim, two different students in the group might present the following grounds: "with smaller classes, teachers are more able to know their students and provide individual assistance" and "with smaller classes, teachers are more able to be inventive and energetic, and that improves student achievement."

The remaining members of the group might present the backing for each of these grounds: "We found three university studies that compared the achievement of students in classes with more than thirty students with the achievement of students in classes with fewer than twenty students. In each case, the students in the smaller classes had higher rates of achievement by between 20 and 45 percent" and "We also found a university study that found that teachers with fewer students were more confident and more relaxed and their students reported better relationships with their teachers and with their peers. The study also showed that the quality of teaching was superior in smaller classrooms."

The structure of a claim supported by grounds and backing fits neatly with the notion of a thesis statement followed by topic sentences, each of which is further supported. This is depicted in figure 3.11.

Claim (Thesis statement)
    Grounds 1 (Topic sentence 1)
        Backing 1a (Support 1a)
        Backing 1b (Support 1b)
        Backing 1c (Support 1c)
    Grounds 2 (Topic sentence 2)
        Backing 2a (Support 2a)
        Backing 2b (Support 2b)
        Backing 2c (Support 2c)

**Figure 3.11: Framework for claim with grounds and backing.**

## Primary Students Developing the Concept of a Claim

The idea that claims should be supported can be reinforced even with primary students. Of course, a teacher might not want to use terminology like *claim*, *grounds*, and *backing*. If this is the case, use simplified terminology. (See figure 3.12.)

**New idea:** _____
**Reason 1 why I think it is true:** _____
**What I actually observed:** _____
**Reason 2 why I think it is true:** _____
**What I actually observed:** _____

**Figure 3.12: Framework for new ideas.**

Marzano and Brown (2009) explained:

With students at the elementary level, the concept of grounds to support a claim can be addressed in a rudimentary but powerful manner. We recommend using the term "my new idea" to represent a claim. For example, after observing and talking about the behavior of classroom pets, students might be asked to think of "my new idea"—something about pets that they haven't thought of before. This is tantamount to a claim. To introduce the concept of grounds supporting claims, the teacher would simply ask students to explain why they think their new idea is true. (p. 121)

The concept of *my new idea* can then be expanded to include simplified versions of grounds and backing. Again, Marzano and Brown (2009) noted:

Again, at the elementary level, the idea of backing for grounds can be approached in a rudimentary fashion. Once students have stated their new idea (their claim) and presented the reasons why they think their new idea is true (their grounds), the teacher can introduce the concept that reasons must themselves be supported. Again, the terms *claims*, *grounds*, and *backing* do not have to be used (although we suggest that these terms be introduced as early as possible). To illustrate, students' new ideas and their reasons why their new ideas are true can be recorded on the board or on chart paper. One student might have written the following:

My new idea is that hamsters like to help each other. I think this is true because I saw them take turns running on the wheel and I saw them share the food dish.

Using this as an example, the teacher would ask the student to explain what she actually saw that looked like the hamsters were taking turns running on the wheel. The student might respond that she saw "one hamster would get on for a while, and then the other would try to get on and the one on the wheel would get off to make room." (p. 123)

In short, even very young students can be taught to offer claims along with grounds and backing. The following vignette depicts how a primary teacher might help students present their new ideas along with their reasons and what they actually observed.

*Ms. Redd's physical education class has been using the school's rock-climbing wall. After learning the basics, she asks them to come up with some claims about what the most important muscles are in terms of rock-climbing success. Wilson says he thinks that hand strength and abdominal strength are the most important because after he climbed, those muscles hurt the most. Dillie says she thinks arm and back strength are the most important because those muscles form a "cage" that holds the rest of your body on the wall.*

*After each student comes up with a claim and gives support for it, the class watches a video about rock climbing that features some of the best rock climbers in the world. The video shows the climbers climbing mountains and doing strength conditioning in the gym. It also shows interviews in which the climbers talk about their own strengths and weaknesses.*

*After watching the video and learning a few new techniques from a local climber who comes to class as a guest lecturer, Ms. Redd asks her students to revisit their original claims and determine how accurate they were based on what they learned from the video and the guest lecturer.*

## Summary

This chapter focused on analyzing and utilizing information in the 21st century. Perhaps the most obvious and dramatic way the 21st century differs from those previous is the way in which information is discovered or created and how it is distributed. Students cannot be successful critical thinkers if they cannot properly focus on what is important, navigate digital sources to find information that is relevant and credible, and identify and dismiss arguments that contain errors in thinking. They cannot be successful at considering, developing, and defending their own arguments if they cannot generate reasonable conclusions, present claims, and provide adequate support for those claims.

# Chapter 3: Comprehension Questions

1. How might you help students develop keywords to use when searching?

2. What are the defining features of errors of faulty logic, attack, weak reference, and misinformation?

3. Why is it important for students to evaluate both the validity and the truth of deductive conclusions?

4. How does the use of qualifiers facilitate students' work as they generate and defend claims?

# Chapter 4

# ADDRESSING COMPLEX PROBLEMS AND ISSUES

Addressing complex problems and issues is the second category of 21st century cognitive skills in our model. As described in chapter 1, this new century often presents more complex and frequent problems and issues than the 20th century presented to its citizens. In this chapter, we present three types of strategies that, taken together, constitute a useful set of tools that apply to a variety of complex problems and issues: (1) focus, (2) divergent and convergent thinking, and (3) a problem-solving protocol.

## Focus

Focus refers to an individual directing his or her attention to a specific issue over an extended period of time. As we saw in chapter 2, the concept of focus is antithetical to the popular notion of multitasking. Or, to state it differently, multitasking while trying to address complex problems and issues is a recipe for disaster.

### Exposing the Dangers of Multitasking

Given the popularity of multitasking, an important awareness to instill in students is that while multitasking may sometimes be necessary, there are times when it can be detrimental to learning and even dangerous to one's well-being. Perhaps the best way to broach this topic with students is to present anecdotes about the dangers of multitasking such as the following.

In 2002, in Germany, an air traffic controller was manning two different controller stations (not an uncommon occurrence); he was using two different frequencies to provide services to two different planes. He picked up the telephone to inform the airport of the arrival of one of the planes, but was unable to get through because of problems with the telephone system. He became preoccupied with trying to contact the airport and failed to notice that the two planes were on a collision course. He also failed to notice that the ground-based collision warning system was not working. The two planes collided in mid-air, and seventy-one people died (Loukopoulos, Dismukes, & Barshi, 2009).

Teachers might also introduce the dangers of multitasking by highlighting a few of the many studies that have demonstrated that cell phone use while driving is distracting and leads to a large number of traffic accidents. Note the following examples.

- A study by researchers at Carnegie Mellon showed that talking on a cell phone reduces the percent of brain activity associated with driving by 37 percent and that cell phone conversations are more distracting than simply conversing with a fellow passenger in the car (Just, Keller, & Cynkar, 2008).

- A study from the University of Kansas showed that the part of the brain that controls vision becomes less active when visually focusing on something while having a conversation. This illustrates that even when using a hands-free device, a cell phone conversation impairs a driver's ability to focus on the driving task (Atchley & Dressel, 2004).

- The National Highway Traffic Safety Administration (NHTSA) revealed that in 80 percent of car crashes drivers were distracted within three seconds of the crash (Klauer, Dingus, Neale, Sudweeks, & Ramsey, 2006).

On a humorous note, a cartoon like figure 4.1 can be used to provide an initial awareness of the dangers of multitasking.

The First Multi-Tasker

**Figure 4.1: Multitasking cartoon on prehistoric survival.**

Source: Used with permission from cartoonstock.com.

Once students understand the hazards of multitasking, they can be asked to identify situations during which multitasking is not harmful, situations for which multitasking is detrimental to performance, and situations in which multitasking is dangerous. To this end, students might be presented with a list of activities like the following and asked to organize them into three categories of *not harmful*, *detrimental*, and *dangerous*.

- Folding laundry and watching TV

- Listening to an audiobook in the car

- Babysitting a young child and cooking

- Writing an essay for a class while surfing the Internet for birthday presents

- Walking in an unfamiliar city while talking and reading a map

- Driving while talking on the phone

- Reading while you are on hold on the phone or waiting for an appointment

- Balancing a budget while watching television or talking

- Taking prescription medication while filling out a college application

- Creating something artistic like a poem or a painting while talking on the phone

Another option is to have students identify situations in their own lives that fall into these three categories. For example, a teacher might read the checklist and ask for a show of hands as to who has done something similar. Or, for more privacy, a teacher might provide a checklist and then ask students to volunteer funny or telling anecdotes from their own lives that demonstrate the harm of multitasking.

As mentioned previously, given the demands of the 21st century, there will be times when students will have to multitask. On these occasions, strategies can be employed to mitigate the potentially negative effects. Refer to the following strategies (Small & Vorgan, 2008).

- **List tasks, and give each a priority level:** For example, if Charity needs to do a number of things—make lunch for her little brother, study for a calculus exam, take photos for her photography class, chat online with a friend who recently moved far away, and complete an application for a summer job—she might list these activities in order of their priority:

  a. Make lunch for her brother (because he is going to be hungry very soon)

  b. Study for her calculus exam (because her brother will quietly eat lunch, and she will not be distracted)

  c. Complete an application for a summer job (because the application has an upcoming deadline)

  d. Take photos for her photography class (because by that point in the afternoon her mom will be home to watch her brother, and she can leave the house)

  e. Chat online with a friend (because her friend moved to a different time zone and won't be home until later in the evening)

- **Assign a reasonable amount of time to each task, and schedule time during the day for each one:** For example, because Charity's list begins with lunch, she would schedule her day in order of the events listed from the time of lunch. She might allot the most time to studying for calculus because that exam will be very difficult and the least amount of time to completing the job application because she knows she has most of it finished already.

- **Get enough sleep, and take power naps:** For example, if Evan has swimming practice for two hours before school, a long day of classes, and an hour of swimming after school, he might take a short nap after afternoon practice to refresh his body and mind before he begins homework. He should then make sure he gets to bed early that night so that he can repeat the same process the next day.

- **Alternate tasks (a large task can be broken into smaller bits that are then accomplished at different times—this is not multitasking):** For example, if Uri has a large amount of reading for language arts class, some math problems, and a social studies assignment to complete, he might begin by breaking his large amount of reading into four shorter sections. He might then read the first section, complete the math problems, read the second section, complete his social studies assignment, read the third section, and save the last section until after dinner.

- **When interrupted, pause for a moment to remember where you are on your current task, and note where you want to pick it up again:** For example, if interrupted while reading, John might skim the last few pages he has read before leaving the task and jot down a few sentences to remind himself of where he should pick up when he returns.

- **Reduce clutter:** For example, if Courtney works at a desk in her room, she may want to put books she is not using on a bookshelf, her phone and magazines on her nightstand, past homework assignments in a file folder, and photographs of the previous weekend in a drawer so as to keep her workspace clean and free of potential distractions.

- **Create a routine, and stick to it:** For example, if Colin normally studies until 8 p.m. on weekday nights, but discovers that his favorite television show is moving to 7 p.m. instead of 8, he might record the show and watch it according to his normal routine as opposed to altering his study routine at the risk of not completing his work.

- **Slow down:** This reduces errors that have to be fixed later. For example, when doing math problems, Sierra might want to take a little extra time and check her work to make sure each answer is right as opposed to completing the problems in a rush and moving on to something else.

The following vignette depicts how a teacher might introduce the dangers of multitasking.

> *Ms. Burns asks her students to read a passage silently. She tells them there will be a quiz when they finish. While they are reading, she turns on some music. Another teacher comes in the classroom, and the two of them have a conversation during which she puts on a clip of a film they are discussing. Her students are distracted, and, not surprisingly, they do poorly on the quiz. She gives them another reading passage the next day in class but allows them to read silently. This time their scores are much better, and she initiates a discussion about why they think that might be.*

## Enhancing Focus

Clearly, 21st century students should be wary of the potential pitfalls of multitasking. In addition to this awareness, 21st century students should understand and cultivate the ability to focus. As described at the beginning of this chapter, focus is the ability to direct all of one's attention to a specific issue over an extended period of time. At an extreme level, focus has been associated with the *flow experience*.

Csikszentmihalyi (1990) explains that people experience *flow* when they are totally absorbed in experiences that challenge and interest them. In a flow experience, a person loses track of time, forgets about other tasks or worries, and focuses solely on what he or she is doing. While not an everyday occurrence, nearly everyone has experienced flow at some point in time. Brophy (2004) summarized the eight characteristics of a flow experience:

1. The activity has clear goals and provides immediate feedback.

2. The activity provides frequent opportunities for making decisions.

3. Action and awareness merge; we feel single-mindedly focused.

4. All irrelevant stimuli (such as worries or other tasks) disappear.

5. We feel in control.

6. There is a loss of self-consciousness; there is a sense of growth, of being a part of something larger than oneself.

7. Time is perceived to pass more quickly.

8. The activity becomes worth doing only for its own sake.

Many artists report experiencing flow when they are working at their best. For example, Csikszentmihalyi's doctoral research focused on a group of male artists. These men "spent hour after hour each day painting or sculpting with great concentration. They obviously enjoyed their work immensely, and thought it was the most important thing in the world" (Csikszentmihalyi, 1988, p. 3). However, once these artists finished a painting, they lost all interest in it. Very few of them expected their works to make them rich or famous. This baffled Csikszentmihalyi. Why would these men work so intensely when it seemed that there was no reward? Csikszentmihalyi concluded that it was the pleasure of the flow experience that motivated them.

Athletes experience flow as well. Pelé, a soccer player from Brazil, described his flow experiences during soccer games: "[On those days I felt] a strange calmness I hadn't experienced in any of the other games. It was a type of euphoria; I felt I could run all day without tiring, that I could dribble through any of their teams or all of them, that I could almost pass through them physically. I felt I could not be hurt" (as cited in Eby, n.d.).

While flow might be considered an extreme example of focus, it can be presented to students as a behavior that enhances one's personal satisfaction. At a very basic level, this concept of focus might be presented to students to help them control and increase their attention. To this end, teachers can provide the guidelines in figure 4.2 to students.

---

• **Be conscious of a wandering mind, and refocus it on the task at hand:** For example, if you have noticed that you tend to walk around the room when your mind wanders, use that as a signal, and catch yourself after or just before you get up. In order to refocus your mind, review the last few things you looked at, and remind yourself of something more pleasurable, like getting to go out with your friends after studying.

---

**Figure 4.2: Guidelines to increase student attention.**                    Continued on next page →

- **Make an effort to pay attention:** For example, when meeting many new people, you might make an effort to listen and recall at least one thing associated with each new person and his or her name. That extra personalization helps you remember who you have met.
- **Minimize distractions by turning off gadgets and closing email programs and the like:** For example, when studying at the library, you might leave your phone at home and make up your mind not to check email or look at any websites until you have studied for three hours.
- **Take frequent breaks:** For example, when studying for a final exam you might get up once every forty-five minutes and take your dog on a short walk to the end of the block and back.

Visit **marzanoresearch.com/classroomstrategies** to download a reproducible of this figure.

Finally, a concrete process for enhancing focus like the one in figure 4.3 can be presented to students.

**Step 1:** Before you engage in a new activity—one that is challenging—stop and remind yourself that focus is the key to success. For example, before you sit down to do your chemistry homework, remind yourself that thinking about a friend's party will not help you study.

**Step 2:** If you don't feel strongly motivated to work on this new task:

- Change your inner dialogue to statements that make you want to work hard.
- Change your physical sensations to those that make you want to work hard.
- Change your mental pictures to those that make you want to work hard.

To a great extent, this second step is about creating a mental set that is conducive to success. Such a mental set involves inner dialogue, physical sensations, and mental images that are conducive to learning. For example, if you would rather be riding your bike than doing your chemistry homework, you might try reminding yourself of the poor grade you got on the last test and how bad it felt. Getting a good grade feels much better, so focus on that feeling rather than on not wanting to do the assignment.

**Step 3:** Next, set a specific goal for what you want to accomplish or have happen. By definition, when you are not attending to a specific goal, you are not focused. A concrete goal provides focus. For example, you might complete homework while keeping the goal of a good test grade or class grade in mind, while a golfer might make putts while keeping his or her target score in mind.

**Step 4:** As you are engaged in the activity:

- Keep reminding yourself about the goal.
- Keep monitoring your inner dialogue.
- Keep monitoring your physical sensations.
- Keep monitoring your mental pictures.

Focus requires constant monitoring. For example, if you find you are cold while doing homework, put on a sweatshirt so that your thoughts can remain on the task. If you begin to get frustrated because the assignment is difficult, mentally picture yourself doing well on the test and feeling good. Tell yourself you will get it; you just need to focus and keep trying.

**Step 5:** When you have completed the activity, ask yourself if you accomplished what you set out to do. If the answer is yes, acknowledge your success. If not, ask yourself what you did well and what you would do differently. Even if you have accomplished your goal, it is useful to ask these questions. Once you have answered them, put the incident behind you, and move on to your next challenge.

Visit **marzanoresearch.com/classroomstrategies** to download a reproducible of this figure.

**Figure 4.3: Process for enhancing focus.**

The last step in figure 4.3 is the self-evaluation component of the strategy. This component helps students learn from their actions. Once they have analyzed what they did and did not do well, students can put the experience in the past. Even if they failed, they have learned something. After step five has been completed, there is little need for students to continually review their actions, particularly if they have failed. Learning involves failure, and it does no good to dwell on failures once students have identified what they would do differently in the future. For example, if a student was not able to complete a homework assignment because she didn't understand the work well enough, she should see the teacher for assistance and then put the incident behind her. It would do no good for her to become upset and convinced she will fail the test.

The following vignette depicts a teacher guiding students through a strategy for enhancing focus.

> *Ms. Greene asks her students about what they really love to do, and she asks how they feel when they are doing it. Gene says, "I love to play chess. I love getting my head into a game and having the whole world disappear." Other students volunteer other responses, and then Ms. Greene asks how time passes when they are doing something they love. Everyone agrees that, generally speaking, it seems to go by quickly—it seems to flow. She asks Gene if he is planning on playing chess for a living, and he laughs. "No," he says. "I just really like to play." The students agree that when they do something they really like, they don't do it because they think it will make them rich or popular but simply for the experience. Ms. Greene then asks them how they feel when they are engaged in a task they are intimidated by or one they don't particularly like. Among other things, students note that they are easily distracted, that their mental self-talk becomes negative, and that time seems to go slowly. Some note that it helps them to complete homework when they are also chatting with friends online or downloading music. Ms. Greene introduces the notion that while these other tasks might appear to make the primary task at hand easier or more tolerable, they are also contributing to poor overall performance. She uses real-world examples of the dangers of multitasking in order to help them see that the real goal is not to distract themselves to get through a task, but rather to change how they perceive the task and learn to focus on it until it is complete. After they have become aware of the physical sensations and thought patterns associated with tasks they enjoy and tasks they do not enjoy but recognize as purposeful, she introduces a step-by-step process designed to help them minimize distractions and complete tasks they normally do not enjoy in a more productive way.*

## Fostering Powerful Dispositions

What we refer to here as focus is a precursor to developing dispositions that enhance one's ability to address complex problems and issues. David Perkins (1984, 1985, 1989) and Teresa Amabile (1983) referred to specific dispositions that can be exemplified for students and applied to a variety of situations. Here we consider three dispositions.

1.  **Engage intensely in tasks even when answers or solutions are not immediately apparent:** Few things of consequence are ever accomplished without prolonged periods of failure and even periods during which solutions seemed impossible. A powerful way to introduce this disposition is to provide students with examples such as the following.

    - Thomas Edison tried over six thousand different carbonized plant fibers in his attempt to invent the lightbulb.

    - Junot Díaz worked on one novel eight hours a day every day for five years. It wasn't working, and after a near nervous breakdown he wanted to give up. Sometime later, however, he pulled out his writing again, hoping for just one good thing in the seventy-five pages he had produced, but he found nothing. Still, he started again. Two years later, the book had promise, and three years after that it was finally finished. It won the Pulitzer Prize (Diaz, 2009).

    To help students practice this disposition, a math teacher might present his students with seemingly massive estimation challenges such as "How many people are eating lunch in the world right at this moment?" At first, the students might not think finding an answer is even possible, but with some time and focus they will see that they can find solutions and answers even when they thought they could not.

2.  **Push the limits of your knowledge and abilities:** This disposition involves working well beyond your comfort zone. To introduce this disposition, students can be presented with examples such as the following.

    - Orville and Wilbur Wright were not scientists. They had little formal training and worked largely on their own. Their success is attributed to working as a team and pushing one another to their limits. They argued about how to best design their flying machine, defending their positions passionately while still trying to see the other's point of view. They rejected prominent beliefs about the impossibility of flight because they believed in their own theories. They used all the knowledge and ability they had, but their commitment to pushing the limits is what ultimately led to their success.

    - Jack Chen has completed many marathons and, since 2009, four triathlons, including a half Ironman Triathlon. He is also blind, having lost his sight in a botched eye surgery when he was sixteen. He began by running marathons and eventually started training for triathlons—never mind that he had never learned to swim. The training pushes him past his limits each day; he gets up before 5 a.m. to ride his bike and run on the treadmill, and some days he gets up even earlier to swim laps at a pool in New York City before going to work (Knapp, 2010).

    To help students practice this disposition, a teacher might challenge her students to create a community service program that rivals one at another school. At first they might not think themselves capable of it, but upon seeing personal progress and the good they are capable of doing, students might be willing to focus and put forth more effort than before.

3.  **Generate, trust, and maintain your own standards of evaluation:** This third disposition is strongly related to creativity because creativity requires doing things

differently than what has been done in the past. This often requires one to persevere in the face of opposition. Examples like the following can be used to introduce this disposition to students.

- Warren Buffett is famous for his investments in profitable, high-quality companies. The key to Buffett's success is having unusually high standards for the companies in which he chooses to invest. He wants to be able to buy, "at a rational price, a part interest in an easily understandable business whose earnings are virtually certain to be materially higher, five, ten, and twenty years from now" (as cited in Hagstrom, 1999, p. 190). Buffett admits that there are only a few companies who can meet his exacting standards, but his experience has shown that having high standards is a good strategy for success.

- Roger Bannister, a track-and-field athlete, was the first person to run a mile in under four minutes. His personal standards of excellence drove him to achieve a feat that some doctors of his time deemed to be physically impossible. Interestingly enough, soon after Bannister broke the four-minute barrier in 1954, several other athletes replicated his accomplishment. By holding high personal standards, Roger Bannister achieved something many thought impossible (Larson & LaFasto, 1989).

To help students practice this disposition, a teacher might ask them to imagine an assignment as a finished product. When they begin actually working on it, the teacher might continually remind them about how they initially imagined the outcome. He might encourage them not to settle for less just because the work is hard.

These dispositions are each robust enough that they should probably be presented to students independently as the occasion arises. For example, if students have been given an assignment that requires them to develop and defend their own standards, they can be presented with the third disposition. The teacher might first explain the disposition and offer examples of people who have demonstrated it. Next, the teacher might describe times in his or her own life when she has used it. Finally, the teacher might help students understand how the disposition could be used in the task they are currently addressing.

## Divergent and Convergent Thinking

The ability to shift between divergent and convergent thinking is an invaluable tool when addressing complex problems. In this book, we use the following definitions for divergent and convergent thinking.

- **Divergent thinking:** The process of thinking without limitations or constraints while generating a wide variety of numerous and original ideas

- **Convergent thinking:** The process of using real-world limitations or constraints as filters and finding a single best solution or idea

Both divergent and convergent thinking are needed when addressing complex problems and issues. For example, assume that a student is faced with the following real-life problem.

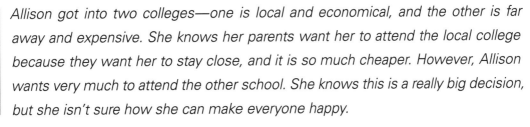

*Allison got into two colleges—one is local and economical, and the other is far away and expensive. She knows her parents want her to attend the local college because they want her to stay close, and it is so much cheaper. However, Allison wants very much to attend the other school. She knows this is a really big decision, but she isn't sure how she can make everyone happy.*

Given the obstacles (her parents wanting her to stay close and not being able to afford the expensive school), it might be best for Allison to think divergently at first. For example, she might think of all the following ideas, and, no matter how silly they seem, write them down:

- I could find out if I could get a government loan to cover the cost.

- I could promise my parents that I will work during college, get a good job after graduation, and pay them back the difference between the two schools.

- I could find out about scholarships from my school counselor.

- I could find out about government grants or fellowships.

- I could just go to the college my parents can afford.

- I could defer entrance for a year, live at home, and work full time to save for school.

- I could find out how much my advanced-placement credit is worth from high school. If it is enough, I might be able to enter as a sophomore and graduate in three years instead of four. That might make up the cost difference.

With a wide variety of options identified, Allison would shift to a more convergent way of thinking in order to select the course of action with the greatest chance of succeeding. For example, she might decide that going to the local college will be her last-resort choice—what she will do if nothing else pans out. She knows that the difference in cost between the two schools is significant, so telling her parents she will pay them back doesn't seem very realistic, either. Her parents might not have enough to let her borrow in the first place, and she can't realistically guarantee she could pay them back. She decides that finding out about scholarships, grants, and fellowships will be her first step; if she could find one of those, she wouldn't have to pay the money back. Next, she will investigate the option of loans, and she will see how much college credit she already has from advanced placement high school courses.

Gerard Puccio, Marie Mance, and Mary Murdock (2011) have a very robust model of divergent and convergent thinking that can be applied in a variety of situations. The model is illustrated in figure 4.4.

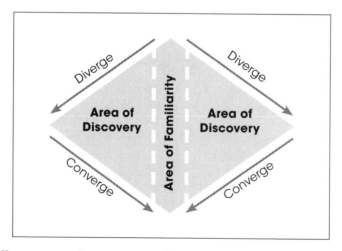

**Figure 4.4: Model for divergent and convergent thinking.**

Source: Puccio et al., 2011. Used with permission.

They also list the following principles for both divergent and convergent thinking (Puccio et al., 2011, p. 87). Divergent-thinking principles:

- "Defer judgment.

- Go for quantity.

- Make connections.

- Seek novelty."

Convergent-thinking principles:

- "Apply affirmative judgment.

- Keep novelty alive.

- Check your objectives.

- Stay focused."

This model is used in Puccio et al.'s (2011) creative problem-solving process, but they noted that it is the core of any effective thinking process for both individuals and groups. First, the diamond branches out during the divergent-thinking phase. The idea behind this is to stretch your thinking—to push your mind past what is merely familiar, and make new discoveries or gain new insight. When the diamond converges, that is, when it shifts away from moving outward in an exploratory manner and begins to focus on a central point, convergent thinking is used. During this phase, the most useful or promising options are selected through a process of synthesizing and evaluating information. By first using one kind of thinking and then the other, a dynamic balance is created, whereby inventive ideas can be formulated and adapted, if necessary, to create better solutions than could be generated using ordinary or common ideas (Puccio et al., 2011).

Puccio's guidelines for divergent and convergent thinking certainly interact as a set. However, they can also be presented and exemplified independently so that students have a firm grounding in each.

## Guidelines for Divergent Thinking

As described previously, divergent thinking is the process of discovering new ideas through sustained and original thinking. The following guidelines (Puccio et al., 2011) assist students in divergent thinking.

### *Defer Judgment*

Deferring judgment simply means delaying evaluation or judgment of an idea—suspending disbelief. Once evaluation enters our minds, ideas stop flowing. The use of deferred judgment can increase our awareness of and respect for possibilities, help us become more open and receptive to new things, expand the number of useable choices, and understand a new way of looking at things. Parnes and Meadow (1959) showed that when two groups were asked to generate ideas, the group that was asked to only write down its good ideas (essentially, evaluate as you go) only generated half as many ideas as the group that was told to write down every idea it had. For example, Max might hear Danni's suggestion that he run for student council and be tempted to disregard it right away because he has never run in any kind of election before. However, Max might defer judgment and tell Danni he will think about it. After he learns what student council members do and talks to his parents and teachers about the idea, he might decide that he would like to run after all.

It is important to provide students with concrete examples of deferring judgment. For example, in 1962, during the Cuban Missile Crisis, Robert F. Kennedy led an executive committee (ExComm) that was tasked with advising the president, John F. Kennedy, about possible solutions to the crisis. Although many of these advisors had strong opinions about what should be done, they all agreed to refrain from judging their options and instead focused on generating alternative solutions.

The following vignette depicts a teacher introducing the concept of deferring judgment.

> *Mr. Linetzky has noticed that his students can be quite judgmental about which ideas are good ones and which aren't. In order to help students generate more ideas and refrain from jumping to conclusions about them, he has them gather in small groups and tells them they are going to have a contest. Each group has two minutes to come up with as many ideas as possible for how to cross a river using no bridge and no floatation device of any kind. "It doesn't matter what the idea is, only that you write it down," he tells them. The contest and timed aspects of the exercise, he knows, will shift their focus and keep them from immediately judging any idea.*

### Go for Quantity

Going for quantity involves generating as many ideas as possible. As Linus Pauling noted, "The best way to have a good idea is to have a lot of ideas" (as cited in Puccio et al., 2011, p. 88). Making an effort to generate as many ideas as possible increases the probability that one of your ideas will be good. Parnes's (1961) research showed that the final third of a list of ideas usually reflects the most original thinking; the more ideas you generate, the more original your thinking becomes. For example, instead of generating a single list of ideas in one class period, a teacher might give students a little bit of time each day to meet with their classmates or group members and continue to generate ideas.

Concrete examples of going for quantity should be provided to students. For example, Georgia O'Keeffe, Pablo Picasso, Paul Cézanne, and Salvador Dali were all artists who went for quantity. Instead of trying to create a masterpiece every time they began, they created large bodies of work, from which a number of works emerged as masterpieces. Scientists and inventors work this way too. Thomas Edison, Alexander Graham Bell, and George Washington Carver are examples of scientists who explored and invented with a vast number of ideas, from which they were then able to harvest the best, most promising prototypes (Puccio et al., 2011).

The following vignette depicts a teacher using this strategy.

> *After giving his students two initial minutes to think of as many ideas as possible, Mr. Stafford allows more time for generating ideas. "Don't look at the ideas you've already written," he tells them. "Just keep coming up with more ideas." After a small group discussion, the whole class continues to generate ideas together. At the end of class, he tells his students to continue to think of ideas.*

### Make Connections

Making connections involves piggybacking off other work, comments, or ideas. As a group, people can work together and build off each other to create a larger and more original idea than they would have been able to alone. Making connections increases the likelihood of getting unusual responses or solutions, encourages flexible thinking, helps elaboration and extension of original ideas, and helps in the cross-fertilization of ideas. For example, if students come up with two or three ideas they really like, they might try finding a way to combine them instead of voting on which idea is best.

Students should be provided with examples of making connections. This happens in the real world on a daily basis. For example, a woman who is living with an elderly father might see how hard it is for him to get around and that his limited mobility gives him a sense of isolation. She might ask some of her neighbors to help out by visiting with him while she is gone. It might turn out that several families in the neighborhood are dealing with a similar circumstance. After meeting and discussing different schedules and ideas, the neighbors discover that they can help many of the family members with limited mobility feel less isolated, and they can also carpool and help one another with things like doing home repairs and filling out insurance forms. By talking with many different people and making connections, the woman found a superior solution to her problem and the problems of others in the neighborhood.

The following vignette depicts a teacher introducing this strategy.

> *Ms. Berringer's class is working in small groups, coming up with ideas for balancing a given budget. She has asked the students to write each idea on a sticky note and then place the notes on their desks. After brainstorming is over, she asks them to look at all the sticky notes they have written. She says, "Don't think about which are the best ideas right now. Instead, think about how to combine them. Do some go together? If you combine some of them, do they become stronger overall ideas?"*

### Seek Novelty

Seeking novelty involves intentionally looking for new interpretations of a concept. For example, if someone asked you to make a list of all the birds you could think of, you might not include Larry Bird, Senator Robert C. Byrd, or the Boeing 747 unless you were seeking novelty. For example, a teacher might encourage students to seek novelty by using a few different grab bags full of nouns and verbs and selecting two or three and reading them aloud. "What would happen if . . . ?" would be the only guide students would have to make connections between the randomly chosen words. For example, if a teacher challenged students to describe how they can clean their bedrooms using the nouns and verbs chosen at random (nouns *ski*, *safety pin*, and *slipper* and the verbs *pull* and *jump*), one student might provide the following example: "I would attach a dust cloth to the *ski* and use it to clean the high places like the ceiling fan. Then I would use the *safety pin* to help clean small spaces like between the tiles in the bathroom. I could put a wet cleaning cloth on the bottom of a *slipper* and clean the floor by *pulling* myself around the room using my bed and my desk. Then I could *jump* from my bed to the doorway to keep the floor from getting dirty."

Students should be provided with examples of seeking novelty. For example, the employees of Pacific Power & Light Company suffered numerous injuries climbing telephone poles in the winter to shake the ice off power lines. During a brainstorming session to resolve this issue, it was suggested (jokingly) that the company might train bears to climb the poles. An individual suggested placing honey pots atop the poles to attract the bears, and someone else postulated using helicopters to place the pots so high. At this point, an employee who had served as a nurse in Vietnam observed that the downdraft from a helicopter must surely be forceful enough to knock the ice off the power lines, and it turned out that flying helicopters over frozen power lines removed the ice far more efficiently (and safely) than the previous method (Puccio et al., 2011). Note that the previous example also includes making connections. Indeed, in many cases the process of divergent thinking employs more than one of these guidelines simultaneously.

The following vignette depicts a teacher introducing this strategy.

> *Ms. Baxter's students are in the process of divergent thinking. She asks them to keep in mind the novelty or originality of ideas as they are generated. Then she says, "When you have written all your ideas down, rank them on a scale of one to four—four being very novel and one being conventional. Think carefully about these novel ideas. Don't dismiss them just because they are unusual. In fact, really try to take these ideas seriously, and find a way for them to work."*

## Guidelines for Convergent Thinking

Puccio et al. (2011) noted that when engaging in convergent thinking, you must "turn your energy away from generating alternatives and focus on examining what has been created and on making decisions about how it will be used" (p. 96). The following guidelines assist students in convergent thinking.

### *Apply Affirmative Judgment*

Affirmative judgment sets the tone for the convergent-thinking process. This judgment must be positive and open-minded in order to sustain the progress made in divergent thinking. This mission of affirmative judgment is not to throw out bad ideas or to find fault. Rather, it is to carefully consider the positives and negatives of each idea. For example, when looking at the pool of ideas collected during the divergent-thinking phase, students might be encouraged to write a list of positives associated with each idea before moving on to discuss the negatives. When there are more than twenty ideas to evaluate, it might be more practical to have a two-step convergent process, that is, first have students select the ideas that intuitively seem the strongest and then have the students more closely evaluate the short list of ideas by looking at the positives and negatives.

A teacher might use the following examples to illustrate affirmative judgment: an artist selecting pieces to include in her show at a gallery does not individually point out the defects of each piece of work. Rather, she views them all with an eye to selecting the very best to be included in the show. In the same way, judges at a culinary competition, instead of finding fault with every dish, look for the few dishes that stand out from the crowd.

The following vignette depicts a teacher introducing this strategy.

> *Ms. Prem's class has recently finished a brainstorming session during which they came up with many ideas for solutions to a hypothetical prison-overcrowding problem she presented to them. The solutions range from instituting early parole to*

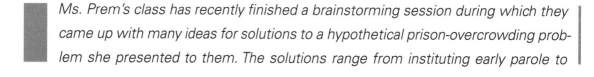

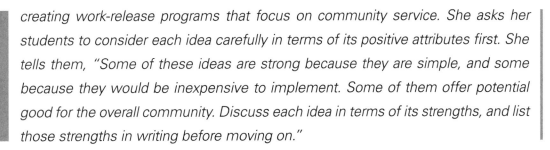

*creating work-release programs that focus on community service. She asks her students to consider each idea carefully in terms of its positive attributes first. She tells them, "Some of these ideas are strong because they are simple, and some because they would be inexpensive to implement. Some of them offer potential good for the overall community. Discuss each idea in terms of its strengths, and list those strengths in writing before moving on."*

### Keep Novelty Alive

Keeping the novelty alive means evaluating ideas with an open-minded curiosity about unexpected outcomes and an eye for protecting the novelty that led to the generation of the idea during the divergent-thinking phase. It is also about remaining open to the unexpected. For example, students might be encouraged to look at their most unusual or creative ideas and dedicate a bit more time to discussing them. Unusual ideas often have unexpected outcomes. Students might be encouraged to consider those outcomes and decide whether they would be more or less beneficial than other outcomes.

The following example can help a teacher introduce the guidelines for keeping novelty alive: Percy LeBaron Spencer was a scientist working with magnetron tubes. One day he found the chocolate bar in his pocket completely melted. This led him to investigate how magnetron tubes affected other substances that were susceptible to melting. Eventually, he concluded that the waves that the tubes emitted were able to heat many foods far faster than conventional ovens, and the microwave oven was born (Puccio et al., 2011).

The following vignette depicts a teacher introducing this strategy.

*Mr. Ludwick's class has generated a pool of ideas for solving a hypothetical dispute between a state and local government. Students have ranked their ideas according to which ones they believe are the most likely to solve the dispute in the best way possible for both sides. Mr. Ludwick asks his students to look again at some of the ideas they ranked as being the most novel and compare them with other ideas they have ranked as being among the best. "I'd like you to think a bit beyond this single dispute," he says. "What will happen not just in the short term but in the long term? Do you think some of these solutions might lead to further disputes down the road?"*

### Check Your Objectives

Checking your objectives involves being aware of what success looks like. For example, after discussing many ideas for how their school might help fight local poverty, students might choose one and then review that idea by checking it against their objectives. They might find that while the idea would work well, it would only work with a very specific portion of the population, and the objective was to help the greatest number in need as possible. Given this new insight, students might go back to their original pool of ideas and select another.

The teachers should provide concrete examples of checking objectives. For example, car engineers focused on the core goal of making it easier to enter and exit a minivan and were able to come up with the simple idea of adding a second sliding door (Puccio et al., 2011).

The following vignette depicts a teacher introducing this strategy.

> *Ms. Braja's art class has been working on designs for a mural they will paint on one of the largest walls in the school. They have three final designs, and Ms. Braja asks the students to look at each design and check it against their original objectives. "We wanted something that would be bright and bold in color so as to improve the appearance on the north side of the building. We wanted something that carried a positive message, and we wanted something that represented our school in some way. Look at these designs, and consider how well each meets these criteria."*
>
> *After doing this, her students realize that one of the designs does not actually say much about their school, and another, while it is positive and represents the school well, does not have the bright and bold appearance they wanted. They decide to go with the third design, which best meets all three criteria.*

### Stay Focused

Staying focused involves thoroughly investigating all alternatives to ensure the best one (as opposed to the easiest or most expedient) is chosen. Students must balance their intuition with critical analysis. For example, students might be encouraged to write down the idea they are immediately drawn to and discuss it. Next, they might carefully consider the idea that another student was drawn to. After discussing all immediate solutions, students might be encouraged to look at the other ideas in the pool to see if any of those might provide the best of the benefits discussed without the drawbacks also discussed.

The teacher can provide students with examples that illustrate the guideline of staying focused. For example, William Wordsworth spent forty years rewriting and revising his long poem "The Prelude," which many consider a masterpiece (Puccio et al., 2011).

The following vignette depicts a teacher introducing this strategy.

> *Mr. Calhoun's students have discussed a pool of ideas, and they have quickly decided that two of the ideas are the best. When Mr. Calhoun asks the students why they think so, Gerry says both ideas are the simplest and easiest to implement. "That doesn't mean they are the best ideas, though," Mr. Calhoun says. He asks them to take some time and look at some of the other ideas. When the students take the time to do so, they see that other ideas in the pool offer better long-term solutions, are more original, and would require fewer resources. Ultimately, they have an in-depth discussion about the pros and cons of many of the ideas; after thoroughly vetting them all, the students make a much more informed choice than they were initially prepared to make.*

These guidelines help both individuals and groups address complex problems and issues. Deferring judgment and affirming judgment both encourage creative thinking and discourage negative self-talk in the individual, and they create a positive atmosphere for students working in groups by discouraging immediate dismissal or judgment of any idea. This allows group members to feel confident in speaking up and sharing ideas. Students' ability to engage in effective problem solving will be greatly enhanced if teachers clearly identify the kind of thinking to be used for the task at hand, that is, either divergent or convergent thinking, and then ask them to follow the associated guidelines to enhance individual and team problem-solving efforts.

## The Practice of Divergent and Convergent Thinking

Once students have an understanding of the guidelines for divergent and convergent thinking, they should practice those guidelines using tasks provided in programs like Odyssey of the Mind. Odyssey of the Mind is an educational program that challenges students with problems that require divergent and convergent thinking. The problems fall into five main categories.

1. **Mechanical or vehicle:** Students use multiple power sources to build mechanical devices or vehicles that they drive or use to perform some task or overcome some obstacle.

2. **Classics:** Students use sources of classic art, architecture, or literature to complete unique tasks like writing an extra chapter to canonized books or in some way bringing a painting to life.

3. **Performance:** Students present performances that include required elements and are based on a specific theme. Previous themes have included animals expressing human emotions and objects going through metamorphosis.

4. **Structure:** Using balsa wood and glue, teams devise contraptions usually designed to hold as much weight as possible.

5. **Technical performance:** Combining two of the previous categories, this category requires students to create a performance based on a devised mechanism. Past challenges have included playing a new kind of musical instrument or writing a music score for a performed play.

You can visit www.odysseyofthemind.com for more information, and visit www.odysseyofthemind.com/curriculum.php for classroom activities.

Some similar programs are:

- **Destination ImagiNation (www.destinationimagination.org)**—This organization works domestically and internationally to encourage students to use creativity and teamwork to solve open-ended problems and compete in tournaments.

- **Creative Education Foundation (www.creativeeducationfoundation.org)**—This organization focuses specifically on solving local problems and connecting to the community.

- **International Center for Studies in Creativity (www.buffalostate.edu/creativity)**—This graduate program in creativity includes a page of freely available resources that has both video and print material useful for promoting creativity in the classroom.

## A Problem-Solving Protocol

Ultimately, problem-solving strategies must be applied to the messy and often ill-defined problems that are encountered in everyday life. To this end, the following eight-step process can be presented to students.

1.  **Determine whether you really have a problem:** Is the goal truly important to you, or is it something you can ignore? By definition, a problem occurs when an individual has a goal but some obstacle or constraint is an impediment to that goal. In some situations, the goal we are striving for is really not that important to us, and it might be just as easy to temporarily ignore it. For example, if your goal is to go to a movie tonight but you do not have enough money, you are involved in a problem situation—at least on the surface. You have a goal, and there is an obstacle in the way; however, going to a movie probably is not critically important. Consequently, involving yourself in a detailed and stressful process of trying to overcome the obstacle (lack of money) simply might not be worth it.

2.  **If you determine that you really do have a problem, take a moment to affirm the following positive beliefs:**

    *   There are probably a number of ways to solve it, and I will surely find one of them.

    *   Help is probably available if I look for it.

    *   I am perfectly capable of solving this problem.

    Using these statements, we become conscious of our inner dialogue. If we are thinking about all the reasons we cannot solve a problem, we will have little mental energy left with which to actually solve it.

3.  **Start talking to yourself about this problem:** Verbalizing your thoughts will help you think deliberately. Even though verbalizing thoughts might seem clumsy, it requires you to slow down and become aware of your thought patterns. This in itself will help your conclusion be more thoughtful.

4.  **Start identifying the obstacles in your way and possible solutions for overcoming each obstacle:** Solving a problem means finding a way around each obstacle. This step is at the heart of good problem solving. How you define the obstacle or the constraint that is the impediment to the goal affects everything else you do to solve the problem.

5.  **For each of the possible solutions you have identified, determine how likely it is to succeed:** Consider the resources each solution requires and how accessible they are to you. The most straightforward solutions might in fact be unreasonable because they require resources that are difficult to obtain.

6.  **Try out the solution you believe has the best chance of success and fits your comfort level for risk:** Some solutions might be likely to work but might also carry a high degree of risk; some solutions might be so risky that they are not worth trying. The risk should be determined in each circumstance so that you can determine if it fits within your tolerance. Excessive risk causes tension and will ultimately distract you.

7.  **If your solution does not work, clear your mind, go back to another solution you have identified, and try it out:** Another critical step in the problem-solving process is being willing to abandon a solution that is not working well. Sometimes this requires letting go of your original thinking about the problem and starting over.

8.  **If no solution can be found that works, revalue what you are trying to accomplish:** Look for a more basic goal that can be accomplished. This is a strategy good problem solvers use when no solution can be found—they identify another goal that *can* be reached. Revaluing turns unsolved problems into opportunities.

The preceding problem-solving process is a robust one that is designed for real problems students might encounter in their lives and, therefore, should be practiced on such problems. To this end, a teacher would provide opportunities for students to select problems of importance to them and apply the process. Students would be asked to record their reactions to the process in a journal and then periodically report in class. Since problems may be intensely personal, the teacher should be the only one who reads the journal and provides feedback to students. Additionally, the teacher should not require students to comment on the presented problem they are addressing when they report. To further facilitate the process of applying the problem-solving strategy and discussing its utility in class, the teacher should apply the strategy to a personal problem of her own at the time of the students' reports. The teacher, then, can begin discussions by sharing her insights and inviting students to share their thoughts. Candidness on the part of the teacher will elicit candidness among students.

The following vignette depicts the eight-step problem-solving process.

> Ms. Chance tells her students that her son really wants to sign up for swim team with a winter club. "He normally swims in the summer. It's a big time commitment, but in the summer that isn't a problem. In the winter, things are much busier. She asks her students, "Is there something that you have been struggling with that might or might not be a problem for you?" She gives them the day to meditate on the subject.
>
> In class the next day, she asks if anyone would like to share a problem they have identified. Franklin says he has been struggling with the coach on his soccer team. "I thought it was just something I had to deal with, but when I thought about it, I saw that it really is a problem," he says.
>
> After some class discussion on other students' problems, Ms. Chance says that she too has decided that her son participating in a winter swim team does pose a problem. She asks her students to think about their problems. "If your problem is one you really can't solve, think about where you could go for help. However, remember that most of you are capable of solving your problems."
>
> Two days later, Ms. Chance says, "Over the weekend I started to talk to myself about the problem with my son. I wasn't really sure what my possible solutions were or what my thinking was. I just started talking out loud about it. I discovered that I have been assuming there would be no one to help us. That is probably not true." She asks her students to do the same thing with their problems, and when they have, she invites them to discuss any insights.
>
> Franklin says, "I discovered that I have been blaming myself for my problem with my coach. I was thinking maybe I'm not a very good player; when I think about it,

*though, I know I am." After discussing other students' insights, Ms. Chance asks them to start thinking about their problems in more specific ways.*

*"What exactly are your obstacles? What exactly is in the way?"*

*A few days later she shares her own insights. She says, "There are two main obstacles: getting him to practice before school each morning and getting him home after school two nights a week. Traveling to meets on the weekends might be an obstacle as well." She asks her students to share their own insights.*

*Franklin says, "My major obstacle is that I'm not getting very much playing time because my coach won't put me in the game. I have to find some way to get my coach to let me play more, or I have to figure out why he isn't letting me play."*

*After some discussion with other students, Ms. Chance asks them to consider possible solutions to their problems and what resources they will need. "How available is each resource? Are some easier to obtain than others?" she asks.*

*She begins the next class discussion by saying, "I figured out that there are three main solutions to this problem: I could refuse to let him sign up, I could try to put together a car pool in which someone else drives him in the morning and I contribute by driving team members home at night, or I could try to get money together to buy my son his own car." She discusses the resources necessary for each solution and then opens up the discussion for her students.*

*Franklin and some others share their insights, and Ms. Chance assigns the next step—trying out the solution that is at a tolerable risk level and seems the most likely to work. After they do this, the class comes together for another discussion about the outcomes.*

## Summary

This chapter addressed the cognitive skill of solving complex problems and issues. Both here and in chapter 2, the dangers of multitasking while trying to complete unfamiliar, complex, or high-stakes tasks were discussed. Students are not wired differently than adults, and the prevalence of things like chatting online while completing homework and surfing the web, as well as the reduction in reflective time, are taking a toll on an entire generation. Students must learn to focus on one issue for a longer period of time if they are to see its complexity, synthesize new information with old, and gain new and relevant insights.

This chapter also included a discussion about divergent and convergent thinking. Divergent thinking comes at the beginning of a problem-solving process and involves opening the mind to many original ideas. It involves the suspension of judgment as well. During convergent thinking, all ideas are considered and evaluated in a way that preserves the novelty and creativity of the divergent-thinking phase. Finally, we discussed a process for addressing problems outside the academic sphere. As students grow into citizens of an increasingly diverse and complex society, the problems they will face (in both professional and social circles) will be unique and complex, and only students who are equipped to solve them will succeed.

# Chapter 4: Comprehension Questions

1. Why is it a good idea to discourage students from multitasking with tasks that require complex thought?

2. What role does self-evaluation play in the process of enhancing focus?

3. What is the underlying dynamic between convergent and divergent thinking?

4. What is the role of affirmative judgment when students are using convergent thinking?

# Chapter 5

# CREATING PATTERNS AND MENTAL MODELS

Creating patterns and mental models is our final category of cognitive skills important to the 21st century. In this chapter, we address six types of strategies for creating patterns and mental models: (1) identifying basic relationships between ideas, (2) creating graphic representations, (3) drawing and sketching, (4) generating mental images, (5) conducting thought experiments, and (6) performing mental rehearsal.

## Identifying Basic Relationships Between Ideas

Cognitive psychologists tell us that the basic unit of thought for human beings is the proposition (Kintsch, 1974). In basic terms, a *proposition* is what we would think of as a single clause. More technically and more accurately, a proposition is a statement that can be affirmed or denied. The following are examples of eight basic propositions:

1. Tina walks.

2. Tina is pretty.

3. Tina eats fruit.

4. Tina is in Denver.

5. Tina gave a toy to Julia.

6. Tina hit Lindsay with a pillow.

7. Tina runs fast.

8. Tina was overcome with sorrow.

Herbert Clark and Eve Clark (1977) have asserted that the preceding eight structures represent the basic forms of all propositions in any language. They are the basic units of thought expressed linguistically.

Thinking in propositions comes quite naturally. Again, human beings do not have to be taught to think in propositions as they are born with this disposition (Chomsky, 1965). However, thinking becomes more complex when propositions are strung together to form sets of related ideas. For example, consider the following sentence: Mary called Bill after he left for work, but he didn't get the call because his cell phone was off.

This one sentence contains four propositions: (1) Mary called Bill, (2) Bill left for work, (3) Bill didn't get the call, and (4) Bill's cell phone was off. While all four of these propositions are quite simple, it is the relationship between propositions that produces the network of ideas. Specifically, the relationship between the first and second proposition is one of time—the first proposition occurred after the second. The relationship between the third and the first proposition is one of contrast—Mary called him with the intent of talking to him; however (or in contrast), Bill did not receive the call. Finally, the relationship between the fourth and the third proposition is one of causality. The fourth proposition is the reason the third proposition occurred. The relationship between these four propositions might be diagrammed as depicted in figure 5.1. When we read the preceding sentence and understand it, we have translated or *parsed* the sentence into its basic propositions and their relationships.

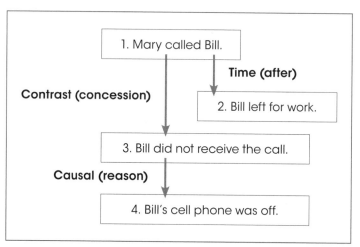

**Figure 5.1: Relationships between propositions.**

Just as we are hardwired to understand basic propositions, so too are we hardwired to understand the basic relationships between them. However, when complex sets of ideas are being examined, it is sometimes useful to engage students in a detailed analysis of the relationship between ideas. To this end, Robert Marzano, Patricia Hagerty, Sheila Valencia, and Philip DiStefano (1987), identified four types of basic relationships that can be used to help students engage in detailed semantic analysis.

1. **Addition:** One idea is similar to or adds to another idea in some way. (He is tall, and he is handsome.)

2. **Contrast:** One statement does not go with or subtracts from another statement in some way. (He is tall, but he is not a good basketball player.)

3. **Time:** One statement is stated as occurring before, during, or after another statement. (She left before he left.)

4. **Cause:** One statement is the cause or condition for another statement. (He went home because she went home.)

Figure 5.2 illustrates these relationships and identifies various signal words that signify these relationships.

Each type of basic relationship can be subdivided into more specific types of relationships.

**Subtypes**

*Addition*

1. **Equality:** He is tall, **and** he is handsome.
2. **Restatement:** I am tired. **In fact**, I am exhausted.
3. **Example:** He does many things well. **For example**, he is excellent at cards.
4. **Summation:** He does many things well. He cooks. He sews. **In all**, he is an excellent homemaker.

*Contrast*

1. **Antithesis:** I will be there, **but** I won't be happy.
2. **Alternative: Either** it will rain **or** it will snow.
3. **Comparison:** Bill is tall. In **comparison**, his brother is short.
4. **Concession:** I don't like violence. **Nonetheless**, I'll meet you at the fights.

*Cause*

1. **Direct cause:** He won the race **by** maintaining his concentration.
2. **Result:** Bill went home. **Consequently**, the party ended.
3. **Reason:** He went to the store **because** he needed food.
4. **Inference:** Mary is going on a long trip. **In that case**, she should plan well.
5. **Condition: Unless** you stop, I will leave.

*Time*

1. **Subsequent action:** They went to the game. **Afterward**, they went to the dance.
2. **Prior action:** They went to the game **before** they went to the dance.
3. **Concurrent action:** Bill thought about Mary **while** Mary thought about Bill.

The following are signal words associated with each specific relationship.

**Signal Words**

*Addition*

1. **Equality:** and, moreover, equally, too, besides, furthermore, what is more, likewise, similarly, as well, in addition, besides, at the same time
2. **Restatement:** indeed, actually, in actuality, in fact, namely, that is, that is to say, another way of saying this
3. **Example:** for example, first, second, third, one, two, three, for a start, to begin with, next, then, finally, last but not least, for one thing, for another thing, another example would be
4. **Summation:** altogether, overall, then, thus, in all, therefore, all in all, in conclusion, in sum, in a word, in brief, briefly, in short, to sum up, to summarize

*Contrast*

1. **Antithesis:** but, yet, or rather, what is better, what is worse, contrariwise, conversely, oppositely, on the contrary, else, otherwise, on the other hand
2. **Alternative:** alternatively, either . . . or, neither . . . nor, rather than, sooner than
3. **Comparison:** in comparison, in contrast, like
4. **Concession:** however, anyhow, besides, else, nevertheless, nonetheless, only, still, though, in any case, in any event, for all that, in spite of that, all the same, anyway, though, at any rate, regardless of this

**Figure 5.2: Subtypes and signal words for basic relationships.**          Continued on next page →

*Cause*

1. **Direct cause:** by, due to, owing to, through
2. **Result:** consequently, hence, now, so, therefore, thus, as a consequence, for all that, as a result, whereupon, accordingly, the result was, this is the reason
3. **Reason:** because, because of, in that, so that, since, so on account of, for the fact that
4. **Inference:** else, otherwise, in that case, then
5. **Condition:** now that, providing that, supposing that, considering that, granted that, admitting that, assuming that, presuming that, seeing that, unless . . . then, as long as, in so far as, if, where . . . there, when . . . then, no sooner

*Time*

1. **Subsequent action:** afterward, next, since, then, after that, later, in the end, shortly, subsequently, so far, as yet, before, until, finally
2. **Prior action:** after, earlier, initially, in the beginning, originally, at first, previously, beforehand, formerly, before that, before now, until then, up to now, by now, by then
3. **Concurrent action:** simultaneously, while, meanwhile, meantime, at this point, at the same time

Marzano et al. (1987) recommend the symbols in table 5.1 for the four basic relationships as students diagram relationships between ideas.

## Table 5.1: Symbols for Propositional Relationships

| Relationship | Symbol |
|--------------|--------|
| Addition | = |
| Contrast | ≠ |
| Time | → |
| Cause | ⇒ |

Addition is indicated by the equal sign. Contrast is signaled by the not equal sign, time by an arrow with a single line, and cause by an arrow with a double line. As students read information or listen to information presented orally, they can diagram the basic relationships.

It is important to note that diagramming basic relationships between ideas does not have to follow a sentence-by-sentence format. For example, assume that elementary students are watching a video about Martin Luther King Jr. After watching the video, one student might focus on an addition relationship and diagram it as follows:

He was a minister. = He was a social activist.

Another student might focus on an important causal relationship and diagram it as follows:

He promoted nonviolent protest ⇒ He was awarded the 1964
to achieve civil rights.        Nobel Peace Prize.

When discussing relationship diagrams with students, the teacher can ask them to identify any of the signal words that provided clues regarding the relationship they identified.

With secondary students, relationship diagrams can include a discussion of the subtypes of basic relationships. For example, instead of a student simply noticing that a causal relationship exists, the student might also identify whether the relationship is direct cause, result, reason, inference, or condition as specified in figure 5.2 (page 95). The following vignette depicts how relationship diagramming can be used with secondary students.

*Mr. Carrington's students are diagramming interesting relationships on the topic of famous inventions. Bart writes about Alexander Fleming and then uses key words to identify relationships: "Fleming knew there was a need for medicine that would prevent infection without exacerbating wounds, so he tried to find it (reason). He used Petri dishes to culture bacteria for his experiments, and after he neglected to wash them, mold began to grow (subsequent action). As it did, it killed the bacteria, and consequently, Fleming discovered the antibiotic properties of penicillin (result). He wrote about his discovery in 1928, but no one funded or supported his research (antithesis). However, by the late 1930s, penicillin was being produced and used in mass quantities (concession). It was a good thing, too, because it saved the lives of many soldiers during WWII (reason). Since Fleming won the Nobel Prize for being messy, I guess it's good to be a slob sometimes (inference)!"*

## Creating Graphic Representations

A very powerful and popular way to help students generate patterns and mental models is to use graphic representations, also known as graphic organizers. Graphic organizers allow students to see and make crucial connections between ideas.

Moving beyond standard graphic organizers, Thinking Maps (Hyerle, 2009) have become quite popular in schools throughout the United States and abroad. Thinking Maps are eight distinct visual patterns linked to specific thought processes. When implemented throughout a school, Thinking Maps create a common visual language for teaching and learning used by all teachers and students. As an example, we highlight two of the Thinking Maps. Visit www.thinkingmaps.com for more information about implementing Thinking Maps.

### Circle Map

A circle map is used for defining in context. For example, before viewing a controversial painting, students might fill in a circle map to show the artistic context in which the artist worked and the political frame of reference he used. After viewing the painting, students could use another circle map to fill in the context in which they viewed the art, as well as their frame of reference for interpreting it. See figure 5.3 (page 98) for an example.

Each shape represents how mental parameters are created when people try to define things. The frame of reference around the circle map provides the opportunity for asking questions such as: "What is your cultural background? What are your life experiences, and how do your religious, social, political, experiential, and emotional points of view affect how you make sense of something in context?" The circle map and frame of reference are used to help students see the importance of context and its effect on how we understand things.

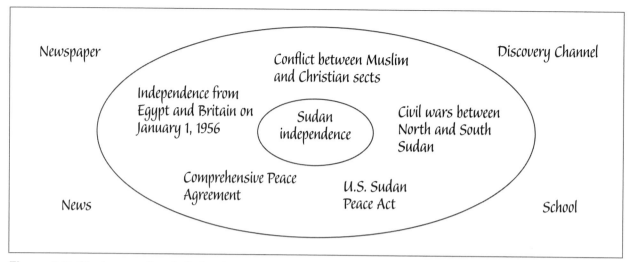

**Figure 5.3: Circle map for defining in context.**

Source: Used with permission. Thinking Maps® is a registered trademark of Thinking Maps, Inc.

## Bubble Map

Bubble maps are used for describing with adjectives. They offer a flexible way to explore the various attributes of something in more depth. The frame of reference can be used with a bubble map to cite textual evidence to validate the descriptors and further show the influences on a student's thinking. See figure 5.4 for an example.

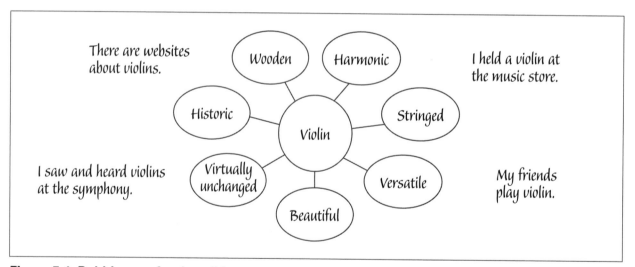

**Figure 5.4: Bubble map for describing.**

Source: Used with permission. Thinking Maps® is a registered trademark of Thinking Maps, Inc.

## Problem and Solution Map

The problem and solution map, as well as the others presented in this section, can be used to augment Thinking Maps. The problem and solution map helps students think through the basic structure of a problem. Problem solving involves the following elements:

1.  Identifying the problem and desired outcome (or goal)

2.  Identifying obstacles and constraints to solving the problem

3.  Generating multiple solutions

4.  Picking the best solution and trying it out

5.  Reflecting on the outcome

If the chosen solution fails to solve the problem or achieve the goal, students should return to step four and try an alternative solution.

The problem and solution map is effective in guiding students through the problem-solving process and documents their thinking as they identify goals, obstacles or constraints, and possible solutions. If the first solution fails to achieve the goal, this record can be useful for selecting alternative solutions.

For example, if a group of students wanted to raise money for a charitable cause, their teacher might guide them through the problem-solving process using a problem and solution map like that shown in figure 5.5.

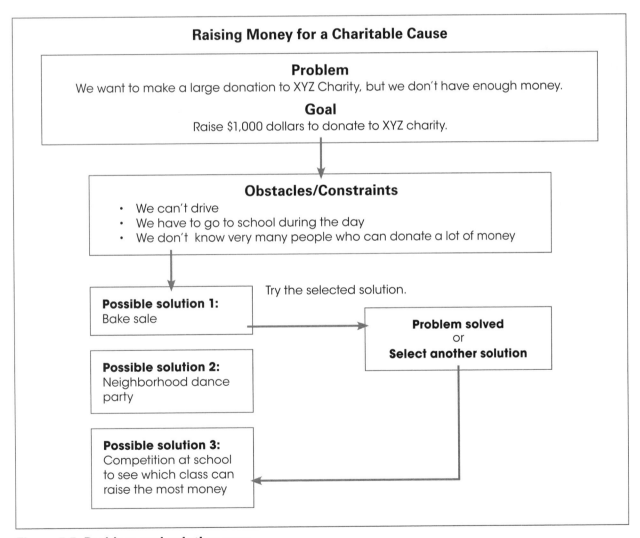

**Figure 5.5: Problem and solution map.**

## Experimental Inquiry Map

The experimental inquiry map helps students think through the basic structures of generating and testing hypotheses. Many times, when students think of conducting experiments, they expect to be given instructions about materials to gather and steps to follow. Experimental inquiry, however, begins when students observe something that they are unable to explain and are interested in investigating further. Experimental inquiry involves the following elements:

1. Observing and describing something that has occurred

2. Attempting to explain why it occurred, using background knowledge, theories, or rules

3. Making a prediction based on the explanation

4. Designing and conducting an experiment to test the prediction

5. Evaluating the results

If the results do not support the explanation and prediction generated in steps two and three, students should revise their explanations and predictions or conduct another experiment.

To illustrate the use of the experimental inquiry map, assume that a student had observed that when he gets ice out of the freezer with wet hands, it sometimes sticks to his skin. He knows that frozen water has free electrons that seek to bond with free hydrogen atoms, so he explains this phenomenon by saying that the water in the ice is forming a bond with the water on his hands. He predicts that this bond is unique to wet skin and will not occur between ice and a wet, nonskin material, like a paper towel. He designs an experiment to test his prediction: first he puts his wet hands into a bucket of ice, and then a wet paper towel into the bucket of ice. He finds that, contrary to his prediction, the ice sticks to both. He revises his prediction to reflect the results of the experiment and designs another experiment to test his new prediction. Figure 5.6 depicts how a student might use the experimental inquiry map to plot this investigation.

## Decision-Making Map

The decision-making map helps students think through the process of making a decision. To use the decision-making process, students need to understand alternatives and criteria. Alternatives are the different options that one is deciding between. Criteria are the things that are important to the person making the decision. Stated simply, the decision-making process involves the following steps:

1. Describing the decision to be made

2. Generating a list of alternatives

3. Selecting criteria that will influence the decision

4. Evaluating the alternatives in light of the criteria

5. Making the decision

If a clear choice does not emerge, the student may choose to narrow the list of alternatives or add one or more additional criteria.

For example, if a student has been asked to select the most influential historical figure of the 20th century, he would generate a list of alternatives, which might include Albert Einstein, Mohandas

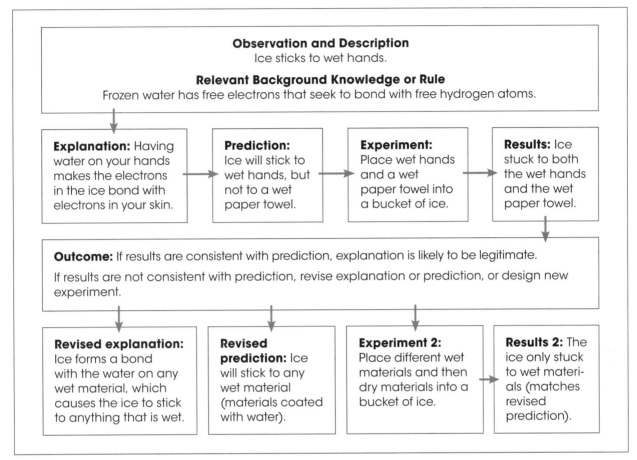

**Observation and Description**
Ice sticks to wet hands.

**Relevant Background Knowledge or Rule**
Frozen water has free electrons that seek to bond with free hydrogen atoms.

**Explanation:** Having water on your hands makes the electrons in the ice bond with electrons in your skin.

**Prediction:** Ice will stick to wet hands, but not to a wet paper towel.

**Experiment:** Place wet hands and a wet paper towel into a bucket of ice.

**Results:** Ice stuck to both the wet hands and the wet paper towel.

**Outcome:** If results are consistent with prediction, explanation is likely to be legitimate.

If results are not consistent with prediction, revise explanation or prediction, or design new experiment.

**Revised explanation:** Ice forms a bond with the water on any wet material, which causes the ice to stick to anything that is wet.

**Revised prediction:** Ice will stick to any wet material (materials coated with water).

**Experiment 2:** Place different wet materials and then dry materials into a bucket of ice.

**Results 2:** The ice only stuck to wet materials (matches revised prediction).

**Figure 5.6: Experimental inquiry map.**

Gandhi, Franklin D. Roosevelt, Sandra Day O'Connor, Bill Gates, Nelson Mandela, Mother Teresa, and Winston Churchill. Criteria that would influence the decision might include: *advocated for civil rights, contributed to the knowledge of the world, brought about peace, affected a large number of people,* and *made contributions that have lasting effects.* To evaluate the alternatives in light of the criteria, the student might use a decision-making map like the one in figure 5.7 (page 102).

To use the map, the student would assign each alternative a rating for each criterion and then add the ratings together to create a total for each alternative. Students should understand that the decision-making map is a tool to help them represent the reasoning behind their decisions. They are not bound by the results that are generated on the map. If they disagree with the top choice as shown on the decision-making map, they may choose to repeat the process with more or different criteria, or fewer alternatives.

As an extension, students can also rate the importance of each criterion using the following scale:

0. Not important

1. Slightly important

2. Moderately important

3. Highly important

| Criteria | Alternatives | | | | | | | |
|---|---|---|---|---|---|---|---|---|
| 0 — Does not meet the criterion at all<br>1 — Meets criterion slightly<br>2 — Meets criterion<br>3 — Strongly meets criterion | Albert Einstein | Mohandas Gandhi | Franklin D. Roosevelt | Sandra Day O'Connor | Bill Gates | Nelson Mandela | Mother Teresa | Winston Churchill |
| Advocated for civil rights | 1 | 3 | 1 | 2 | 1 | 3 | 2 | 2 |
| Contributed to the knowledge of the world | 3 | 2 | 2 | 2 | 3 | 2 | 1 | 2 |
| Brought about peace | 1 | 3 | 3 | 1 | 1 | 3 | 2 | 3 |
| Affected a large number of people | 3 | 3 | 3 | 2 | 3 | 2 | 3 | 3 |
| Made contributions that have lasting effects | 3 | 3 | 3 | 2 | 3 | 3 | 3 | 2 |
| Total | 11 | 14 | 12 | 9 | 11 | 13 | 11 | 12 |

**Figure 5.7: Sample decision-making map.**

To illustrate, a particular student might rate the first criterion of *advocated for civil rights* as 3—highly important. Examining figure 5.7, we see that Albert Einstein received a rating of 1 on this criterion. To obtain the quality points for Einstein on this criterion, the student would multiply the score for meeting the criterion (in this case a 1) by the importance score for the criterion (in this case a 3). Einstein's quality points for this criterion would be 3 (that is, 1 × 3). However, Mohandas Gandhi would have 9 quality points for this criterion (that is, 3 × 3). In the scenario, the student then sums the quality points for each alternative, and considers the alternative with the highest total of quality points the best selection.

## Inventing Map

The inventing map helps students think through the process of creating a new product. The inventing process involves the following:

1. Identifying a specific need or desired improvement

2. Describing standards that the invention should meet

3. Creating a list of ideas likely to achieve the standards

4. Building a prototype of the idea most likely to work

5. Testing the invention

If the invention does not work or does not sufficiently meet the standards, the student would continue to cycle between the standards and prototype creation, testing until he or she is satisfied with the product.

For example, a student might want to invent something that would allow her to take her dog, Skipper, in the car without having him shed all over the seats. Her standards for this invention might include *keeps dog hair off the seats*, *comfortable for Skipper*, and *easy to use*. The student would then generate possible ideas of how to satisfy the need and meet the standards. Figure 5.8 depicts three possible ideas that the student might brainstorm.

The student would then select the idea that most nearly meets the standards. In this case, the second idea seems to be most likely to meet all three standards, and so the student would create a prototype, perhaps recruiting the help of someone with sewing skills to design and sew a hair-capturing, lightweight dog suit that fastens with Velcro around the dog's neck and down his back. After testing this prototype on her dog during a car ride, the student would evaluate its effectiveness at meeting her standards. If her invention did not meet the standards, she could then either revise her prototype to improve its effectiveness or create a new prototype from one of her other possible ideas.

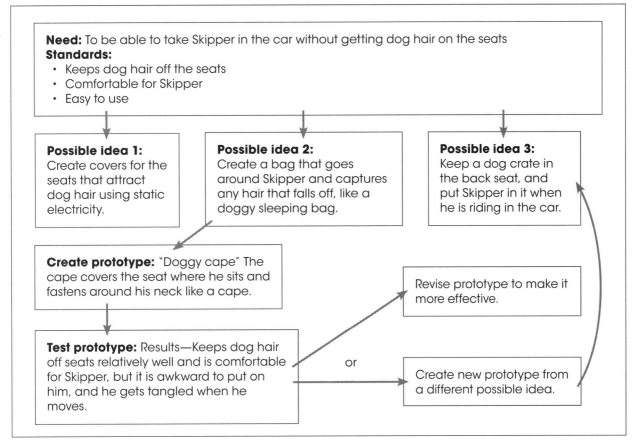

**Figure 5.8: Sample inventing map.**

The following vignette depicts the use of graphic representations.

*Mr. Hart's class is studying the process of a court trial. He has provided his students with the details of the trial of the Chicago Seven and tasked them with deciding how just or unjust the verdict in each case was. To do this, students begin with a bubble map. They place each defendant's name in a bubble in the center, and in the surrounding bubbles, students write which crimes each defendant can legitimately be found guilty of. They then connect the defendant's bubbles to the crime bubbles so they can compare and contrast the defendants. This helps them figure out whether all defendants were guilty of the same crimes or whether some were guiltier than others. They then make a decision-making matrix, listing all the crimes in the criteria column and the defendants in the alternatives column. They then rate each defendant on each crime according to whether or not he committed the crime and how atrocious it was. After using both graphic representations, the students can examine each defendant's case and assess whether the verdict and sentence were just or unjust.*

## Drawing and Sketching

Identifying basic relationships and creating graphic organizers rely heavily on language accompanied by arrows, lines, boxes, ovals, and circles. In this section we address techniques for generating mental models that employ drawing and sketching. This is important for dual processing as discussed in chapter 2 (page 21). Students process information more deeply when they engage in both linguistic and nonlinguistic ways. This technique is also important for students who struggle with writing.

### Pictographs

Pictographs are like graphic representations except that they use stick figures and symbols to represent ideas and content. Virtually every graphic representation discussed previously can be drawn as a pictograph. To illustrate, consider the relationship diagram in figure 5.9 for the following sentences: I was walking down the street when my brother drove by in a brand new car. I was astonished because I didn't know that he had a new car.

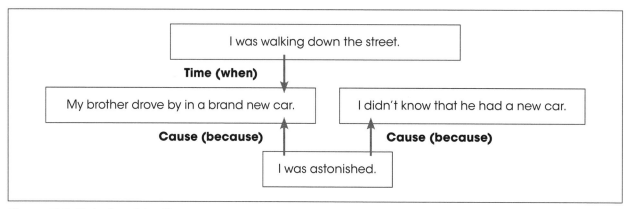

**Figure 5.9: Relationship diagram.**

This same diagram can be created using stick figures and relationship symbols as shown in figure 5.10.

**Figure 5.10: Pictograph for relationship diagram.**

Graphic organizers can also be drawn as pictographs. Consider the context map in figure 5.11.

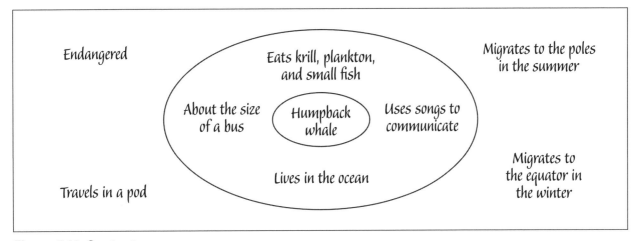

**Figure 5.11: Context map.**

By replacing the text with pictures, the organizer is transformed into a pictograph, as shown in figure 5.12.

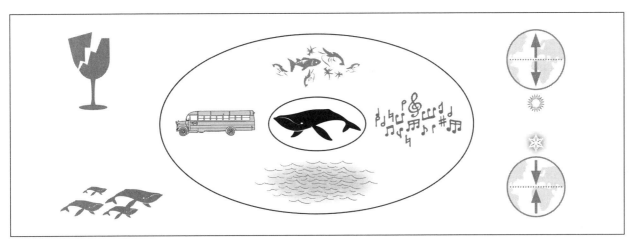

**Figure 5.12: Pictograph for context map.**

## Sketching

Architects and engineers use sketching to explore ideas and stimulate the creative process. Sketching can also be used to generate ideas and to support mental work during complex academic tasks. To illustrate, consider the following examples.

In language arts, sketching is very useful when fleshing out an idea for a composition. A student who is composing a poem might sketch a number of drawings based on the theme of the poem. For example, a student who wanted to write a poem on the theme of silence might begin by sketching a night scene. He might also sketch a scene from a funeral or an awkward moment with a friend. As he adds details to his sketches, he would be able to explore more complex meanings of silence, perhaps coming to the realization that although silence technically refers to an absence of sound, the concept of silence is quite complex and rich with connotation.

In math, sketching can help students conceptualize the multiplication of fractions. A student who is having trouble understanding the algorithm for multiplying fractions might use a sketch to visualize the operation taking place. For the equation ⅛ × ½, he might begin by sketching a half circle and then dividing it into eight equal parts. He would fill in one of those eight sections, and he would then sketch the other half of the circle, which is also divided into eight equal parts. By counting all the parts and observing that one is shaded, he would reach the answer of ¹⁄₁₆.

In science, a student could explore the inner workings of a nuclear reactor by sketching the various structures involved and tracking the flow of water and energy. By sketching the reactor core, the paths that water and steam take in and out of the reactor, and the role of turbines and generators in the process of creating energy, she would support her mental grasp of the complex processes at work.

In social studies, a student designing a community park might create a number of sketches to examine how different designs impact issues such as traffic flow, landscaping, irrigation, and safety. By generating many alternative solutions on paper, the student can more effectively weigh the pros and cons of various plans. He could see that placing the playground close to the parking lot might be more convenient for families with strollers but might also pose a safety risk for children. Flowers and shrubs could add color to the area, but they would require water and maintenance. After consideration, the student might decide that a large mural would be a better way to add color.

## Storyboards

Roger Essley (2008) provides an interesting rationale for storyboarding. By an early age, many students have already become intimidated by writing, labeling themselves as "bad" at it. Consequently, because so much of education is text dependent, these students often come to think of themselves as unskilled academically. Essley focuses on the use of storyboards to help students learn to confidently read, comprehend, and write. Storyboards are simply sheets of paper with designated boxes in which students draw various elements of a story. They can be used to draw the chronological events of a story like the one in figure 5.13 about moving.

**Figure 5.13: Chronological events of a story.**

Teachers can also provide more guidance in crafting storyboards. Figure 5.14 illustrates how a teacher can ask students to provide specific details in a story (*Snow White*) and drawings that show characterization and an understanding of cause and effect.

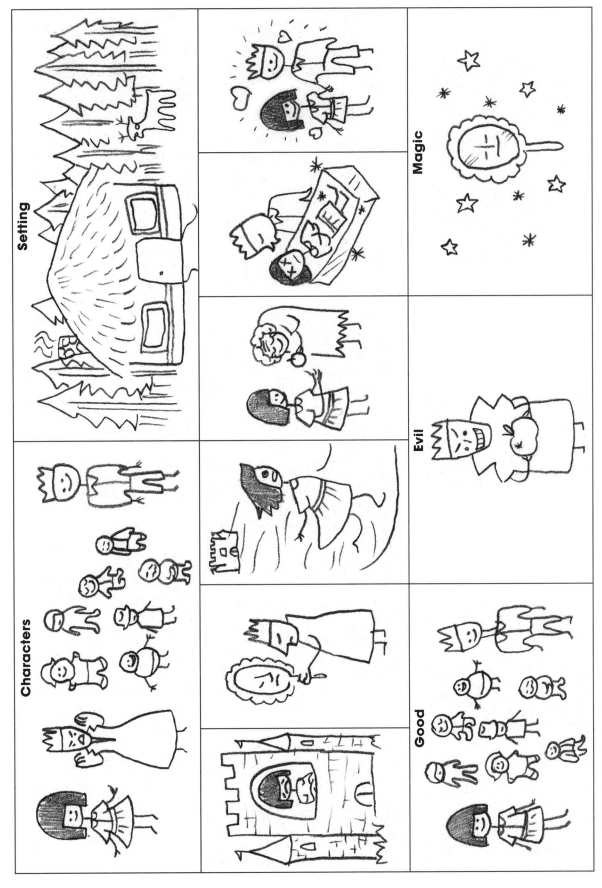

**Figure 5.14: Crafted storyboard.**

Figure 5.14 (page 107) shows a more detailed storyboard. Two boxes are at the top of the board—one box is labeled *characters*, and the other is labeled *setting*. Students draw the characters in the story as well as something that represents the story's setting. Below the two boxes are six smaller boxes in which students draw the major events of the story in a chronological fashion. Finally, there are three boxes along the bottom, labeled *good*, *evil*, and *magic*, respectively. Students draw the heroes, the villains, and the characters with magic in the appropriate boxes. Another way to use storyboards is to include a close-up insert: students first draw a whole scene and then the details of one part of that scene. This can help students focus on the main characters or ideas of a story. This is depicted in figure 5.15.

**Figure 5.15: Close-up storyboard.**

Storyboards can even help students become comfortable with informational content such as the parts of speech. Figure 5.16 depicts a storyboard used to help students with the parts of a sentence.

**Figure 5.16: Parts-of-a-sentence storyboard.**

In the first square of figure 5.16, the student writes *the horse*; he or she connects a visual of the noun with the word representing it. In the second, the student draws the horse jumping and writes *the horse jumped*. The student has gone one step further by linking a noun to a verb both linguistically and nonlinguistically. In the third square, the student draws a horse jumping over a gate and writes *the horse jumped over the gate*. In the last square, the student draws a horse jumping over the gate at night and writes *the horse jumped over the gate at night*. Now the student connects modifiers to both the drawing and the sentence. The teacher can use these increasingly complex pictures to demonstrate how language works.

Essley (2008) also noted that an entire class can use storyboards. There are six steps to the process.

1. **Read:** Students read a story or a passage either silently to themselves or as a group.

2. **Discuss and draw:** Ask students to summarize what they read by drawing the most important parts of what was read in four (for example) squares.

3. **Share notes:** Students literally look at one another's cards and drawings. They discuss them and pick the ones they think best represent the story.

4. **Create cards:** Students or the teacher can then create cards based on the discussion to use for the whole-class storyboard.

5. **Retell and revise:** Students come up to the storyboard and retell the events depicted in the squares. If students stumble over squares, the squares may be revised.

6. **Review before next reading:** For any extended reading, this is an excellent way to aid comprehension.

The following vignette depicts a teacher using a drawing or sketching technique with her students.

Ms. Strand's math students have been learning the graphing process. She knows that while they are grasping the relationship between the x-axis and the y-axis on an intellectual level, they are not grasping how highly applicable the information on a graph can be. She provides a graph with a line that shows only that as x increases, y increases as well. "I want you to draw this," she says. "Think about the relationship between x and y and what else shares this relationship; then, create a picture that shows your x and y and how they relate."

One student draws a picture in which a person is striking out in a baseball game. In the next frame, he is at a batting cage, and in the next frame, he is at another game, only this time he is hitting the ball. "The more I practice baseball, the better I get," he says. When the students have finished, Ms. Strand continues to draw graphs demonstrating different relationships between x and y, and she asks students to create more pictures.

## Generating Mental Images

As the name implies, mental images require students to generate images in their minds. The students do not generate anything tangible. That is, they do not create any graphic representations or figures or drawings. Mental images are more than just mental pictures. They can also include smell, taste, touch, sound, kinesthetic sensations, and even emotions. As discussed in chapter 2, a vivid mental image complete with sensory detail closely mimics our experience of the real world. For example, assume that a student is trying to create a mental image of the characteristics of life aboard a submarine. The student would first create a visual image of the submarine. He might imagine touching the outside of the steel shell before entering with other crew members. He might imagine the smells inside: food cooking in the galley, coffee officers on duty are drinking, and perhaps the less pleasant smells of fellow crew members (fresh water for showering is scarce on board a submarine). The student might imagine the boring flavors of rations after thirty days at sea or the claustrophobic feeling of being closed in a metal cylinder many miles under the surface of the ocean. He might be able to imagine the fear associated with being hunted or chased and the exhilaration of seeing the sky and the smell of fresh air when the crew returns to port. The brain deeply processes information learned using mental imagery, and students are more likely to remember it.

Mental images can be very symbolic in nature. For example, assume that students were trying to create a mental image for the scientific concept of *entropy*, which is the measure of disorder in a system. The student might imagine looking at an empty room through a thermal imaging camera. In the center of the room, a cup of hot coffee sits on a table. The coffee would appear red because it is hot, and the rest of the room would appear blue because it is cooler than the coffee. The student could associate this mental image with *low* entropy, since the system at this point is very organized (hot things in one place, cooler things in other places). As the coffee cools, the student could picture the thermal image shifting from red and blue to green all over as the heat transfers from the coffee to the room and the system equalizes, thus becoming more disordered and *high* in entropy.

Teachers can also introduce mental images by guiding students through the creation of images. This is sometimes referred to as guided imagery. Guided imagery can help students learn to use all five of their senses, not just their sight, to create vivid mental pictures. The following vignette depicts how a teacher might use guided imagery.

> *Mr. Lewis's class has been studying the behaviors of various animals. He asks his students not to just write down facts about them but to imagine living in a similar way. "Imagine being a penguin," he says. "Close your eyes and imagine sitting in the freezing cold. It's snowing and the wind is blowing, and you are huddled up next to all the other penguins to stay warm. When your baby is born, you have to huddle over him to keep him warm all the time, or he will die. That's a lot of pressure! Now imagine you are getting hungry, but you have nothing to eat. And you have to stay like that for weeks! And when you can go eat, you have to walk hundreds of miles first!" He guides students through visualization with many of the animals they are studying so that they can get a better understanding and appreciation for each animal.*

## Conducting Thought Experiments

Philosophers and scientists have been conducting thought experiments since the time of Galileo. Although thought-experiment theorists do not completely agree on one specific definition or classification system for thought experiments, there is some common agreement that can provide guidance for teachers using thought experiments with students in the classroom.

A thought experiment is essentially a "what if?" question that has been extrapolated in the imagination. James Brown (1991) said thought experiments are "visualizable; they involve mental manipulations . . . they are often (but not always) impossible to implement as real experiments either because we lack the relevant technology or because they are simply impossible in principle" (p. 1). Peg Tittle (2005), in her collection of philosophical thought experiments, explained that "conducting a thought experiment is engaging in hypothetical reasoning. Like a regular experiment, a thought experiment involves setting up a situation and then paying close attention to what happens" (p. x). With a thought experiment, however, the situation plays out in the experimenter's mind.

Thought experiments have a rich history. Here we present some classic thought experiments. As a way of introducing the concept of thought experiments, some of these classics might be presented to students along with some of the history behind them.

## Philosophy

Locke's *Voluntary Prisoner* (Tittle, 2005) supposes that a man falls asleep, very much wishing to be in the company of a particular person he adores. While he is asleep, someone comes in and moves his bed into a locked cell where that person is. Upon waking, the man sees this person and is so overwhelmed with joy that he decides to stay in the cell. Is he free?

Paley's *Watch* (Tittle, 2005) postulates that a man is walking along the beach and encounters a stone. He picks it up and observes it. When asked how the stone may have come to be, he replies that it may have lain there forever, for all he knows. There is no real absurdity in the statement. But suppose he encounters a watch. After inspecting the watch in the same manner, can the man make the same statement?

## Physics

Einstein used a thought experiment to help him think through his theory of relativity. He imagined himself running to catch up with a beam of light. He got the idea from reading Maxwell, who said that a changing electric field creates a magnetic field and a changing magnetic field creates an electric field and that a wave traveling through the electromagnetic field with velocity $c$ is light. Einstein wondered what it would be like to catch up to the front of a beam of light. He thought it might be like running alongside an incoming wave from the end of a pier toward the shore. He figured that if he ran at the same speed as the wave, the wave would appear constant; that is, it would not appear to change. The contrast between Einstein's thought experiment and Maxwell's theory led Einstein to question Maxwell and eventually to develop the theory of relativity (Brown, 1991).

Galileo conducted a famous thought experiment in response to Aristotle's hypothesis that heavier bodies fall more quickly than lighter ones. He imagined a cannonball attached to a musket ball. According to Aristotle's thinking, which said that lighter things fall at a slower rate than heavier things, the musket ball would fall at a slower rate than the cannon ball, thus creating drag and slowing the combination down. However, the added weight of the musket ball should also make the set heavier, which would make it fall faster, according to Aristotle. Since both could not be true, Galileo concluded that Aristotle was wrong (Brown, 1991).

## Biology

In *The Origin of Species*, Darwin imagined giraffes' necks that were different lengths. Because some would be better able to reach food (leaves in the tops of trees) they would survive while shorter-necked species would gradually die out. He used this to illustrate natural selection (Brown, 1991).

Agassiz used a thought experiment with lobsters to illustrate his point that scientific taxonomies (species, genus, family, and so on) are not arbitrary. He imagined a world where lobsters, but no other articulated creatures (such as crustaceans, spiders, or insects) existed. His thought experiment argued that you would still need all the different levels of distinction to classify the lobster, whether the other types were there or not, thus illustrating the necessity of scientific classification structures (Brown, 1991).

---

One common place to encounter thought experiments in everyday life is movies. Here we present examples of classic philosophical thought experiments that correspond to popular movies.

Putnam's *Brain in a Vat* (Tittle, 2005) thought experiment asks the thinker to imagine that a scientist has discovered a way to keep people's brains alive in a vat of special chemicals. Not only can the scientist keep the brains alive, but by sending electrical signals to the brains, he can cause each one to think that it is really a person living life in the world. If this were the case and everyone in the world was just a brain in a vat, is there any way that we would be able to know that this was the case? In the film *The Matrix* (Silver, Wachowski, & Wachowski, 1999), the main character discovers that his real body is hooked up to a machine that sends electrical impulses to his brain that make him think he is living in the real world. The movie follows him as he discovers this reality and finds that the real world is actually far less appealing than the fictitious Matrix world, except for the fact that it is indeed real.

Nietzsche's *Eternal Recurrence* (Tittle, 2005) thought experiment asks the thinker to imagine that one night a powerful being appears and says, "The life that you have lived, up to this point, you are destined to live over and over again for eternity. You will never go past this point, but will always return to the beginning of your life and live it over and over and over again." His intention is for the thinker to consider whether he would be happy about this or sad. The movie *Groundhog Day* (Albert & Ramis, 1993) examines this question from the point of view of a person who is doomed to live one day over and over again. It depicts his mixed emotions and the different ways that he reacts to the continuously recurring circumstances.

Goldman's *Book of Life* (Tittle, 2005) thought experiment asks the thinker to imagine that he finds a book that tells the story of his life. He reads about his childhood, his memories, and his experiences. Wanting to know the future, he turns to a future entry, but it only says, "He is reading this book." He tries to contradict the book by closing it and putting it away. However, his curiosity gets the better of him, and he decides to look at the book again. But when he does, he finds that it is the time of the future entry that he looked at previously. The intention of the experiment is that the thinker considers the idea that someone else is the author of his or her life. If someone is writing your story, are your choices really choices, or are you forced to follow the story being written? In the movie *Stranger Than Fiction* (Doran & Forster, 2006), the protagonist discovers one day that a disembodied voice is narrating the events of his life. The voice belongs to a writer who is working on a book in which the protagonist will eventually die. The movie depicts the emotions that the main character feels at finding that someone else has anticipated and written everything he does.

For younger students, the concept of thought experiments can be illustrated through the use of age-appropriate movies and comic books, which, although not based on specific classical thought experiments, are nonetheless built around "what if?" questions. For example, many comic books and the movies that they inspire examine the question, What problems and dilemmas might a character with superhuman powers face? Additionally, many films for children are built around other "what if?" questions.

- *Cars* **(Anderson & Lasseter, 2006):** What if cars acted like people?

- *Toy Story* **(Arnold, Guggenheim, & Lasseter, 1995):** What if toys came to life?

- *Tron* **(Kushner & Lisberger, 1982):** What if you could enter a video game?

Fairy tales in which the hero or heroine is placed in a situation and his or her emotional response and actions are imagined in the form of a narrative may also be used as examples of thought experiments. The oral tradition of storytelling gives the storytellers the power of the experimenter as they use their discretion to tweak different parts of the story based on how the thought experiment plays out in their minds. This tweaking by different storytellers over the centuries has led to multiple versions and endings to many of the classic fairy tales. The following are some different variations of classic fairy tales.

Everyone knows the story of *The Three Little Pigs* (Jacobs, 1890); three pigs are saved from the wolf because one among them was smart enough to build a strong house made of brick. However, in some versions, the penalty for building a flimsy house turns out to be death, as the wolf eats the first two pigs after blowing their houses down. Storytellers also examine the wolf's punishment for trying to eat the pigs. In some stories, the wolf falls down the brick house's chimney into a pot of boiling water and subsequently the pigs eat him. In other stories, he simply runs away and never bothers the pigs again. One entertaining version of the tale, by Jon Scieszka (1996), stars a wolf who feels that he has been falsely accused of blowing the pigs' houses down and proceeds to make the case that he had a cold and merely sneezed while paying neighborly visits to each pig. He also claims that the first two pigs were actually killed when their houses fell on them, and not because he ate them. In this story, the wolf ends up in jail.

*Cinderella* (Grimm & Grimm, 1903) is a tale of a girl who goes from rags to riches. It features her new stepmother and two horrible stepsisters who torment her. In disguise, Cinderella meets the prince of her kingdom at a royal ball. They fall in love, but she runs away before her disguise wears off, and his only clue to her identity is a glass slipper she leaves behind. The prince searches far and wide, eventually finding her and rescuing her from her stepfamily. The tale varies in that in some versions Cinderella's father is deceased, while in others he is absent or present but unwilling to interfere with his new wife's affairs in raising the children. A more important variation is the appearance of the stepsisters. They are often portrayed as ugly, and Cinderella is portrayed as beautiful, thus depicting physical beauty as representative of inner beauty or virtue. However, some versions portray both Cinderella and her stepsisters as beautiful in order to focus on the idea that outward beauty can mask selfishness and greed. Still other versions feature an ugly Cinderella who is transformed into a beautiful princess because of her goodness and the prince's love for her.

For more information on fairy tales and their variants throughout history, the website www.surlalunefairytales.com is an excellent resource.

Given the complexity of thought experiments, it is best for teachers to set them up. The following are thought-experiment questions a teacher might ask for various subject areas.

## Math

"What if I gave you a penny one day and doubled your money every day after that?" This experiment could be used to introduce the idea of exponential growth.

"What if there were only three numbers?" This experiment could be used to introduce students to the concept of base 3 systems (or any system other than base 10).

## Science

**Biology:** "What if you could invent an animal? How would its digestive system work? What about its other body systems?" This experiment might be used to compare the body systems of different animals.

**Physics:** "What if a specific law of physics didn't apply (such as gravity or the conservation of matter)? How would that affect other laws?" This experiment might be used to explore cause and effect and the interrelated nature of the laws of physics.

## Social Studies

"What if the Tigris and Euphrates rivers had not existed?" This might be used to investigate the interrelated nature of climate as well as to investigate how climate affects people.

"What if Alexander the Great had died as a child?" This might be used to investigate the small or large effects people have on one another and on history. It is possible that history would have unfolded very differently, but it is also possible that another person would have walked in his shoes, and virtually nothing would be different.

"What if another country had developed nuclear weapons first? How would World War II have ended? How would life be different today?" This is another good one to consider in terms of cause and effect. This is particularly relevant because it is likely that a different path in history would change things for students dramatically.

## English or Language Arts

"What if Virginia Woolf had been born in 1982 instead of 1882? How would this have changed her voice?" This can be used to introduce women's rights topics as well as the progression of the novel in the last century.

"What if Shakespeare had died of the plague? How would that have affected the English language (Shakespeare introduced about 1,700 words and many common expressions into the English language)?" Thought experiments with Shakespeare could be quite inventive and explore many different topics, given how few facts about his life can be verified.

## Foreign Languages

"What if English used English words but followed the grammar rules of Spanish (adjectives follow nouns, and so on)? How would it sound?" This could be a fun way to explore the sentence structures of foreign languages.

---

Even when a well-designed thought experiment is presented to students, a great deal of teacher guidance is frequently required to make sure that students rely on their mental images to conduct the experiment. Once students have independently engaged in their thought experiments, the teacher would then have students interact in small groups and then as an entire class. The following vignette depicts how a teacher might use thought experiments in class.

> *Mr. Ginsburg's class has been studying the concepts of freedom and morality in a society. He asks his students to record their answers to questions such as, Should citizens of a nation be required to fund the care for the elderly, the poor, and the sick? Students also have to answer more practical-based questions such as, Should the education system test students from an early age and place them in different*

*tracks the way they do in countries like Germany, each of which has a different level of rigor and each of which has a different focus (academic versus vocational)? After they have recorded their answers, Mr. Ginsburg asks them to close their eyes. He then says, "Imagine you are about to be born into a world that works according to your answers to these questions. You have no idea though who you will be. You might be born into a wealthy family or a poor one. You might be born healthy, or you might not. You have absolutely no idea what your societal position will be or what your personal advantages or disadvantages might be. Are you still happy with your answers to the questions?"*

## Performing Mental Rehearsal

All the previous depictions of mental models have dealt with informational knowledge, technically referred to as declarative knowledge. Mental rehearsal is applicable to procedural knowledge—knowledge relating to skills and procedures.

Mental rehearsal has a rich history in the world of sports. Athletes use mental rehearsal for many different purposes, such as learning and practicing specific skills and learning and practicing new strategies for motivation, goal setting, emotion regulation, and maintaining positive attitudes. For example, when learning or practicing a specific skill, a soccer player might mentally rehearse the series of moves used to "bend" a soccer ball, or a basketball player might imagine shooting free throws. To help his team learn new plays, a football coach might lead his players in mental rehearsal of a blitz or a corner route to help each player understand where to go and what to do. An Olympian might use mental imagery to motivate herself and set goals, picturing herself standing atop the podium receiving a gold medal as her national anthem plays and her countrymen cheer for her.

For athletes learning a new skill or sport, mental rehearsal can be an effective way to practice, since it is not "muscularly detailed" enough to hurt them if they have details of the technique wrong, but it can prevent them from forgetting what they have just learned during a session with their trainer or coach (Hutson, 2009). Hutson (2009) noted that it can also make athletes more flexible since it helps them form an abstract representation of a skill, thus making it easier to perform the same skill under varying circumstances (for example, using a tennis backhand with a different racquet or on a different court). Consider the following examples of athletes using mental rehearsal.

Michael Johnson, an Olympic track champion and world-record holder, used mental rehearsal to visualize competing in the 1996 Olympic games. He said, "I'd visualized the 1996 Olympics down to the millisecond, I'd crafted a decade of dreams into ambitions, refined ambitions into goals, and finally hammered goals into plans" (as cited in Harwood, Cumming, & Hall, 2003, p. 292).

Sylvie Bernier, an Olympic diving champion, is famous for her use of mental rehearsal and visualization. She would rehearse all ten of her dives in her head every night before going to sleep.

> I started with a front dive, the first one that I had to do at the Olympics, and I did everything as if I was actually there. I saw myself in the pool at the Olympics doing my dives. If the dive was wrong, I went back and started over. For me it was better than a workout. I felt like I was on the board. (as cited in Orlick, 2008, p. 105)

Bill Russell, an NBA basketball player who won eleven championships with the Boston Celtics, described how he used visualization to create instant replays in his head of moves that he saw other players make:

> Every time one of them would make one of the moves I liked, I'd close my eyes just afterward and try to see the play in my mind. In other words, I'd try to create an instant replay on the inside of my eyelids. Usually I'd catch only a part of a particular move the first time I tried this; I'd miss the headwork or the way the ball was carried or maybe the sequence of steps. But the next time I saw the move I'd catch a little more of it, so that soon I could call up a complete picture. (as cited in Russell & Branch, 1979, p. 74)

Mark Plaatjes, gold-medal winner in the men's marathon at the 1993 World Championships in Athletics in Stuttgart, Germany, stated:

> I had received some information and pictures on the contours and flow of the marathon course prior to arriving in Germany. When I got to Stuttgart, I felt completely comfortable and absolutely familiar with the course. There's no doubt that I was the most motivated runner in my marathon race, but I was also the most prepared. (as cited in Ungerleider, 2005, p. 5)

Real-life stories about the use of mental rehearsal can be a powerful way of introducing the concept to students. There are a number of research-based generalizations regarding the use of mental rehearsal. Consider the following components of effective mental rehearsal.

## Combining Physical Practice

Mental practice works best when you do it in combination with physical practice. The majority of the research on the effectiveness of mental practice in comparison to physical practice concluded the following: mental practice alone is "more effective than NP [no practice] and less effective than PP [physical practice]" (Morris, Spittle, & Watt, 2005, p. 32). However, a combination of mental practice and physical practice has been shown to be "as effective as . . . or even more effective than, physical practice alone" (Wulf, Horstmann, & Choi, 1995, p. 262).

For example, a teacher in a physical education class might implement this generalization by alternating physical-practice sessions, in which students dribble a soccer ball, with mental-practice sessions. During mental practice, she might ask students to picture the side of their foot tapping the ball just lightly enough to keep it moving in front of them. She would ask them to feel the cadence of their body as they time their steps and alternate their kicks, tapping the ball with their right foot and then their left, while jogging down the field. She would then have them engage in physical practice of the same skill.

## Using Proper Timing

Mental practice works best early or late in the learning process. Grouios (1992) pointed to research that suggests that "mental practice is especially effective during the early stages of learning or during the later stage, although individuals apparently must achieve a minimum proficiency level before MP [mental practice] can be effective. It appears that a novice is unable to concentrate on the appropriate movement responses." This means that people just learning a skill can benefit from mental practice because it allows them to practice what they have learned but is not muscularly detailed enough to lead to bad habits. Individuals more skilled in a process can use mental rehearsal for more sophisticated practice to study details of a technique or to prepare themselves mentally for competition.

For example, an art teacher might implement this generalization while teaching his students to throw pottery on a wheel. During the early stages of learning, when students are still trying to keep their hands steady against the pressure of the spinning lump of clay, he might direct them to visualize their hands feeling strong and pressing the clay into the correct form. Once they are more proficient with the basic techniques and are able to focus more on artistic design, the teacher might direct the students to use visualization to calm themselves and steady their hands before performing delicate carving work on a larger vessel.

## Giving Clear Instructions

Teachers need to give clear instructions about how to mentally rehearse a skill. Teachers should explain to students what mental practice is, why it is helpful, and exactly what they want students to think about. The research also suggests that using as many different formats as possible for instructions increases the quality of mental practice. For example, a teacher might tell students what to do, give written instructions, use a film or video to show them what to do, and demonstrate what students should do during mental practice. Instructions should also explain the subparts of mental rehearsal (for example, activating all five senses, paying attention to emotions). Research shows that clear instructions presented in multiple formats lead to better mental practice and therefore better physical performance (Grouios, 1992).

For example, an athletics coach who wants his students to mentally rehearse performing a layup in basketball might introduce mental practice of this skill to his students by first showing them a video of a professional athlete performing the skill. Then he would ask students to create a mental instant replay of the video. Next he might provide students with written instructions about doing a layup and model visualizing the feel of the gym floor under his feet, the cadence of steps leading to the basket, what he is looking at, the smell of sweat, and how it might sound when his shoes squeak on the floor. Finally, he would help them imagine how it might feel to do a layup during a game with the crowd cheering and other players shouting.

## Including Context

Mental rehearsal should include the context of the performance. Students should focus on placing themselves in the environment in which they will be physically performing a skill, and they should actually *feel* themselves performing the movements of the skill. They should feel that they are in control of the image and that it is clear and vivid. Paying attention to how a task feels is most important (rather than worrying about doing the task exactly right).

For example, a teacher in a music class might implement this generalization by asking his students to imagine themselves onstage at their upcoming vocal performance. He would help them picture the auditorium, from the color of the seats to the way the lights will shine down from the ceiling. He asks them to imagine breathing deeply and producing clear tones. The students should be able to almost hear the melodies and harmonies as they picture themselves giving a flawless concert followed by thunderous applause.

## Practicing in Slow Motion

Start slow, and then speed up. Because learning a complex skill may lead to information overload during mental practice (too many things to think about at once), mentally practicing a skill in slow motion can help students get used to mental rehearsal. Watching a slow-motion film clip of someone performing a motor skill, then mentally practicing that skill in slow motion, and finally mentally practicing at normal speed can help students manage the amount of information they have to keep track of during mental practice.

For example, in a physical education class, students might rehearse the motions involved in using a tennis backhand, first by watching a video of an expert executing the skill, then listening to a teacher's verbal explanation and watching him or her model the process, and then watching a slow-motion film clip of the techniques involved. Then the teacher would lead them in guided practice to imagine executing a backhand, slowly at first, and then speeding up to normal speed. This would be followed by a session of actual practice where students could try out and practice what they had rehearsed mentally.

Finally, it is important to remember that mental rehearsal can also be applied to mental skills such as playing chess. A chess player might rehearse different moves and outcomes in his head, playing out different scenarios to practice the visualization required to be excellent at this game. A number of mental skills from academic subject areas can be enhanced through mental rehearsal. For example, the process of conducting an experiment in science lends itself to mental rehearsal in that there are steps to follow.

The following vignette depicts how a teacher might use some of the aspects of mental rehearsal with academic skills.

> *Mr. Highland's class has been preparing for a statewide exam. The students have reviewed various study skills, and Mr. Highland reviews them with his students by asking them to mentally visualize the day of the exam.*
>
> *"I want you to close your eyes and imagine sitting at your desk the day of the exam," he says. "What are you wearing? Are you hungry or full? What is the weather like outside? Imagine the test being handed out. How do you feel? Are you nervous or calm? The test begins, and you read over the first questions, finding you know the answers to each of them. You feel confident until you come across a question you don't know the answer to. You're stuck, but instead of guessing, you look over the multiple-choice options; you find that you can rule out two of the four options. You aren't sure what the right answer is, but you know what it is not. You consider the remaining two options carefully. You look at the prefixes and suffixes of each word and consider what they might tell you. You realize you know the meaning of the root of one of the options, and, as it does not relate to the question, that it is probably not the correct answer. You choose the remaining option and move on."*
>
> *He guides the students through visualizing the use of the study skills they have learned and encourages them to repeat the process independently.*

## Summary

This chapter was about the cognitive strategy of creating patterns and mental models. Creating graphic representations can help students connect ideas and see patterns and processes. Using drawing and sketching techniques, students can use their creativity to see information and relationships, which can help reluctant or struggling readers and writers become more confident. Creating vivid mental images is a powerful way to remember information and deepen understanding, and mental rehearsal can greatly enhance performance whether it is in an athletic, artistic, or social endeavor. Finally, thought experiments can help students gain new and original insights. Creating mental models using any of these strategies takes advantage of the deep connection between the mind and body, and this connection will help 21st century students perform well in virtually all arenas of their lives.

# Chapter 5: Comprehension Questions

1. How does parsing sentences into propositions help students identify important relationships between ideas?

2. Explain the reasoning behind asking students to create mental images. What advantages do mental images have over graphic representations and drawing and sketching?

3. How can thought experiments be used to help students gain new perspectives?

4. Why can mental practice sometimes be more effective than physical practice?

# Part II: Conative Skills

## Chapter 6

# UNDERSTANDING AND CONTROLLING ONESELF

As described in chapter 1, conative skills have both affective and cognitive dimensions. Citizens of the 21st century will face an increasingly more complex world, and the ability to approach this world calmly and rationally will make them successful. As Goleman (1995) noted, people are well served if they cultivate "a neutral mode that maintains self-reflectiveness even amidst turbulent emotions" (p. 47). Understanding and controlling oneself is the centerpiece of maintaining self-reflectiveness even in the face of turbulent emotions. In this chapter, we address three types of strategies that are useful to this end: (1) becoming aware of the power of interpretations, (2) cultivating useful ways of thinking, and (3) avoiding negative ways of thinking.

## Becoming Aware of the Power of Interpretations

It is natural to believe that our interpretations are reality. For example, a student might see another student frowning at her from across the classroom. She might immediately conclude that the other student is angry with her. In fact, however, the other student might be thinking of an unpleasant chore he must perform while he gazes out the window right above her head. She has interpreted the event as reflecting on her personally, when in fact it has nothing to do with her.

The nature of interpretations can be introduced to younger students using books such as *White Is for Blueberry* by George Shannon (2005), *Not a Box* by Antoinette Portis (2007), and *Duck! Rabbit!* by Amy Krouse Rosenthal and Tom Lichtenheld (2009). In a limited manner, even cartoons like *Calvin and Hobbes* can help younger students become familiar with the role of interpretation.

To begin exploring the nature of interpretation, a teacher might lead a brief discussion with students. It is important to manage these discussions in such a way that they do not challenge students' religious beliefs. For example, a discussion exploring the nature of interpretation on the topic of sports or sports teams is likely to be lighthearted, but a discussion on the topic of religion can get heated very quickly, especially if the class is comprised of students with very different religious orientations. Indeed, nearly all religious beliefs could be seen as different interpretations rather than absolute truths, and this notion is likely to offend students and their families. That being noted, discussions that develop the awareness that perceptions are not necessarily reality are powerful foundations for understanding and controlling oneself. Students can begin this process by understanding and examining the nature of misperceptions.

## Understanding Misperceptions

Human interpretations quite frequently cause misperceptions. For example, students may perceive a student who is not very talkative as stuck up when in fact she is simply shy. This is a misperception because her peers are creating a false conclusion about her character based on a simple observation of her behavior. One way to introduce the concept of misperceptions is to use visual illusions. Here are just a few examples of the many sources teachers may use for visual illusions. Visit **marzanoresearch.com /classroomstrategies** for live links to these illusions and more.

- *The Ultimate Book of Optical Illusions* **(Seckel, 2006):** This book has many illusions both in color and black and white.

- *Masters of Deception* **(Seckel, 2004):** This book contains work by artists such as M. C. Escher, Salvador Dali, and Octavio Ocampo.

- **Optical illusions (www.optillusions.com):** This site has many illusions both in color and black and white.

- *Anamorphic illusions* **(www.designioustimes.com/design/pavement-drawings-creative-art.html):** Julian Beever creates sidewalk art that appears three-dimensional, but the illusion only works from one specific angle. The entire project looks distorted if the viewer stands somewhere else.

Figure 6.1 depicts a visual illusion that illustrates how human beings might have difficulty perceiving what actually exists. In this case, the two horizontal lines are the same length but they appear to be different lengths.

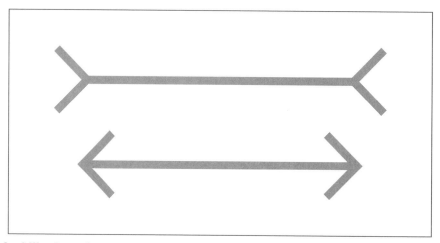

**Figure 6.1: Optical illusion of arrows.**

Source: Müller-Lyer, 1889.

Teachers can use visual illusions like the one in figure 6.1 to introduce the idea of misperceptions in an intriguing way. A teacher might use an optical illusion to begin a discussion on voting, pointing out that many people vote based on general misperceptions, such as President Barack Obama being a Muslim, or specific misperceptions, such as former President George W. Bush having halted all stem cell research.

Once students understand the nature of misperceptions, they can examine them in real life and in literature. As a real-world example, take the small town of Cold Harbor, Virginia. It makes no sense at first that a small town in Virginia nowhere near the water would be called Cold Harbor. However, during the Civil War, *cold harbor* was a term that meant there was a place soldiers could stay (harbor) but that hot meals were not prepared (cold).

On a large scale, misperceptions can lead to disaster. Investigations into the 2010 British Petroleum (BP) oil spill in the Gulf of Mexico report that many misperceptions were at fault. These misperceptions included everything from one employee misreading data about pressure in the well to upper-level misperceptions about who exactly was responsible for managing the safety of the well (Carroll, 2010).

Misperceptions can also be approached from a humorous perspective. All kinds of blogs and websites attest to the funny misperceptions kids have. For example, a four-year-old girl named Brittany had an earache, and she wanted to take some medicine. She tried and tried to get the lid off the bottle, but her efforts were in vain. She brought the bottle to her mom, who explained that the lid to the bottle was childproof, and an adult would have to open it for her. With an expression of amazement Brittany said, "How does it know it's me?" (Head Jammer, 2010).

Probably the most powerful activity students might engage in is to examine misperceptions in their own lives. Students might have had times in their lives when others misperceived them or times when they might have developed misperceptions about someone else. Since this type of self-analysis might be difficult for some students, it is best if the teacher begins the discussion by describing a time when he or she was misperceived or misperceived others. Then students might be asked to share other examples.

The following vignette depicts a teacher addressing misperceptions.

> *Ms. Pierce's class has been looking at how data can be perceived in different ways. She begins class by showing her students a few optical illusions to get them thinking about multiple perspectives, and then she uses a personal example of misperception to introduce the concept. She says, "Just recently my sister and I were looking at the number of total hits for her website for the week. We were excited at first because it appeared as though ten thousand people had visited that week. When we looked a bit closer, however, we saw the story was somewhat different. It turned out that about two thousand different people had visited the site over the week, and roughly the same number had returned each day for five consecutive days. Ten thousand was the total number of times the site was visited, not the total number of different people who visited." After students share some similar stories of misperception, they begin to look at why people need to be very careful about studying the data when they see news headlines like "Detroit Is the Most Dangerous City in the United States."*

## Exploring Cultural Interpretation

Even though students don't often recognize it, where they are from, their religious, cultural, and family traditions, and their local and national histories profoundly affect how they view the world. Teachers can help students understand the role cultural interpretations play in our perceptions of the world. This begins with small things, such as the foods that societies enjoy or shun. For example, sea slugs are a common dish in China. In Japan, horse meat is occasionally served in a style similar to sashimi, and toasted grasshoppers are often eaten in Mexico. Conversely, many cultures perceive foods like marshmallows, peanut butter, corn on the cob, and hot dogs as odd.

Exploring cultural interpretation could also involve examining different social customs. In China, people use their middle fingers to point, a gesture that could be interpreted as rude in the West. In many Muslim countries, showing the soles of your feet is considered offensive, whereas in the United States most people think nothing of lying barefoot on a lawn chair at a crowded swimming pool. In Sri Lanka, flowers are connected specifically with mourning and would not be a good gift to bring for a host.

Finally, cultural interpretations of concepts like human rights often differ in deep and important ways. For example, while women in some Muslim countries wear burkas to honor their religion, many women in Western countries see the burka as a violation of women's rights. While some countries like Israel require military service for every citizen for a certain period of time, some Americans argue against any kind of draft under any political circumstance.

There are a number of books that students can study that portray different cultural interpretations. For elementary students:

- *Brothers in Hope: The Story of the Lost Boys of Sudan* (**Williams, 2005**)—This book addresses the difficult subject of the mid-1980s civil war in Sudan in a picture book for grades 3–5.

- *Cora Cooks Pancit* (**Gilmore, 2009**)—This book is about a young girl cooking dinner with her mom and learning a bit about her Filipino heritage.

For middle school students:

- *Faraway Home* (**Taylor, 1999**)—This book is about a thirteen-year-old Jewish boy sent to Ireland by his family during WWII for protection. He makes new friends and tries to blend in, but the war reaches Ireland too.

- *Sunrise Over Fallujah* (**Myers, 2008**)—This book is about a young man who feels compelled to join the army after September 11. He is sent to Iraq as part of a Civil Affairs unit, the purpose of which is to build trust with the Iraqi people.

- *Tangled Threads: A Hmong Girl's Story* (**Shea, 2003**)—This book is about a thirteen-year-old girl who leaves a Thai refugee camp with her grandmother for Rhode Island, where she joins the rest of her family, each member of which is struggling in some way with living with both the older Hmong traditions and America's alluring culture.

For high school students:

- *Three Cups of Tea* (**Mortenson & Relin, 2006**)—This book is about Greg Mortenson's experience building schools in rural Pakistan and Afghanistan.

- *A Thousand Years of Good Prayers: Stories* (**Li, 2005**)—This book of short stories explores the effects of the Cultural Revolution on modern Chinese, both in China and in the United States.

- *Reading Lolita in Tehran* (**Nafisi, 2003**)—This book is about a secret women's book club in Iran in which members read Western classics.

There are also websites that provide annotated lists of books and videos that introduce perspectives from other cultures. Visit **marzanoresearch.com/classroomstrategies** for live links to the following websites.

- Morton Grove Public Library's Webrary (www.webrary.org/kids/jbibasianamericans.html)

- Seattle Public Library (www.spl.org/default.asp?pageID=audience_teens_bmm_ readinglist&cid=118235534833)

- The Horn Book (www.hbook.com/resources/books/asianpacific.asp)

- Documentary Educational Resources (www.der.org)

One activity in which students might engage is to explore different cultural interpretations within their own families. For example, someone who grew up in New Orleans might have attended jazz funerals that concluded with a small celebratory parade. He might think a more somber and quiet funeral odd.

The following vignette depicts how a teacher might explore cultural interpretations.

*Ms. Antoinette's elementary class has been studying different cultural perspectives. Together, they read a picture book about the civil war in Sudan and a young boy traveling to a refugee camp. When the story is finished, Ms. Antoinette asks her students to pick one part of the story that stuck out to them and compare that element to their own lives.*

*Sarah says she was struck by the detail that none of the boys had shoes. "My mom is always yelling at me to wear shoes when I go outside or to the swimming pool," she says. "It always seems like such a hassle, but I never considered not having any shoes at all."*

## Choosing an Interpretation

Once students understand the nature and power of perceptions, they are better able to explore the possibility of choosing their own interpretations at any given time. While this is not self-evident, it is quite logical once one becomes aware of the fact that perceptions are not necessarily reality. The act of consciously choosing one's own interpretation of events at any point in time might be the most powerful and useful skill regarding understanding and controlling oneself.

A teacher can begin a discussion about how human beings have the power to change their interpretations by showing students a visual illusion like the one in figure 6.2 (page 126) that is based on perception. After everyone understands how to "see" both illusions, the teacher might relate this shift in perception to real life with an example of his own. He might explain that for a long time he believed his father always favored his brother over him and his other siblings, but one holiday his sister shared her perception that their father had always favored him. He might explain that after having listened to his sister's point of view, his interpretation of his father's feelings changed, as did his behavior toward his father.

Choosing an interpretation can also be practiced using literature and art. Students might select a character from a story and consciously interpret his or her actions in different ways. For example, a

**Figure 6.2: Visual illusion of a woman's face or a man playing the saxophone.**

Source: Shepard, 1990. "Sara Nader" Illustration from the book *Mind Sights* by Roger N. Shepard. Copyright © 1990 by Roger N. Shepard. Printed by permission of Henry Holt and Company, LLC.

teacher might find that students' varied interpretations of a character like Mr. Rochester in *Jane Eyre* are affecting their overall opinion of the book. She could thoroughly outline Mr. Rochester as both the romantic hero and the ill-tempered captor and design an activity in which her students attempt to see Mr. Rochester in a role they hadn't previously considered. After doing so, students can discuss how the different interpretations affected how they perceived the story.

Art is a perfect vehicle for providing practice in choosing an interpretation. For example, a teacher might show students an image of an iconic painting like *The Scream* by Edvard Munch and ask what they think is happening and why. One student might say she thinks the man is screaming because he is having a nightmare, and she might point out the way the painting is blurry and wavy and dreamlike to support her interpretation. Another student might say he thinks the man is a ghost, and he is screaming because he is haunting someone. Each student would be asked to describe his or her initial interpretations along with an alternative interpretation. Students would also be asked to explain what they learned about the painting or the painter by examining alternative interpretations.

Perhaps the most important way for students to apply interpretation shifting is to analyze negative interpretations in their own lives that are creating discomfort for themselves or others. For example, a particular student who views his sister as selfish might consciously change that interpretation to think of her as passionate or ambitious. He would then interact with his sister from this new, more positive interpretation and keep track of the results. The following vignette depicts how a teacher might set up this type of assignment.

*Ms. Orson's students have been studying the role of interpretation in human interaction. She challenges them to identify a negative interpretation they have of a person in their own lives. "Write down who this person is," she says, "and describe*

*your interpretation of him or her. Consider other ways you might interpret his or her actions. Sometimes it helps to write down a few specific actions that led you to your original perception." She encourages students to try this first with someone they are not very close to because sometimes the perceptions we have of those we are closest to can be the most difficult to change. "For example," she says, "you might choose a neighbor or a teammate; if you have previously viewed that person as being nosy, you could decide to view him or her as caring and concerned. Once you have identified your new perception, remind yourself to interact with the person you have chosen in this new way." She also asks students to keep a journal in which they write down the results of each new interaction they have with the person they have chosen. She says that at the end of the term they will be given the opportunity to look back at all their entries and see if anything has changed.*

## Using a General Strategy for Managing Interpretations

With a basic understanding of the nature of interpretations, students can be presented with a general strategy for managing their interpretations. It is particularly important to manage interpretations when involved in a highly volatile or negative situation. Such a strategy includes the following questions:

1. What is my current interpretation of the situation?

2. What is the most likely outcome given my current interpretation?

3. Do I want a different outcome?

4. How must I change my interpretation to obtain a different outcome?

As the fourth question in the set illustrates, the ultimate purpose of the strategy is to provide students with a sense that they can positively affect any situation. To illustrate, assume that a student finds herself in a class where she believes the teacher does not like her. This has the effect of diminishing her desire to work in the class. As a result of the first two questions, the student realizes that this interpretation of the teacher will most likely result in a poor performance. Given that she wishes to do well, she consciously decides to behave as though the teacher does not dislike her. Rather, she chooses to believe the teacher is simply not very outgoing or demonstrative, even shy. With this new interpretation, the student begins to initiate interaction with the teacher as opposed to avoiding her. In response, the teacher begins to interact with the student.

This process is best introduced if the teacher provides a personal example for each step. The following vignette depicts how a teacher might present the first step to students.

*Mr. Silver's class has been discussing a recent event in the community, a car accident that killed several students; this event has affected everyone. Mr. Silver says, "When I was young, a bridge collapsed, and my aunt and uncle were killed. For a long time, my family did not talk about them. When I was older, I realized that this bothered me. I asked myself informally what my interpretation of the situation was. It became clear that I was still sad about what happened, and I was angry with my parents for refusing to talk about my aunt and uncle."*

*He then leads his students through the same process. "Think about this recent accident and how you have been feeling," he says. "Think about why you feel that way, and try to write down in words how you are interpreting this event." He gives them some time to do this, and in another discussion he asks if anyone would like to share what they wrote.*

*Jamal says, "I've been really confused. I'm a religious person normally. I trust and have faith in God, but Martine was a good friend of mine. He was smart; he had his whole life in front of him, and I just don't understand it at all. It makes me not want to go to church anymore or to pray."*

*After other students have volunteered responses, Mr. Silver leads them to the second step, asking them to consider over the next few days and then write down the likely outcome of their current interpretations. "Do you see good or bad things coming if you continue to think this way?" he asks.*

## Cultivating Useful Ways of Thinking

Once students understand the power of interpretation, they can actively seek to cultivate ways of thinking that have demonstrated positive results. Here we consider four powerful ways of thinking, each of which was introduced in chapter 2: (1) the growth mindset, (2) resiliency, (3) positive possible selves, and (4) optimism. These four useful ways of thinking overlap a great deal in that they all enhance self-efficacy; however, there are some important distinctions. A teacher might select one of these useful ways of thinking and focus on it throughout the year, or the teacher might address all four throughout the year under the general heading of useful or powerful ways of thinking. In all cases, the basic message is the same: students can cultivate ways of thinking that help them better understand and control themselves.

### The Growth Mindset

As we saw in chapter 2, the growth mindset is the fundamental belief that intelligence is changeable and dependent on effort as opposed to innate ability, while the fixed mindset is the belief that intelligence, like height or eye color, is determined at birth and cannot be changed. Dweck and Molden (2005) have shown that students with a growth mindset take on challenges, value knowledge over grades, and see failure as a learning opportunity rather than a personal defeat. Although the fixed theory of intelligence can be deeply ingrained, with encouragement, students can move out of a fixed and into a growth mindset.

A good way to help students see this is to provide examples of the value of effort. Many accomplished people are assumed to have achieved their goals because of sheer talent when in fact they have achieved their goals because of effort and perseverance. In his book *The Talent Code*, Daniel Coyle (2009) discusses a trip around the world he took for the purpose of visiting various hotbeds of talent. He went to see where the best of the best came from and what they do differently. Instead of finding people performing at very high levels all the time as he had expected, he saw people struggling. They tried, they failed, and then they tried again. He discovered that these people were always performing at the limit of their ability. They didn't waste time with what they knew they could do and do well; looking good didn't matter. What mattered was getting better, and to do that they pushed themselves. They tried new things and failed as a result, but after trying again and again, they succeeded. There are many examples of people who found success out of failure. Here are a few.

- Rowland H. Macy opened his first store in Boston in 1844, but it quickly went out of business. He tried his hand at business again, opening a dry-goods store, but it also failed. After moving to California, Macy tried to succeed in the dry-goods business there. After only a year, however, his store failed, and he returned to the East. Macy's fourth store in Massachusetts went bankrupt, but his fifth attempt, a shop in New York City, was a success and grew to be the largest department store in the world by the time of Macy's death in 1877. It still exists today in many locations as Macy's department store (Aaseng, 1990).

- Peter Doherty grew up in Australia. He was clumsy and socially awkward and never fit in. He went into veterinary medicine at the age of seventeen and found, after three years of intense schooling, that he was not at all suited to the profession. He went into research because he didn't know what else to do. If he had stayed in his original field, he would never have won the Nobel Prize in Medicine or been named Australia's Man of the Year (Doherty & Zinkernagel, 1996).

- Maury Wills loved baseball. He was very fast, and he was a good pitcher and a good fielder. His major problem was that he had a terrible time at bat—it seemed he couldn't hit a thing. In spite of that, the Dodgers signed him to their minor league team, and Wills was sure he was on his way to greatness. He worked hard, practicing hitting four hours a day, but he remained in the minors with little improvement for eight and a half years. After learning to switch hit, he got his shot at the majors. Wills continued to struggle, however, and he knew that if his hitting didn't improve he would see his dream slip away. His first-base coach discovered Wills really needed more help with his confidence than with his physical game. He dedicated himself to a new mental confidence, and it worked. He finished his first season in the majors, and eventually he broke Ty Cobb's record for stealing bases. He even found a place in the Baseball Hall of Fame (Kersey, 1998).

A teacher can provide students with a basic understanding of the two mindsets by explaining them in grade-appropriate ways. For example, a primary-school teacher might simply give his students a choice of three tasks, each with a different level of difficulty, and ask them to choose one to complete. After they complete the tasks, he might ask why they chose the task and whether or not they feel they learned anything. A middle or secondary teacher might apply the concept of the two mindsets to people facing daunting challenges in real life. She might begin a discussion by asking students whether or not they think Olympic athletes, for example, believe themselves capable of winning gold medals. This is just an initial step in helping students to develop an awareness of which of the two mindsets they tend to use.

Once students have a basic understanding of the two mindsets, the teacher would then engage students in activities that will help them to utilize the different mindsets. Literature is a perfect vehicle for examining the impact of different mindsets. Characters can be analyzed from the perspective of whether they exhibit a growth versus a fixed mindset. For example, a teacher might ask students to examine Miss Havisham and Magwitch in the book *Great Expectations* and compare them in terms of the two mindsets.

A very powerful application of the growth versus fixed mindset is for students to identify those areas for which they have a growth versus a fixed mindset. Individuals can have a growth mindset regarding one area and a fixed mindset regarding another area. For example, a student might have a fixed mindset regarding mathematics but a growth mindset regarding sports. Dweck (2000) offered a number of ways to measure one's self-theories. The following surveys (figures 6.3 through 6.6) have been adapted for use in the classroom. All survey responses labeled *A* indicate a fixed mindset, and all survey responses labeled *B* indicate a growth mindset. The survey questions in figure 6.3 can be used to help students understand their differing mindsets.

---

**Directions:** Identify which statement you agree with most.

1.

    A. There are some subjects in school I am good at, and some I am not good at.

    B. There are some subjects in school I try harder at than others.

2.

    A. Failing is never OK.

    B. Failing can be OK if I learn something.

3.

    A. Some of my peers are smarter than I am.

    B. Some of my peers try harder than I do.

4.

    A. Sometimes trying harder helps, but it doesn't really change how smart you are.

    B. If I wanted to be smarter in certain subjects or sports, I could try harder.

5.

    A. I know I can do well at the things I'm good at.

    B. I know I can do well at anything if I really want to.

---

Visit **marzanoresearch.com/classroomstrategies** to download a reproducible version of this figure.

**Figure 6.3: Growth versus fixed mindset intelligence survey.**

Source: Adapted from Dweck, 2000.

It is probably best to keep all discussions about individual students' mindsets private. For example, students can take this survey, analyze their mindsets, and make notes in a reflection journal that they periodically hand in to the teacher for her comments. However, class discussions about the general topic as opposed to specific student results are also useful.

The surveys in figures 6.4 through 6.6 can be used to examine various aspects of fixed versus growth theories. A teacher might begin by having students examine their fixed theories regarding intelligence. Once students have explored their views on intelligence, they can move to the topic of personality, then morality, and finally world views. This would give students a comprehensive perspective on the effects of fixed versus growth theories in their own lives.

---

**Directions:** Identify the statement you agree with most.

1.

    A. A person can do a few things that might help get people to like him or her more, but no one can much change his or her basic personality.

    B. No matter who you are, you can change your personality, if you really want to.

2.
  A. Some people get along well with other people and some people don't, but you can't change the way you are very much.
  B. Even people who don't seem to get along with others very well can learn how to, if they really want to.

3.
  A. People can change how they act, but it doesn't really change who they are deep down.
  B. People can always change even their basic characteristics.

4.
  A. The basic characteristics of a person are not really changeable.
  B. Someone can always change what kind of person he or she is.

**Figure 6.4: Theories of personality survey.**

Source: Adapted from Dweck, 2000.

Figures 6.5 and 6.6 provide surveys regarding morality and theories of the world.

**Directions:** Identify the statement you agree with most.

1.
  A. A person has a basic moral character that is so ingrained that it cannot much be changed.
  B. A person's moral character is a result of life experiences and choices, and it can be altered.

2.
  A. A person is either honest and morally upright, or he or she is not.
  B. People can change and become morally upright, if they want to.

3.
  A. People have a basic moral fabric.
  B. People can always make different moral choices.

**Figure 6.5: Theories of morality survey.**

Source: Adapted from Dweck, 2000.

**Directions:** Identify the statement you agree with most.

1.
  A. There isn't much one person can do to change the basic dispositions of the world.
  B. The world is always changing, and people are always changing it.

2.
  A. Trends come and go, but the basic ways of the world don't change much.
  B. The world is always in flux, good or bad.

3.
  A. People must learn to adapt to the world the way it is, because it isn't going to change.
  B. If a person doesn't like something about the world, he can change it.

**Figure 6.6: Theories of the world survey.**

Source: Adapted from Dweck, 2000.

The following vignette depicts how a teacher might address fixed versus growth theories throughout an entire year.

> *Mr. Jones begins the school year by getting to know a bit about his students. Along with personal information surveys, he asks them to fill out a survey on how they view the nature of intelligence. He doesn't explain the survey until after they fill it out and score themselves as either a fixed or a growth mindset. Then he starts a discussion about what the two theories mean.*
>
> *Over the next few months, Mr. Jones tells the class stories of accomplished and intelligent people and how they got to be successful, emphasizing the effort and discipline all those people have in common. As a new quarter begins, he asks his students which personality traits they would most like to possess, and who they know who possesses those traits—people with successful personalities. He then gives them another survey, this time based on the growth and the fixed mindset regarding the malleability of personality traits. He notices that more students appear to have moved into a growth mindset, even though they are discussing personality rather than intelligence.*
>
> *Mr. Jones continues to tell his students stories, now about people who made major changes in their lives with regard to a particular personality trait. Some of these people were taught to be angry and violent and learned not to be, some overcame addictions, and others went from being selfish and materialistic to being more kind and giving. In the second half of the year, he continues the process by providing surveys and examples of people who altered their systems of morality and people who changed the world.*

## Resiliency

*Resiliency*, the ability to bounce back from adversity, is another useful interpretation for students to cultivate. Critical to developing a sense of resiliency is the realization that many people who are very successful have also had to learn to handle difficult circumstances. Again, there are many concrete examples of resiliency that teachers can use to introduce the concept to students. Following are some examples of well-known people who have demonstrated resiliency to overcome specific obstacles.

- **Dyslexia:** Tom Cruise, Whoopi Goldberg, Thomas Edison, Leonardo da Vinci, Albert Einstein, Winston Churchill, and Nelson Rockefeller (Levinson Medical Center for Learning Disabilities, 2010)

- **Epilepsy:** Leonardo da Vinci, Alexander the Great, Napoleon Bonaparte, Charles Dickens, Sir Isaac Newton, Michelangelo, and Julius Caesar (Disabled World, 2008b)

- **Clubfoot:** Mia Hamm, Kristi Yamaguchi, and Troy Aikman (Disabled World, 2008a)

- **Bullying:** Robert Pattinson, Sandra Bullock, Tom Cruise, Miley Cyrus, Bill Clinton, and Christina Aguilera (Daily Beast, 2010)

Resiliency also includes the idea that people can actually gain strength and grow through adversity. This is referred to as *positive behavioral adaptation*. Many people who face adversity become stronger people for having done so. Following are more examples of people who have become stronger through adversity.

- **Kevin Saunders:** He worked as a federal grain-elevator inspector in Kansas. One day, an explosion sent him three hundred feet in the air and over a two-story building. His body was so broken that his doctors didn't believe he would survive. He did survive, but he was paralyzed from the chest down. Shortly after his accident his marriage ended, and he was left alone, permanently disabled, and on the verge of bankruptcy. Despite all this, he went on to become one of the world's best wheelchair athletes. He has also written five books and now works as a motivational speaker. He might not be where he is today had that terrible accident not occurred ("Kevin's Story," 2011).

- **Erik Weihenmayer:** Although he lost his vision at the age of thirteen, Weihenmayer has become an accomplished mountain climber, paraglider, and skier, never allowing his blindness to interfere with his passion for life. Erik's feats have earned him an ESPY Award, recognition by *Time* magazine, induction into the National Wrestling Hall of Fame, an Arete Award, the Helen Keller Lifetime Achievement Award, and the Freedom Foundation's Free Spirit Award. He has also carried the Olympic torch. On May 25, 2001, Erik became the first blind man to summit Mount Everest. On August 20, 2008, when he stood atop Carstensz Pyramid in Australia, he completed a seven-year quest to climb the Seven Summits, the highest mountains on each of the seven continents, joining only one hundred others who have accomplished that feat (Adversity Advantage, n.d.).

- **Sidney Weinberg:** He was one of eleven children and came from a family of Polish immigrants. He left school at fifteen and worked selling evening newspapers; his back was covered in scars from knife fights he was in during that time. He lied his way into a janitorial position at a brokerage company that paid three dollars a week and worked his way up from there, ironically playing on his humble beginnings. He found that people liked and promoted him because of his background, figuring he had learned how to put his head down and work hard. Throughout his career, he went out of his way to tell people that they needed to explain things in simple and clear terms to him because he was, after all, just a poor kid from Polish parents. That poor kid was a senior partner of Goldman Sachs by the time he was forty (Gladwell, 2008).

As the teacher presents examples of resiliency, she can lead a discussion of its characteristics. Some of the more important characteristics of resilient people are:

1. They can tell positive from negative influences, and they can limit the power of those negative influences in their lives.

2. They have a clear sense of what they want and do not want for themselves in the future.

3. They do not feel resigned to an unsuccessful future, no matter how much adversity they have encountered.

4. They have an ability to make and adapt specific plans to reach their short- and long-term goals.

Teachers can reinforce the characteristics of resiliency by discussing the resilience of local personalities or characters in books and movies. For example, a teacher who volunteers with an organization that assists people who are physically disabled might ask someone he knows there to come speak to his students about the difficulties she faces doing even ordinary things. After listening to the speaker, he might ask students to identify some characteristics the speaker discussed or displayed that contribute to her resiliency.

Ultimately, students must examine their own resiliency. The survey in figure 6.7 can be used to this end. The more positive a student's responses are to each question, the more resilient the student tends to be. Prior to presenting the survey to students, a teacher might wish to explain and exemplify important concepts like *ambiguity*, *intuition*, and *finding meaning in bad experiences*.

---

**Directions:** Rate yourself on a scale of 1 to 5 on the following (a score of 1 means *I strongly disagree*, and a score of 5 means *I strongly agree*).

1. I am curious; I ask a lot of questions. I want to know how things work, and I like to try new things and new ways of doing familiar things.
2. I solve problems using logic, creativity, and common sense.
3. I find humor in difficult situations.
4. I can handle a lot of ambiguity and uncertainty.
5. I generally learn valuable lessons from my experiences.
6. In general, I see obstacles as opportunities for growth and change.
7. I believe I have good intuition, and I use it.
8. I am stronger and better for the difficulties I have faced in my life.
9. I have found meaning and benefit in bad experiences.
10. I am always myself, but I can adapt to different circumstances.

---

**Figure 6.7: Resiliency survey.**

Source: Adapted from Seibert, 2005.

Students should be asked to complete the survey privately by recording their responses in a notebook that only they see. After the teacher has read all of the responses, she might then select a time to lead the class in a discussion of what various responses might imply in terms of a person's resiliency. While students' individual responses should be kept private, a whole-class discussion of the general interpretation of the survey can be very useful. Such a discussion might end with students being asked to identify those aspects of their lives in which they wish to become more resilient. The following vignette depicts this.

> *Ms. Gordon has been discussing the concept of resiliency with her class, and she asks her students to take a brief survey that can help them get a good idea of their own levels of resiliency. Then she leads the class in a discussion about the results. "Sometimes we aren't quite as resilient as we want to be in certain areas," she says. "I used to be an active rock climber, but I hurt my knee, and after surgery I didn't go to physical therapy like I should have, and now I never climb anymore. That is something I would like to change."*
>
> *She asks her students to consider similar areas in their own lives. Jana says, "I used to dance a lot. I danced in school plays and all kinds of things. However, my*

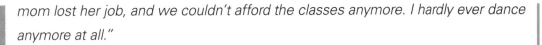

*mom lost her job, and we couldn't afford the classes anymore. I hardly ever dance anymore at all."*

*After students have identified areas in their lives in which they are particularly resilient and areas in which they are not so resilient, they begin to discuss how they can improve their overall resiliency.*

## Positive Possible Selves

As described in chapter 2, possible selves are the ways students picture themselves in the future. If students have positive images of themselves, they tend to work to actualize positive possible selves. If students do not have positive images of themselves in the future, they tend to be less goal oriented and less enthusiastic about their future possibilities. To introduce the concept of future possible selves, it is useful to provide examples of people who have followed a dream they had at a very early age. Consider the following examples of such stories.

- **Alexander McQueen:** He began making dresses for his sisters when he was very young. He told his mothers and his sisters even then that he would be a fashion designer. He was an apprentice at various tailors and theater costumers in Great Britain as a teenager, and he soon earned a master's degree in fashion design. His graduation collection was purchased in its entirety by a very influential fashion stylist, and he became a very successful fashion designer from there—even becoming one of the youngest designers ever to earn the title of "British Designer of the Year" (Camber & Nathan, 2010).

- **Stevie Nicks:** She believed she was born to be a musician. Her grandfather was a country music singer, and he taught her to sing so that they could perform duets when she was just four years old. When she was sixteen, she got a guitar for her birthday, and she wrote her first two songs. She said, "I knew I was never going to be a good person to get up at 8 and be at an office at 9 and drive in traffic at 5:30. I knew instinctively, as a pretty little girl that I wasn't gonna be happening for the office scene" (Stevie Nicks in Her Own Words, n.d.).

A teacher can introduce the concept of positive possible selves using the preceding stories or personal stories, if applicable. For example, a teacher might tell his students how his brother said from the time they were little kids that he was going to be a fireman just like their dad. He might tell them about how his brother wore a fireman-style raincoat every day for almost a whole school year.

Once students understand the concept of positive possible selves, they can be asked to develop their own. Daphna Oyserman, Kathy Terry, and Deborah Bybee (2002) described a series of activities teachers can use to this end.

- **Accomplishment introductions:** Students introduce themselves in terms of something that they would like to someday accomplish. For example, students might sit in a circle and take turns introducing themselves using their own first name and the last name of a person who is accomplished in an area of interest to them. If a student wants to be a ballet dancer, she might introduce herself using her own first name and the last name of *Bussell*, in honor of one of her favorite dancers, Darcey Bussell. Then the class names or guesses the accomplished person's full name and what he or she is known for (clues can be provided). Finally, the student introduces herself with her own last name, and the next student takes his or her turn.

- **Life images:** Students choose from pictures portraying people in the domains of work, family, lifestyle, community service, health, and hobbies. For example, the teacher might provide magazines and ask students to pick out images of people engaged in physical-fitness activities. Then the teacher would ask students to imagine what they would most enjoy doing to keep themselves fit. One student might choose an image of a scuba diver, while another might choose an image of a skier. While discussing the images, the students might share that these are activities they can see themselves engaged in because they are unique to the kind of climate they would most like to live in. The images they collect might even be used to create collages that represent a typical day in the life they want to have in the future.

- **Timelines:** Students draw personal timelines from the present to as far into the future as possible. The teacher might ask them to include specific forks in the road (choices that have consequences) and roadblocks (obstacles such as discrimination or lack of financial resources). For example, a student who wants to become an actor might create a timeline with a fork in the road after high school when he will have to decide whether to go to Los Angeles and start auditioning or apply to arts colleges and receive theater training. The obstacle identified might be getting the support of his parents, who very much want him to be a football player instead.

- **Possible selves research:** Students look for information to find out what the requirements or prerequisites are for achieving their possible selves. For example, a student who wants to join the Federal Bureau of Investigation (FBI) might find out what would be the best major in college, what her grade point average would need to be, what community service or previous experience is necessary, and what other skills are necessary as well as other factors, such as having no prior association with drugs. Students can use Internet sources, personal interviews, or even biographies of people who are similar to their possible selves. For example, the student who wants to join the FBI might look for technical information such as education requirements on a government website and look for more practical information such as skills that make a candidate unique by reading about specific agents and the skills they had that made them successful. After researching, students can compare their possible selves.

- **Information interviews:** Students contact adults who occupy positions in the community that are similar or connected to their possible selves and interview them to collect information. For example, a student who wants to be a baseball player might contact the community's local minor league team and interview a player.

Positive possible selves can also be approached from a short-term perspective. In such cases, students focus on an imminent event. Students might write down their best hopes for the outcomes of the event and also write down their worst fears. For example, a student who is anticipating an upcoming audition for a school play might write that getting the part of the lead character would be her best hope, while forgetting her lines or fainting onstage during the audition would be her worst fear. This activity can be extended by having students write out what they intend to do to make sure that their best hopes are achieved. For example, a student who is anticipating a choir concert might want to make sure he gets plenty of rest and avoids overexertion of his voice in the days before the concert.

The following vignette depicts how a teacher might reinforce the concept of short-term positive possible selves.

 *Ms. Rutherford teaches in a small arts school, and important performances are coming up for many of her students. She asks them to visualize and write down the best outcome possible for these performances. Luke hopes to dance well*

> *enough to impress choreographers at professional dance companies and professors at college arts schools who will be in the audience. When they have identified and detailed their best hopes, Ms. Rutherford asks them to write down the things that will help and hinder the achievement of these best hopes. Luke knows that he needs to get enough sleep, practice regularly, and visualize success. He knows that meditation also helps him. Finally, he cannot risk an injury and therefore needs to stay off his skateboard.*

## Optimism

A final useful way of thinking to cultivate in students is an optimistic explanatory style. As described in chapter 2, explanatory style is "the manner in which you habitually explain to yourself why events happen" (Seligman, 2006, p. 15). Martin Seligman (2006) identified three important characteristics of one's explanatory style: (1) permanence, (2) pervasiveness, and (3) personalization. These are described in table 6.1.

### Table 6.1: Explanatory Styles

|  | Optimistic | Pessimistic |
|---|---|---|
| Permanence | **Temporary:** Temporary circumstances in my life cause the bad things that happen to me. | **Permanent:** Permanent elements of my life cause the bad things that happen to me. |
| Pervasiveness | **Specific:** When a bad thing happens in one area of my life (like losing a job), it doesn't affect other parts of my life. | **Universal:** When a bad thing happens in one area of my life (like losing a job), it ruins my whole life. |
| Personalization | **External:** A bad thing happened to me because of other factors. | **Internal:** A bad thing happened to me because I didn't do something right. |

*Permanence* speaks to the degree to which a person believes good or bad things to be attributable to temporary circumstances in life versus permanent circumstances. For example, a person with a high degree of permanence regarding bad events might attribute a car accident to always having been a bad driver or always having bad luck, whereas a person with a low degree of permanence might see a car accident as having been the result of trying to drink coffee and drive at the same time. A person with a high degree of permanence for good events might see a promotion as having been the result of being organized and dedicated for many years, and a person with a low degree of permanence might see a promotion as being the result of having had an unusually good idea on a recent project.

*Pervasiveness* speaks to the degree to which a person believes good or bad things affect other parts of life. For example, a person with a high degree of pervasiveness for bad things might find himself more cautious and frightened while driving after a car accident but might also find himself more cautious and frightened when walking along a busy street, when skiing, or even when someone else is driving. A person with a high degree of pervasiveness for good things might find himself or herself more confident at work following a promotion and might also be more confident on a first date or when giving a speech.

*Personalization* speaks to the degree to which a person believes good or bad things to be attributable to his or her personal qualities or actions. For example, a person with a high degree of personalization for bad events like the break up of a relationship might attribute the breakup solely to his or her own self-centeredness or inability to commit, but a person with a low degree of personalization might see a breakup as having been completely the fault of the other person. A person with a high degree of personalization for good events might see something like a good date to be attributable to having been relaxed and charming, while someone with a low degree of personalization might see a good date as having been attributable to the other person being able to converse well and find topics of common interest.

Seligman (2006) offered his ABCDE reflection strategy as a way to develop an optimistic explanatory style.

1. **Adversity:** The first step includes making a factual description of an adverse event. It does not include any personal feelings or interpretations. For example, after getting off the phone with a friend, Stacy says to her mother, "Jenna cut our phone conversation short because she was going to a movie with another friend." Stacy is not describing any more than what happened.

2. **Beliefs:** The second step includes expressing beliefs and opinions about the factual event. Sometimes our interpretations are logical, and sometimes they are not. Logic and context are not parts of our beliefs; only our individual interpretation of an adverse event is what is important. Students should consciously separate the factual events from their feelings about the event and examine both. For example, Stacy tells her mom, "Jenna thinks I'm boring and doesn't like talking to me." Jenna said no such thing to Stacy. However, Stacy believes that because Jenna cut their conversation short, Jenna thinks she is boring and doesn't like her.

3. **Consequences:** The third step involves taking into account a person's beliefs and feelings about the adverse event and how the person reacted as a result. For example, the next day Stacy might tell her mother that she felt hurt and sad about Jenna cutting the phone conversation short, so she told Jenna she didn't want to be friends anymore. Stacy's mom might ask if she told Jenna about how she felt or if she simply said she didn't want to be friends anymore. "She already thinks I'm boring," Stacy replies. "So it didn't matter how I felt. I just said I didn't want to be friends." Seligman included two techniques to help people ensure better consequences.

   a. **Distancing**—Distancing is the ability to separate oneself from a situation and see it from another point of view. This helps people see that their perceptions are not necessarily true and that acting on those perceptions alone might cause harm. For example, if Stacy had been able to distance herself from the adverse event, she might have understood that Jenna might have a very different point of view and very different feelings than the ones Stacy has assumed. Stacy might have asked Jenna directly how she felt instead of just saying she no longer wanted to be friends.

   b. **Distraction**—Distraction is the process of getting yourself to stop thinking negatively about an adverse event. This can sometimes be difficult. Physical cues such as saying "stop" out loud or looking at a picture of a stop sign can help. Conscious attention shifting can help as well. For example, focusing on another object or activity in the room, going for a run, or reading a magazine are all things that can shift one's focus off an adverse event. Scheduling a later time to think about the event can also help shift focus.

4. **Disputation:** Disputation involves carefully considering each belief about an adverse event and then arguing against it—playing devil's advocate. It is the process of vetting beliefs and looking for misperceptions. Following are four methods of disputation.

a. **Evidence**—Look for things in the event that would refute your beliefs. For example, Stacy might talk with her mom about her decision to tell Jenna she no longer wanted to be friends. "I've been thinking, and I don't feel good about it," she says. "She called me before she went to the movies." Her mom replies, "She probably doesn't think you're boring, if she is calling you. Normally no one calls people whom they believe to be boring, right?" Stacy admits this is true. "Me and Jenna have been friends for more than two years. That's a long time to be friends with someone you find to be boring."

b. **Alternatives**—This involves finding other possible explanations for how or why an adverse event occurred in the way it did. For example, Stacy thinks about the days before the call. "I didn't want to see that movie, and I told Jenna that," she says. Her mom then notes that no one can change the times movies start, and Stacy admits that it is likely that Jenna had to cut the conversation short.

c. **Implications**—This involves considering the adverse event, the beliefs, and the consequences. When looking at implications, we are trying to see how our actions will affect our relationships. For example, Stacy's mom asks her to think about how Jenna might have felt at school when Stacy said she no longer wanted to be friends. "If she didn't think you were boring, do you think she might have been confused?" Stacy is able to see that she might have been mistaken and that she doesn't want to lose her friend. She might apologize and explain to Jenna how she was feeling.

d. **Usefulness**—This involves considering the degree to which the initial beliefs about an adverse event are productive and helpful. Many beliefs are damaging to us and should be discarded. For example, the belief that Jenna considered Stacy boring is not useful to Stacy in terms of herself or her friendships. If she can recognize this belief as a useless one and discard it, she is more likely to have positive interactions in the future.

5. **Energization:** The purpose of this reflection is to understand how the strategy helps in dealing with adverse events. For example, Stacy might note that using the strategy kept her from losing a friend and made her feel a lot better.

Seligman's ABCDE strategy is detailed and powerful. The model in its entirety is depicted in figure 6.8. Because of the complexity of Seligman's model, it is best approached in small increments. For example, a teacher might introduce and guide students through one step at a time over a period of a term, semester, or an entire school year.

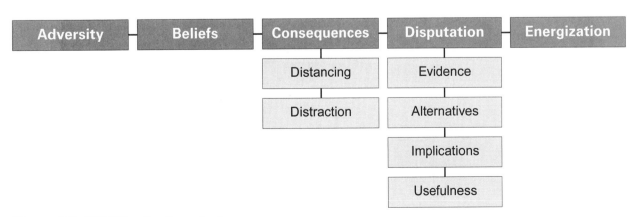

**Figure 6.8: ABCDE reflection strategy.**

Whether a teacher focuses on the growth versus fixed mindset, resiliency, positive possible selves, or optimism, it is important to keep the conversation alive throughout the year. Teachers can accomplish this by capitalizing on situations in the news in which positive (or negative) ways of thinking are evident and using movies, literature, and personal examples. The following vignette depicts how a teacher might keep reminding students of these types of thinking.

> *Mr. Barnes brings in an article he found in the newspaper over the weekend to show to his students. They have been studying the growth versus fixed mindset, and he likes to bring in periodic reminders of how effective a growth mindset can be. "This article is about a man who was told in school that he was learning disabled," he says. "He had always loved art and drawing, though, and no matter what his teachers or anyone else said, he kept drawing and painting. He didn't go to college, but he did find an agent, and he just had a showing of his work at a major gallery in New York."*
>
> *Mr. Barnes asks his students if they have found any recent examples. Brian has brought in a quotation from a state senator. The senator said that he wanted to be a physicist but he gave it up because he knew he wasn't smart enough. "I thought it was interesting that someone as successful as a state senator could display a fixed mindset," he says.*

## Avoiding Negative Ways of Thinking

Just as students should cultivate positive ways of thinking, they should also avoid negative ways of thinking. Here we address two general categories of negative thinking: (1) emotional thinking and (2) worry.

### Emotional Thinking

Emotions are a natural and important aspect of life. To develop an understanding of emotions, students should have a working knowledge of the various types of emotions they will experience in their lives.

There are many lists describing the types of emotions a student might experience. For example, Reinhard Pekrun (2009) provided the following list of emotions that are associated with learning:

- Enjoyment
- Hope
- Pride
- Anger
- Anxiety
- Shame
- Boredom

In the book *A Handbook for Classroom Management That Works*, Marzano and colleagues (2005) provided a list of six basic feelings that can be explored even with relatively young students: *sad*, *glad*, *mad*, *afraid*, *ashamed*, and *surprised*.

The first step in fostering an understanding of emotional thinking is to help students understand the nature of emotions. It is helpful for students to describe particular emotions in their own words. A teacher might start such a discussion by using a personal story. For example, a teacher might begin a discussion about the emotion of anger by telling the class about a friend who recently called and asked if he wanted to go to next week's football game with him. He was really excited about it all week, and then on Saturday his friend told him he had given the tickets to his boss instead. He might explain that he was mad because his friend gave away the tickets and didn't even tell him about it until the night before the game. He might also explain the physical sensations such as sweating and fidgeting that he feels when he gets mad and how his thoughts change.

Of course, a teacher must take great care when addressing the emotions of fear and shame, because discussions about these emotions have the potential to embarrass students, who might later regret what they shared. With young children, it is probably best for the teacher to give examples from his or her own life. Another effective strategy is to use characters from literature or from current events as a way of teasing out the behaviors associated with feeling afraid and ashamed. For example, after reading a story about a boy who stole his brother's baseball mitt, a teacher might ask students how they think the boy felt before he stole it, while he was stealing it, and after he stole it. She might ask them to explain their interpretations using the boy's actions in the book.

With older students, more terms for emotions can be used. For example, *unhappy*, *distraught*, and *melancholy* are all words associated with sadness. Students can identify the many synonyms for the six basic emotions and the slight differences in meaning between them. For example, *sad* has a slightly different connotation than *distraught*. Students can then order the synonyms from mild to strong expression of emotion.

To help students develop a deep understanding of emotions, a teacher might ask them to gather information about the nature and effect of emotions. For example, students might gather information on situations that incite emotions like anger, or they might gather information on which emotions people commonly report difficulty controlling. The following list provides resources students can use to collect information about dealing with the emotions anger and grief.

Websites:

- Conflict Resolution Network (www.crnhq.org) helps to create safe schools and civil communities by making conflict resolution education universally available.

- School Mediation Associates (www.schoolmediation.com) is a site featuring school conflict resolution and mediation information, book excerpts, discussions, news, and links.

Books:

- *The Anger Control Toolkit* (Shapiro, 1994)

- *Student Workshop: Angry? Ten Ways to Cool Off* (Sunburst, 1999)

- *Expressing Anger: Healthy vs. Unhealthy* (Schloat, 1999)

- *Defusing Anger and Aggression: Safe Strategies for Secondary School Educators* (Colvin, 1999)

- *Helping the Grieving Student: A Guide for Teachers* (Dougy Center, 2003)

- *35 Ways to Help a Grieving Child* (Dougy Center, 1999)

Once students have a sense of the various types of emotions they experience in life, they should learn how strong emotions affect human experience. For instance, anger is a very strong emotion that often leads people to make regrettable choices. As discussed in chapter 2 (pages 27–28), Goleman (1995) noted that the body literally reacts to a strong emotion more quickly than the brain does, causing the amygdala to release adrenaline. Goleman (1995) identified three signals that this amygdala hijack is happening or has happened: (1) strong emotional reaction, (2) sudden onset, and (3) regret for actions on later reflection.

Finally, it is important that students understand that emotions can be contagious. That is, when one person is feeling a strong emotion, the other people around him or her begin to feel it too. Goleman reported on a study (Sullins, 1991) in which volunteers were asked to fill out a simple checklist about how they felt. They were then paired with another person and left alone in a room for two minutes. During that time, the two volunteers only sat, facing one another; there was no talking or communicating of any kind. Afterward, they filled out another checklist about how they felt. Pairs intentionally included one person who was emotionally expressive of emotions by nature and one who was more passive. Goleman noted, "invariably the mood of the one who was more expressive of emotions had been transferred to the more passive partner" (p. 115). The study indicated that when a person is around someone who has strong negative emotions he or she can feel strong negative emotions as well. Conversely, being around someone who has strong positive emotions can have a positive effect. If students are aware of this, they become capable of surrounding themselves with people who are positive rather than negative influences.

Perhaps the most powerful way to emphasize the power of emotional thinking is to provide examples of people who let their emotional thinking translate to regrettable actions.

- **Zinedine Zidane:** He was the captain of the French soccer team and a worldwide soccer role model who was to retire after the 2006 World Cup final game against Italy. About one hundred minutes into the game, the score was tied, and Italy's Marco Materazzi was defending Zidane. They were seen exchanging words. It is believed that Materazzi insulted Zidane's sister, and Zidane lost control, headbutting Materazzi in the chest. He was kicked out of the game, and France lost the World Cup to Italy 5 to 3. Zidane had a long and successful career in soccer, but the lasting image of his career (seen by 28.8 billion viewers in 213 countries) will be the moment he lost control and drove his head into another player, possibly costing his team the 2006 World Cup (Berlin, 2006).

- **Mike Tyson:** He met Evander Holyfield in the ring for a second time on June 28, 1997. Holyfield had won the first match, and Tyson wanted to settle the score. In the second round, Holyfield headbutted Tyson, and Tyson was left with a gash over his eye. Headbutting was something Tyson had complained about during and after the first fight, and the act fueled his anger. Just before the start of the third round, Tyson bit Holyfield on the right ear, actually severing a small part of it. The referee docked him two points and told Tyson outright he did not believe him when Tyson tried to claim the injury was the result of a punch. The docked points appeared to fuel Tyson's rage even more, and he took another bite out of Holyfield's left ear. After the second bite, he was disqualified from the fight. It was later announced that he would receive no payment and would be fined three million dollars. His license was also suspended for over a year, and he narrowly escaped a jail sentence. To this day, the incident clouds Tyson's entire career, and he has stated publicly that he regrets it (Weinberg, 2009).

- **Serena Williams:** She and Kim Clijsters competed in tennis at the U.S. Open in 2009. After losing the first set, Serena was penalized for throwing her racquet on the court. On match point, she was penalized again for a foot fault, which made her so angry that she said something inappropriate to the lineswoman, who then complained to the chair umpire about verbal abuse. Serena was assessed a code violation point penalty for the comment, which gave Clijsters the match. Serena was later fined $10,000. She issued a statement apologizing to everyone involved, saying she regretted her actions ("Clijsters Wins," 2009).

- **Steven Slater:** He was a JetBlue flight attendant in August 2010. Allegedly, a passenger had been rude to Slater at the start of a flight from Pittsburgh to New York's John F. Kennedy International Airport, and when they reached Kennedy, she hit him in the head with her luggage. It isn't entirely clear what happened at the beginning or the end of the flight, but what is clear is that Slater completely lost his temper. It is reported that he began drinking a beer, cursed over the intercom, and made a grand exit down the emergency slide. Though he was elevated to folk-hero status following the incident, he was charged with criminal mischief, reckless endangerment, and trespassing—all felony counts that carry a maximum penalty of seven years in prison (Mayerowitz, 2010).

There are also humorous scenes in movies that can be used as examples of people who could not calm down. We've summarized some examples. (See YouTube for clips of these scenes or others; a teacher should screen any clip that will be used in class to ensure it is appropriate.)

- *Father of the Bride* (Baum, Meyers, Rosenman, & Shyer, 1991): George Banks is angry about the cost of his daughter's wedding. He goes to the supermarket to buy hot dogs and hot dog buns, and his anger gets the best of him.

- *Sleeping Beauty* (Disney & Geronimi, 1959): Rose's fairy godmothers get angry with each other over her dress, and there are consequences for what happens. (There are also a lot of other Disney-movie scenes in which people lose their tempers. In *Cinderella* [Disney, Geronimi, Jackson, & Luske, 1950], the stepsisters get angry with one another and wind up tearing Cinderella's dress; in *The Little Mermaid* [Ashman, Musker, & Clements, 1989], Ariel's father loses his temper and destroys all her treasures.)

- *Jerry Maguire* (Brooks, Mark, Sakai, & Crowe, 1996): Jerry Maguire is fired and fails to retain most of his clients. Needless to say, he has a bad day at work, and he doesn't leave gracefully.

- *Ferris Bueller's Day Off* (Jacobson & Hughes, 1986): Cameron is angry at his father and feels very hurt. He completely loses his temper and kicks his father's car (his father's most prized possession) repeatedly. It winds up crashed in the woods behind the house.

- *Anchorman: The Legend of Ron Burgundy* (Apatow & McKay, 2004): Ron Burgundy gets very upset after losing his dog.

Once students understand how thinking under strong negative emotions like anger or fear can generate behavior they might regret later, they can start to identify situations in their own lives when they engaged in thoughtless or regrettable behavior. This is best done if the teacher begins by sharing examples in his or her own life. For example, a teacher might tell his students that his wife knows he is afraid of snakes and so she put a rubber one in their grill and then filmed him opening the lid, screaming, dropping the charcoal, and running away. He might explain that when he first saw his wife filming it he was angry and started an argument, but after some time he realized that he had overreacted and that it really was a fairly funny joke.

Another option is for students to identify situations in their lives when they are prone to thoughtless behavior. For example, one student might share that she generally gets frustrated when shopping with her mom because her mom always picks out the ugliest clothes and never likes anything she likes. She might say they often get in a fight about it, but then she feels bad later because she knows her mom is trying to do a nice thing by taking her shopping.

Students can develop control over their strong emotions simply by knowing something about them. Johnson and Johnson (2005) listed the following characteristics of anger.

- **Anger is usually a defense:** For example, a student who lashes out and insults another student without provocation is usually doing so because of some personal insecurity. Perhaps she feels that she is not pretty and her clothes are not stylish enough. Consequently, she lashes out in hopes of diverting attention from herself and in hopes of intimidating others so that they won't make fun of her.

- **Anger occurs when people don't get what they want or when they are confused, frustrated, or attacked:** For example, a student who steals a ball or another toy from another student might do so because he feels his friend is neglecting him by paying attention to too many other people, and he feels hurt and frustrated.

- **Anger carries a sense of righteousness:** People tend to believe they are right and someone else is wrong. For example, two students who got into a fight and were sent to the principal's office would likely both feel that they were being unjustly punished. One student might feel that he was insulted and that the other student started the fight while he was merely defending himself. Conversely, the other student may feel that he was only expressing an opinion and did not deserve to be hit for it.

- **There is a narrowing of perceptual focus and priorities when people get angry:** For example, a student who starts a fight is thinking only about how angry he is. He forgets completely that if he is sent to the principal's office again he will be suspended, and his father then will ground him for the weekend, causing him to miss an event he has been looking forward to.

- **There is a demand aspect of anger:** People want what they want. For example, a student might be willing to resort to violence because he is angry and thinks he can force another student to be nice to him.

- **There is considerable physiological arousal that demands expression in anger:** For example, we can often distract ourselves when we are bored, confused, or mildly amused, but anger is difficult to forget about. It is also much more difficult to hide than other emotions.

The ultimate goal of understanding the nature of emotion is for students to be able to mitigate negative influences and control negative emotions. Teachers can present the following steps (Goleman, 1995) for dealing with the amygdala hijack.

1. **Label the emotion:** Attaching a word to a feeling decreases activity in the amygdala. For example, a student who feels that another student insulted him might pause for a few moments and simply put a name to the emotion he is feeling—frustration, anger, embarrassment, or hurt.

2. **Perform an emotional audit:** An emotional audit requires complete emotional awareness and awareness of the consequences of potential actions. There are five parts.

a. **What am I thinking?**—For example, the student who feels he has just been insulted and has identified anger and embarrassment as his primary emotions might also become aware of the thoughts associated with those emotions. He might be thinking, "I can't believe he insulted me in front of all of these people!" Or he might think, "Where did that come from? I've never done anything to him, and now he goes out of his way to insult me?"

b. **What am I feeling?**—Thoughts and emotions are integrated with movements and physical feelings. Our angered student might realize at this point that because he is feeling angry and embarrassed, he is clenching his teeth and making fists. He might also notice that his heart is beating faster.

c. **What do I want now?**—This process activates executive functioning. In a manner of speaking, it puts the brain back in control. By considering what might or might not come next, a student is able to see different courses of action and choose the best one instead of reacting without thinking. For example, the student who has just been insulted might consider hitting the student he is upset with, but he might also consider delivering an insult of his own, making a funny comment that would defuse the tension, or ignoring the student and walking away.

d. **How am I getting in my way?**—This step helps students learn from past mistakes. For example, the student who is angry might remember a previous occasion when he was angry, think about what he did that was not effective, and focus on avoiding the same outcome.

e. **What do I need to do differently now?**—At this point, the student makes a plan to deal with his or her emotions. Having become aware of his thoughts, physical reactions, options, and previous mistakes, the student who feels he has been insulted might decide to walk away, seek advice from a teacher on what to do, and make a plan to talk to the person who insulted him once he has cooled down.

This strategy is rather complex and is best introduced in parts. For example, a teacher might introduce the concept of labeling the emotion one week and provide some personal examples. Then each week for the next five weeks, the teacher might introduce one step of the emotional audit and provide more examples. Then he or she might ask students to identify times in their lives when they have or have not become victims of the amygdala hijack.

The following vignette depicts a teacher addressing emotional thinking.

> After introducing all five steps of the emotional audit, Mr. Rosen tells his students that while he never consistently struggled with strong feelings of anger, his brother did. "My brother is a great guy, but he is really competitive and would always go way over the top in any kind of game," he says. "It got him into a lot of fights. When we were in high school, he learned to label his emotions and the thoughts associated with them. He learned to connect his physiological responses with his emotional responses, but it was really hard for him to 'turn his brain on' again. I remember several times pushing him out of confrontational situations and telling him, 'You don't

*want to do this. Think about it. Think about what happened last time.' Once he did, he was able to calm down and avoid a fight, but it took him some time to get there."*

*Mr. Rosen then asks his students to think about their own behaviors. "Are there ever times you feel like you can't turn your brain on?" he asks. "Do you ever feel like your body reacts before you can think about it?" He asks them to take some time and write down several instances in which this has happened. He then asks them to look for similarities between the instances they wrote about from their own lives and also similarities with any other experiences other students volunteer to share.*

## Worry

Worry is a special type of emotional thinking that affects everyone. As we saw in chapter 2 (page 29), worry is a chronic condition and not necessarily linked to reasonable or specific events. We define worry as persistent negative thoughts or images associated with possible outcomes of real or imagined scenarios. The topic of worry can be introduced through quotes such as the following (Quote Garden, 2010).

- "If things go wrong, don't go with them." —Roger Babson

- "If you can't sleep, then get up and do something instead of lying there worrying. It's the worry that gets you, not the lack of sleep." —Dale Carnegie

- "People become attached to their burdens sometimes more than the burdens are attached to them." —George Bernard Shaw

- "I am reminded of the advice of my neighbor. 'Never worry about your heart till it stops beating.'" —E. B. White

- "I am an old man and have known a great many troubles, but most of them never happened." —Mark Twain

- "If you see ten troubles coming down the road, you can be sure that nine will run into the ditch before they reach you." —Calvin Coolidge

- "When I really worry about something, I don't just fool around. I even have to go to the bathroom when I worry about something. Only, I don't go. I'm too worried to go. I don't want to interrupt my worrying to go." —J. D. Salinger, *The Catcher in the Rye*

Worry can also be introduced to students by using cartoons like the one in figure 6.9. Students can then be asked to identify things that they typically worry about in their lives. An activity like this is best introduced if the teacher shares some of his or her own personal areas of worry. For example, a teacher might share with her students that she plays on a summer softball team. She says that while she knows it is all played in fun, she gets anxious when she goes up to bat and worries that she will strike out and disappoint her team. This personal example illustrates for students that worry doesn't just arise over big things; it can be a problem with small things as well. She might then ask her students about their sources of worry.

Students can also be asked to explore how worry affects them using a survey like the one in figure 6.10 (page 148). There are a number of sensitive questions in figure 6.10, the answers to which must be

**Pachyderm Insomnia**

**Figure 6.9: Worry cartoon about ability.**

Source: Used with permission from cartoonstock.com.

kept confidential. Students could be asked to complete the survey privately, and after they have completed it, the teacher could lead a class discussion by introducing the common symptoms of worry such as the presence of negative or unrealistic thoughts or expectations.

As is the case with emotional thinking, the ultimate goal of understanding worry is to be able to control it. Here we review a few strategies teachers can use.

Alice Fleming (1992) introduced a four-step process to "put worry to work" (p. 63).

1. **Find out if the problem is solvable:** For example, a problem such as a civil war in another country is a real problem, but there is not much of a chance that a student is going to be able to solve it. However, the problem of how to get to and from school without riding the school bus is solvable.

2. **Figure out what's causing it:** For example, a student with a poor grade in a class might look at her grade report and notice that part of the reason why her grade is low is that she has not turned in any homework assignments. She might also realize that not doing homework might have contributed to the current confusion she feels in the class.

3. **Decide how to solve it:** For example, a student who wants to learn to play the violin but knows her family doesn't have enough money to buy an instrument might decide that she can write a letter to a national nonprofit organization dedicated to preserving music in schools and ask for help.

4. **Do it:** For example, a student who has decided that she needs to improve her grade in a class might make a study schedule for the second half of the semester, amend it as necessary, and follow it.

Do you often:

- Find yourself thinking about bad things that might happen in the future?
- Feel overwhelmed?
- Feel unable to control your anxious feelings?
- Worry about disappointing or not pleasing others?
- Feel trapped in or avoid social situations where it might be difficult to escape if you wanted to?
- Have an ongoing fear of a specific object or situation, such as spiders or heights?
- Fear going to unfamiliar places or talking to unfamiliar people alone?
- Experience racing or disturbing thoughts that you're unable to get out of your mind?
- Habitually do things like check the clock, check the door locks, or wash your hands even though you know it isn't necessary?
- Feel that you must be perfect?
- Use sugar, caffeine, alcohol, nicotine, or prescription or illegal drugs to help you feel less anxious?
- Feel that anxiety interferes with your daily life?
- Fear being out of control?
- Find yourself frequently using words such as *can't*, *should*, and *have to*?
- Push yourself to do more, even when you're physically and mentally exhausted?

**Figure 6.10: Survey on worry.**

The following vignette depicts how a teacher might help students understand the concept of worry.

*Ms. Miller and her students have discussed personal examples of worry and signs of the presence of worry. She asks them to identify something they have been consistently worried about. "Is this something you can do something about?" she asks. "For example, if you are worried about a family member who is serving in Afghanistan, that is a perfectly understandable worry. However, there is not much you can do about it. If you are worried about a relationship with a friend or an upcoming event, you can do something about that." She asks students to identify anything they are worried about, but to select one thing in particular that they can do something about.*

*A few days later she asks them to consider the issue of worry they have chosen and try to figure out what is causing it. "If you are worried that a friend might be upset with you, try to figure out why this might be. Did you do something to hurt his or her feelings? Is there reason to suspect that your friend is not actually upset with you but that something else is happening?"*

*After a few days, they revisit the worry issue again. Ms. Miller says, "Now that you know the issue can be resolved and you know what is causing it, decide exactly what you are going to do. If you are worried your friend is upset with you, you might decide to ask him or her if this is the case. If you are worried about an upcoming performance, you might decide to prepare as best you can so that you can feel confident when the time comes." She asks students to write down each step of what they plan to do, and after they have put their plans in action, she asks them to write down the results and whether or not they are still worried.*

### Test Anxiety: A Special Type of Worry

Many students suffer from test anxiety. One way to introduce the topic of test anxiety is to have students complete a survey such as that in figure 6.11.

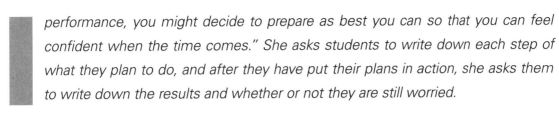

**Directions:** Read each statement, checking those that apply before or during an examination or both. Do you:

_____ Get nervous before an exam?

_____ Get nervous during an exam?

_____ Find it difficult to keep your jitters under control?

_____ Develop a queasy stomach or cold hands, clammy hands, or both?

_____ Sometimes hyperventilate, feeling faint or light-headed?

_____ Often find that the test, at first glance, appears foreign or unfamiliar?

_____ Consider yourself a sensitive person when it comes to other aspects of life?

_____ Have poor or personally unacceptable study habits?

_____ Often blank on exams, exhibiting minimal recall?

_____ Have a personal history of failure on tests?

_____ Worry excessively about the prospect of failure and its consequences?

_____ Have excessive pressure to succeed either from yourself or from other sources?

_____ Often compete with peers, family members, or friends for grades?

_____ Experience test panic due to the realization that you are unprepared?

_____ Fear having to maintain the burden of success?

_____ Have pressing concerns or problems that occupy your mind?

Visit **marzanoresearch.com/classroomstrategies** to download a reproducible version of this figure.

**Figure 6.11: Survey on test anxiety.**

Source: Adapted from Georgia College Counseling Services, n.d.

As with the worry analysis survey, the answers to some of these questions might be embarrassing for students. Consequently, students should answer them privately and then tally their final scores to obtain their degree of test anxiety using the following scale:

12 or more—severe

8 to 11—moderate

4 to 7—mild

0 to 3—slight

The teacher might then lead a whole-class discussion regarding test anxiety. For example, she might tell the students about how upset and worried she was when she had to take the Graduate Record Examinations (GRE) to get into graduate school; she might share that she felt certain she was going to do poorly and that she was sweating the entire time she took the test. After providing a personal example of test anxiety, she can go over a checklist of common symptoms and ask her students to mentally note any symptoms they display before, during, and even after tests. Then she can present specific strategies, such as those in table 6.2.

## Table 6.2: Preparing for Tests

| Before Tests | During Tests | After Tests |
|---|---|---|
| • Maintain good study habits—do your class work.<br>  • Have a clear understanding of homework assignments before leaving class.<br>  • Keep a record of assignments received and completed.<br>  • Make a study schedule and follow it.<br>  • Tell your parents about schoolwork and homework.<br>  • Turn in homework on time.<br>  • Get makeup assignments when returning from an absence.<br>  • See teachers for additional help.<br>• Seek and use past homework assignments, class notes, and available review materials.<br>• Read and follow any directions presented for test review.<br>• Find out when tests will be given.<br>• Get a good night's rest.<br>• Eat a normal breakfast before testing. | • Read and pay careful attention to all directions.<br>• Read each passage and accompanying questions.<br>• Read every possible answer—the best one could be last.<br>• Read and respond to items one at a time rather than thinking about the test as a whole.<br>• Reread, when necessary, the parts of a passage needed for selecting the correct answer.<br>• Don't expect to find a pattern in the positions of the correct answers.<br>• Don't make uneducated guesses. Try to get the correct answer by reasoning and eliminating wrong answers.<br>• Decide exactly what the question is asking; one response is clearly best.<br>• Don't spend too much time on any one question.<br>• Skip difficult questions until all other questions have been answered. On scrap paper, keep a record of the unanswered items to return to, if time permits.<br>• Make sure to record the answer in the correct place on the answer sheet.<br>• Only change an answer if you are sure the first one you picked was wrong. Be sure to completely erase changed answers.<br>• Work as rapidly as possible with accuracy.<br>• After completion of the test, use any remaining time to check your answers.<br>• Keep a good attitude. Think positively! | • Examine your test scores; ask the teacher to explain your test scores, if needed.<br>• Congratulate yourself on identified areas of strength.<br>• Identify areas of weakness which you will want to improve for a better performance next time.<br>• Ask your teacher to suggest areas of study that will help you perform better on the next test. |

Source: Adapted from Tennessee Department of Education, n.d.

Finally, the following are general things teachers can do to help students reduce test anxiety (Landmark School Outreach Program, n.d.) and prepare for tests.

- Help students organize past worksheets, homework assignments, essays, and other class materials to generate (through class discussion) a list of topics that might be on the test.

- Assign sample test questions for homework. These can be teacher-generated questions or student-generated questions.

- Let students fill a note card with information they think they will need during the test and use it during the exam (formulas, for example).

- Provide practice answering short-essay questions by requiring students to write paragraph summaries of sections of their class notes.

- Encourage students to evaluate what topics on the test will be most difficult for them, and use this information to put study topics in order of priority.

- Use past tests and quizzes, and have students correct the questions they answered incorrectly.

The following vignette depicts how a teacher might implement one of these suggestions.

*Mr. Sirens knows that many of his students feel anxious before tests. He decides to help them. First, he clearly states the topics the test will cover. Next, he asks students to review their previous test and quiz scores for each topic. He then provides sample short-answer questions on each topic, and after students answer them, he asks them to rate their confidence level on each topic on a scale of one to four—four being very confident and one being not at all confident. Students then rank the topics.*

*"Put those topics you feel the least confident about on the top of the list," Mr. Sirens says. "When you study for the test, use this list as a guide. If you begin to feel more confident about the toughest topics for you, your overall anxiety level might decrease, and studying the other topics and taking the test might be easier for you."*

## Summary

This chapter focused on the conative skill of understanding one's own interpretations, emotions, and thought patterns. By becoming aware of the power and adaptability of interpretations, cultivating positive and empowering methods of thought, and learning to avoid emotional thinking such as worry, students can develop both self-awareness and self-efficacy. In the 21st century, students will be in constant contact with people who have diverse backgrounds and opinions. Being aware and in control of their own thoughts and actions will be crucial to successful communication in any arena of life.

# Chapter 6: Comprehension Questions

1. Why are optical illusions a good way to stimulate discussion about perceptions?

2. What are the important differences between the growth mindset and the fixed mindset?

3. How can teaching students about resiliency help them to cultivate a sense of self-efficacy?

4. Why is emotional thinking a negative way of thinking?

# Chapter 7

# UNDERSTANDING AND INTERACTING WITH OTHERS

In addition to the conative skills described in chapter 6, which concern understanding and controlling oneself, we present a complimentary set of conative skills that involve understanding and interacting with others. As the global population grows and interaction with others becomes more frequent and complex throughout the 21st century, there will be a greater need for schools to teach these skills. This chapter addresses three categories of skills that can help 21st century students understand and interact with others: (1) perspective taking, (2) responsible interaction, and (3) controversy and conflict resolution.

## Perspective Taking

*Perspective taking* refers to a student's ability to see an issue from multiple perspectives. While this skill has always been foundational for understanding and interacting with others, its importance has been magnified in a century that offers such rich opportunity for interacting with people across the globe. In order to be able to see an issue from multiple perspectives, students must first be aware that different perspectives can and do exist.

### An Awareness of Perspective

To obtain a sense of the power of perspective, teachers can provide students with activities like the following.

#### See Things Differently

Students work in teams to describe verbally or in writing a picture that has been provided. The picture might be of an object such as a dollhouse or of a place such as an amusement park, but each team has a picture of the same object or place taken from a different perspective. In the case of an object such as a dollhouse, some teams might have a close-up and interior picture of a bedroom, and other teams might have pictures of the house from the outside or even pictures of the room in which it sits. In the case of a place such as an amusement park, the pictures might have been taken at different times (perhaps over the course of thirty years). Students then work together to use those descriptions to create or imagine a more complete picture. In the case of photos taken over time, for example, students might put the pictures in order and discuss how they think the park has changed over time (Conflict Resolution Education, n.d.).

### Draw What You See

In this activity, a teacher begins by writing a word such as *ocean* on the board and asking students to imagine being there and then to write about or draw what they see. After they have done so, the students compare their descriptions—some might describe stormy weather and others sunny; some might be detailed and others vague. Some students may have never seen an ocean. Each student's picture and description, and therefore perspective, will be slightly different. This activity can be quite revealing as students have very different associations with words like *wilderness* (Conflict Resolution Education, n.d.).

### Visualize the Whole Picture

A teacher begins this activity by organizing students into four groups and distributing a handout of a picture divided into four quadrants. Each group receives a picture with three of the four quadrants covered up. The visible quadrant is different for each of the four groups. Students in each group discuss what they see and what they think is going on in the picture based on what they see. Then each group verbally describes their visible quadrant to the rest of the class. The groups meet again and discuss what they think might be going on based on what they heard other groups describe (Johnson & Johnson, 2007).

The following vignette depicts how a teacher might use one of these strategies.

> Mr. Talbot has provided his students with a variety of old magazines. He writes the word Africa on the board and asks his students to look through the magazines and create a collage of what they think of when they think of Africa. He tells them they can also draw whatever they like if they can't find what they want in the magazine.
>
> Sheryl creates a collage displaying a beautiful beach and boutiques and restaurants. "My cousin lives in South Africa," she says. "I know most of Africa isn't like this, but this is what I saw when I went to visit her. It is one of my best memories, and that's what I think of first when I think of Africa."
>
> Sol is a very talented artist, and he foregoes the collage to draw a portrait of a woman. "This is my grandmother," he says. "She escaped the civil war in Ethiopia in the 1970s and came here. She always tells me stories about life there."
>
> Adrian has created a collage that shows both a lot of wildlife and conflict among people. "I've never been to Africa," he says. "But I think of two things when I imagine it: the awful conflicts that seem to always be going on there and the nature shows I see on television. I love to watch the shows about the lions and cheetahs especially."

## Perspective Analysis

Once students have an awareness of perspective, they can begin to analyze different perspectives in a more in-depth way. Marzano (1992) provided a concrete strategy referred to as *perspective analysis* to help students do this. During perspective analysis, students scrutinize their opinions on a given issue and the logic behind those opinions. In addition, they consider a contrasting position and the logic behind it. The following five steps are involved in perspective analysis.

1. **Identify a position on a controversial topic:** For example, on the topic of animal research, a student might decide that the advancements made by using animals as test subjects do not justify a practice that he feels is morally wrong.

2. **Determine the reasoning behind the position:** For example, the student might explain that under no circumstances would we allow other humans to be subjected to scientific research that would put their lives, well-being, or general happiness in jeopardy and that the same maxim should apply to animals. He would explain his belief that to harm a living being is wrong, no matter the purpose.

3. **Identify an opposing position:** For example, the student might explain that many people hold the belief that animal research is an important and justifiable practice.

4. **Describe the reasoning behind the opposing position:** For example, the student might explain that proponents of animal research believe it to be justifiable because it ultimately leads to major scientific advancements that save many people's lives.

5. **When finished, summarize a deeper understanding:** For example, the student might explain that after examining specific advancements due to animal research, he understands why people would advocate that the benefits of animal research outweigh the drawbacks. He can see how it saves people's lives, and there is no doubt that is a very good thing, but ultimately he still believes that science should not advance at the expense of ethics.

The steps to perspective analysis can be presented to students as a series of questions such as the following (Marzano & Pickering, 2011, p. 64):

1. "What do I believe about this?"

2. "Why do I believe it?"

3. "What is another way of looking at this?"

4. "Why might someone else hold a different opinion?"

5. "What have I learned?"

Students can use perspective analysis any time they face an issue about which people have different opinions.

The following vignette depicts how a teacher might use perspective analysis.

> *Ms. Norman's students are reading Walter Dean Myers's* Fallen Angels, *a book that can spark controversial conversations about current events. She doesn't want to shy away from that controversy, but she wants to make sure it remains appropriate. She begins by asking students to think carefully about their opinions and to write down justifications for those opinions. When they have articulated their stances, she asks them to role-play and imagine being someone who has a different viewpoint.*

*"What might a different opinion be?"* she says. *"What would be justifications for that point of view?"* When they have thoroughly articulated both sides, students divide into pairs. Each student teams with someone who shares an opinion different from his or her own and discusses the matter using only what he or she wrote down. After the activity, students share what they learned in a class discussion.

## Parallel Thinking

Edward de Bono (1999) has generated a number of strategies that can help students understand the power of perspective and use that power in their interactions with others. One highly useful strategy is *parallel thinking.* Parallel thinking allows a group of students to collaboratively examine an issue from many points of view by exploring each perspective one at a time. De Bono calls this process *sensitization,* because group members become sensitized to other points of view. He identifies six *thinking hats* (symbolized by six colors) that represent six different ways to view any issue or problem. In the whole-group discussion, students all "try on" the same hat at once.

### Blue Hat

The blue hat represents organizational perspectives. When wearing the blue hat, students discuss how the thinking process is working and how to manage the other hats. Blue-hat thinking is used at the beginning of a collaboration to decide the order in which the other hats will be used, the time that will be spent thinking in each hat, and the value of conclusions made while thinking in each hat. It can also be used at the end of collaboration in order to review progress.

### White Hat

The white hat represents neutral and objective perspectives. When wearing the white hat, students examine objective facts and figures without interpreting them. They check for differences between believed facts (what someone thinks is true) and checked facts (what someone has researched and knows to be true). They also investigate the *spectrum of likelihood* for each fact—that is, whether the fact is always true, usually true, sometimes true, occasionally true, or cannot be true. In this stage of the discussion, students gain a solid perspective on what the facts in any matter are, whether those facts are reliable, and under what circumstances and to what degree they are reliable.

### Red Hat

The red hat represents emotional perspectives. When wearing the red hat, students express how they feel about a topic without judgment. These feelings do not have to be validated or justified, and no one is required to provide a logical basis for his or her emotions and feelings. No one is allowed to comment on another person's feelings. The purpose of the red hat is not to reach an emotional consensus but simply to validate different emotions and feelings.

### Black Hat

The black hat represents cautious or careful perspectives. When wearing the black hat, students look for the weaknesses in an idea. This might include assessing the potential risk in ideas, pointing out pitfalls or drawbacks, and considering all the possible outcomes. When wearing the black hat, students try to plan for everything that could go wrong when implementing a particular solution to a problem.

### Yellow Hat

The yellow hat represents optimistic perspectives. When wearing the yellow hat, students look for the positive and valuable aspects of an idea. They assess each idea in terms of how valuable it is and how likely it is to bring about good things.

### Green Hat

The green hat represents creative perspectives. When wearing the green hat, participants generate new ideas. Green-hat thinking is similar to divergent thinking in that the goal is to create new ideas by going beyond the known, obvious, or merely satisfactory ideas or by connecting seemingly unrelated ideas to create novel solutions.

The following vignette describes how a teacher might introduce the six thinking hats to engage students in parallel thinking.

Mr. Moore's class has been studying the effects of a recent earthquake in a developing country. Initial relief efforts are over, but the country will need a lot of help over the long term.

"Just donating to the Red Cross isn't going to be enough," Mr. Moore says. He asks his students to put on their green thinking hats and brainstorm solutions to the problem. "Natural disasters are a part of life, and not every country has the money or the means to recover independently," he says. "How can we help countries like this one with long-term relief?"

The class splits into small groups, and they begin to brainstorm. Students in one group research how the citizens of that country make their living and find that most of the population depends in some way on farming. "Instead of just sending money to the Red Cross, we could think more long term by finding out what kinds of food grow best there year round," they say. "People who know a lot about farming those foods can go over and help them, and we could send seeds and supplies. That way food won't run out, and they can begin to support themselves again."

Another group researches the major cause of death in the recent earthquake. The students find that most of the country's structures are concrete and poorly constructed and that many people died in building collapses as a result. They say, "We think that we should help them rebuild differently. It might be more expensive to help them build sound and flexible structures with steel now, but earthquakes aren't uncommon in that part of the world, and such construction would save lives and money in the long run."

## Cooperative Learning

Spencer Kagan (Kagan & Kagan, 2009) provided a number of activities and strategies that can be used to develop self-awareness, self-control, self-motivation, empathy, and relationships. Here are a few Kagan activities that can be used to reinforce the nature of perspective (for a complete listing see Kagan & Kagan, 2009).

### Sages

With this activity, the teacher polls the class to see which students have special information. For example, one student may have relatives in London whom she has visited, and another might have a parent who is a pilot, and so he knows a lot about large commercial airliners and how they work. The knowledge students have does not necessarily need to tie into classroom content; the point is simply that students are provided an opportunity to share unique things they know and an opportunity to listen and learn from other students. The teacher appoints specific students to be sages, and other students group with one of the sages and listen to what he or she knows about. Each listener then summarizes what the sage said and then moves to hear another sage speak.

### Corners

This activity is intended for younger students. The teacher posts pictures of different animals (such as turtles, puppies, dolphins, or wolves) in each of the four corners of the room. The teacher then asks students which of these animals they would be today if they could. After some time to think, students go to the corner representing the animal they have chosen. They then gather in groups according to the animal they chose and tell one another why they chose that animal; each student summarizes what the previous student said. Students are encouraged to use feeling reasons when they speak. By sharing and summarizing their feelings and the feelings of others, this strategy promotes empathy and encourages students to see the points of view of their peers.

### Fans

Students are assigned teams and given a set of question cards. On each card is an open-ended question such as, If you could go anywhere in the world for a week, where would you go and why?, Who would you vote for in the upcoming election? Why?, or What do you think about the proposed damming of the local river? Is it a helpful or harmful thing for our community? Why?

The first student holds up the cards in a fan, and the second student picks one. He or she reads the question or topic aloud and allows five seconds of think time. The third student answers the question. The fourth student paraphrases what the third student said and then states his or her own opinion. Then students switch roles.

The following vignette depicts how a teacher might use one of the Kagan activities.

> *Mr. Kruger teaches an elementary English learner class, and he knows that his students can sometimes get frustrated and feel left out because of the language gap. In order to encourage them to verbalize their feelings, he puts up four pictures, one in each corner of the room. The pictures display a sunny day on a beach, a thunderstorm over the plains, a gray and foggy day, and a tornado. He asks his students to stand by the picture that most reflects their moods. When they have done so, he asks for volunteers to discuss why their moods are like that particular picture.*

## Connection to Community or Environment

Another way for students to understand perspective is by making connections to the community or local environment. These connections promote collaboration, but they also promote a deeper and increased understanding of the issues and people around them. Students also get the chance to use skills they are learning in a real-world environment. The following three programs have helped students make connections to the community.

### *The Harbor School*

Murray Fisher wanted to combine academic curriculum with restoration projects for a New York area with 85 percent of its residents living below the poverty line. He also wanted to help students feel they were valuable members of society. He partnered with Urban Assembly, a nonprofit that has created twenty-two small, theme-based schools in low-income areas, to create a program that combined academics with rehabilitating the local oyster population. Oysters were important to the local environment, and they had been nearly wiped out. Those that remained were inedible because of high toxicity levels. Several Harbor School students, led by Bart Chezar (who runs a similar program independently), worked to lay down five hundred oyster shells on the floor of Upper New York Bay. One student, Jeptha Sullivan, had a near-drowning experience when he was ten and avoided swimming after that. He found himself diving, however, in order to check on the oysters' progress, and by graduation, he had earned the title of the school's most experienced diver and was planning on going to college to study environmental science. Janique Moore had a similar story. She had never thought about the environment around New York, its harbor, or sea life, but soon was amazed to find herself using words like *salinity*, *turbidity*, and *nitrates*. After the program, she too hoped to study subjects like marine biology or environmental law in college (Kamp, 2010).

### *Common Ground High School*

Common Ground High School, located in New Haven, Connecticut, focuses on connecting the curriculum with the environment. Specifically, the school uses the parks, people, and businesses of New Haven, West Rock Park (in which the school is located), and an environmental learning center and research farm on the campus as learning laboratories for subjects ranging from science to literature. The curriculum is based on six big ideas: (1) interconnectedness—everything is connected, living and nonliving, human and nonhuman; (2) humans and the environment—humans change the environment, and the environment shapes humans; (3) appreciation and curiosity—the environment can fill us with wonder, curiosity, close observation, and good questions, which lead to real learning; (4) learning across disciplines—each and every subject, science, history, English, math, and art, helps us understand the environment; (5) food and health—food and health start with our own choices and connect to bigger issues like poverty, justice, pollution, and climate; and (6) environmental action—we face pressing environmental challenges, local and global, and we are all responsible.

With this philosophy in mind, Common Ground requires a senior project in which students participate in a yearlong Green Jobs Corps. They take on paid internships at local environmental organizations and participate in a yearlong leadership and career-development program. They also compete in the statewide Envirothon competition and participate in an environmental leadership club. Finally, they teach younger students about important environmental issues through after-school, summer, and school-day programs. The school also offers block classes that combine two subjects with authentic real-world-based instruction. Those courses include: biodiversity, which is rooted in West Rock Park and focuses on developing students' understanding of statistical analysis, ecology, and local species diversity;

drama, which is built around an intensive residency with the Elm Shakespeare Company; environmental justice, which is an upper-level science and social studies course that focuses on the environmental challenges facing low-income and urban communities; power, which combines physics and political science to understand energy policy issues in the United States; ecologia, a Spanish and biology course that uses the school's garden as its primary learning laboratory; and food and environment in which students learn the science, politics, and environmental issues behind their food choices (Common Ground, n.d.).

### Howard School District

In 1995, through the Program for Rural School and Community Renewal at South Dakota State University, Howard School District, located in southeastern South Dakota, began receiving funding from the Annenberg Rural Challenge (totaling $150,000 over four years) for projects to connect rural schools with their communities. Its vision has been the development of a sustainable community. They had two main goals: to meet the basic needs of the people who live in the community (food, water, shelter, clothing, and jobs) and to grow and develop within the community's ecological limits. Some of their biggest projects include the Community Cash Flow Study, in which Future Business Leaders of America students investigated how residents spent their money and residents' views of local businesses. Through making residents more aware of the need to spend locally and businesses more aware of community needs, gross sales in Howard increased 41.1 percent and remained fairly steady over the next three years. Other projects include the following: student-taught adult computer-training classes, a state-of-the-art USDA-funded greenhouse and community garden, and a schoolwide study of cancer clusters in the county (Rural Learning Center, n.d.).

## Responsible Interaction

A second skill area that is important to understanding and interacting with others is taking responsibility for the outcomes of interactions. The need for such skills is becoming increasingly apparent. To illustrate, *The New York Times* reported that freshmen college students are increasingly unable to resolve disputes with their roommates. "Students don't know how to negotiate potential areas of friction" and "lack the skills to attend to even modest conflicts," often calling on their parents to solve problems (Moore, 2010). Understanding the nature of assertiveness lays the foundation for responsible communication.

### Assertiveness

According to Marzano (2003), students should become aware of the four major types of behavior commonly exhibited during interaction: passive, aggressive, passive-aggressive, and assertive.

1. **Passive behavior:** People engaging in passive behavior do not directly or honestly articulate their opinions, feelings, and needs. If they express anything, they do so in a way that is apologetic or self-deprecating and therefore send the message that their feelings can be disregarded. This behavior sends the message of "I lose, you win." It devalues the self, and those who engage in it indirectly violate their own rights and present themselves as helpless or as victims. It is difficult to get to know a person who engages in passive behavior, and this can make relationships frustrating. The message is: "I can be discounted and taken advantage of because I am not important."

2. **Aggressive behavior:** A person who engages in aggressive behavior is looking to dominate a relationship—to be a victor instead of an equal partner ("I win, you lose"). Aggressive behavior is often degrading or humiliating. As a result, people distance

themselves from people who behave aggressively, and aggressive people are often disliked. Aggressive behavior is also characterized by inappropriate or excessive expression of emotion, most often anger. The message is: "I am the only important person in this relationship, and you will accede to me no matter what I do."

3. **Passive-aggressive behavior:** People who engage in passive-aggressive behavior demonstrate anger in indirect ways such as being late, not completing assigned work, neglecting responsibilities, and apologizing without changing negative behavior. Those who tend toward passive-aggressive behavior often appear to be confused about their level of responsibility in a given situation and seem surprised when others become upset with them. Essentially, a passive-aggressive person is trying to send a message of anger without being accountable for it. The message is: "You're supposed to know I'm angry and respond to my feelings even though I haven't told you how I feel."

4. **Assertive behavior:** Assertive behavior is the only kind that results in a win-win relationship. Assertive people are able to express themselves and their needs honestly without harming or disrespecting others. Assertive behavior promotes mutual respect and caring. The message is: "I respect myself and value you as a person and our relationship."

The distinction between passive, aggressive, passive-aggressive, and assertive behavior should be introduced to students in concrete ways. One way to do this is for the teacher to provide examples he or she has experienced. For example, a teacher might share with her students that her sister behaved very passive-aggressively when they were growing up by doing things such as saying she didn't want anyone to bother throwing her a birthday party and then acting like she was mad that no one had properly celebrated her birthday. She might say that it was very difficult to tell how her sister really felt or what she really wanted, and then she may point out that her relationship suffered with her sister because of this behavior.

Another way to introduce or reinforce the four types of behavior is to use characters from literature, movies, or television. For example, students might watch clips of reality shows like *Survivor* or *The Biggest Loser* that show someone engaging in one of the four types of behavior as a strategy to win. Characters on shows like *The Office* or *SpongeBob SquarePants* often use aggressive or passive-aggressive behavior in funny ways, and a teacher might introduce the four types of behaviors and ask students to identify each type in an episode or in selected clips.

Once students understand the four types of behavior, they can begin to understand their own behavior and make necessary changes toward assertiveness. In general, assertive behavior is the only type of behavior that produces responsible communication. Any other type of behavior typically dampens the effectiveness of communication in the speaker or the listener. Marzano et al. (2005) described six steps to communicate effectively. Teachers can use these six steps to help students learn to behave assertively.

1. **Keep a journal:** Teachers can ask students to note their own behavior and identify it as one of the four types of behaviors. They can also ask students to estimate (using a percentage) how much time over an average day or week they spend engaging in each of the four types of behavior.

2. **Carefully consider behavior:** Teachers can encourage students to consider the situations that tend to provoke each of the four types of behavior for them. For example, one student might notice that he tends to behave aggressively in situations that involve competition. Students then write down the physical gestures and facial expressions that tend to correspond to each type of behavior.

3. **List effects of behavior:** Teachers can ask students to consider how each type of behavior affects their progress toward short- and long-term goals, their physical health, their relationships with others, their emotions (for example, sadness, anger, happiness, or satisfaction), and their self-esteem.

4. **Spot patterns:** Teachers can encourage students to make connections between their behavior and the people they engage with, the situations that spark different types of behavior, and even things like the times of day that they behave in different ways.

5. **Watch a model:** Teachers can ask students to identify an assertive person from their personal lives, the media, or a historical or fictional context. Students can then investigate that person's behavior, noticing patterns of behavior, how he or she handles difficult situations, body language, facial expressions, and any other revealing behavior.

6. **Visualize assertiveness:** Teachers can ask students to visualize being assertive in a future interaction. Visualizing assertiveness can also be applied to past behavior; students may imagine themselves as having been assertive in situations in which they were not assertive and visualize how they might have done things differently.

The following vignette depicts how a teacher might teach one or more steps.

> Mr. Baio's students have been keeping journals and considering their behaviors and the good and bad effects of those behaviors over the last few months. He now asks them to look over their journals to try to find patterns of behavior. "For example," he says, "maybe you tend to be aggressive with one person and passive with another. Maybe you are more aggressive in certain circumstances, such as when you participate in athletic events. Maybe you find that one of these types of behavior almost always applies to you. See if you can look at the data you've gathered and find some real meaning in it."
>
> A few days later, Keisha says she has noticed that she is almost always passive or passive-aggressive at school, but that at home she has no problem being assertive. Randy says that he is assertive most of the time, but when he is doing something new or meeting new people, he tends to be aggressive.
>
> Mr. Baio gives his students even more time and has more class discussions about patterns over time. He also asks them to look for assertive role models in their lives or in the media. To help them begin looking for good role models, he shows them a few video clips of assertive behavior, and he asks the class to role-play as well.

## Group and Social Responsibility

Responsible interaction is important whenever individuals operate as a group. Erwin (2004) proposed the class meeting as a tool for fostering interaction in groups. Class meetings let students know they are being listened to, but they also help students practice listening to others. They can be held on a regular basis or as the teacher or a student requests. The length of the meeting should vary with the age of the students—age of the students multiplied by two is Erwin's guideline. Erwin noted the following guidelines that should be established before each class meeting.

- **The person speaking must keep to the here and now:** For example, a student who wants to do more activities in groups should discuss why group work would help his or her engagement or understanding of a topic currently being studied, rather than complaining about a past individual assignment being boring.

- **Only one person speaks at a time:** For example, when one student is speaking about a problem, other students should know they need to hold their comments until it is their turn to speak, as opposed to interrupting or telling a friend who is sitting next to them.

- **The person speaking must use "I" statements:** For example, a student who would like the teacher to present some extra-credit assignments should say, "I would like to take advantage of extra-credit assignments" as opposed to "There should be extra credit."

- **The focus is on listening to other group members; no other activity should be going on:** For example, no student should be working on a homework assignment, drawing pictures, or writing notes on unrelated topics during a class meeting.

- **Everyone can participate:** For example, no student should feel he must refrain from participating in the class meeting simply because he does not agree with many of the ideas being expressed.

- **No put-downs—verbal or nonverbal:** For example, if a student does not like an idea another student expresses, he or she must respond only to the idea and not make any kind of personal remarks such as "You always want your own way" or "You never listen to what anyone else wants."

Erwin (2004) pointed out that different meetings can be used for different purposes. The one most pertinent to the present discussion is the *problem-solving meeting*. A problem-solving meeting might be called in the following situations:

- The students want more time to work on an assignment.

- There has been disrespect or teasing in the classroom.

- The students want to raise money for a cause or a field trip.

- A system, such as one for using the classroom computers, needs to be developed.

Erwin (2004) observed that it is important to let students know how much decision-making power they have in these meetings. They should know whether the meeting is simply a discussion on which the teacher will base an ultimate decision or a meeting in which the students will vote to make a change. The following is a suggested format for problem-solving meetings.

1. **State the problem, and define any terms:** For example, a student who feels there has been teasing in the classroom might say, "I feel like there has been a lot of teasing and making fun of people in the classroom, and I think this is a problem because it hurts people's feelings and makes students feel bad."

2. **Describe the desired state:** What is the goal? For example, the student might say, "It would be great if all the teasing stopped and people said nice instead of mean things to each other. If we did that, I think everyone could be happier and work better together."

3. **Describe the present state:** How are things now? For example, the student might say, "I feel afraid to speak up in class a lot because I'm afraid someone will make fun of me. I also don't like to play games in class because people always wind up getting their feelings hurt, and that bothers me."

4. **Examine the current behavior:** For example, the student might say, "Hardly anything is being done about the teasing in the class right now. The teacher doesn't hear a lot of it, and no one sticks up for anyone else."

5. **Evaluate current behavior:** Is current behavior accomplishing goals? Why or why not? For example, the student might say, "I don't think that the teasing will stop or people's feelings will get better if we keep doing what we're doing."

6. **Brainstorm possible plans:** What else can be done to accomplish the goal? For example, one student might suggest everyone just sit with their friends because friends don't tease each other. Another student might suggest that whenever they hear someone teasing another student everyone will speak up and tell him to stop it.

7. **Make a plan:** Students rate the proposed plans by how realistic and likely to succeed they are, and then choose one. For example, of many plans proposed, students might choose three: that each student vow to speak up when he or she hears someone being teased or bullied, that each student vow to take care not to hurt the feelings of other students, and that if any student continues to hurt the feelings of others, the teacher will step in.

## Active Listening

As discussed in chapter 2 (page 32), Rogers and Farson (1957/2007) proposed active listening. The first part of their strategy requires listening for total meaning. *Total meaning* is both the content of the speaker's message and the feelings the speaker expresses. For example, while discussing baseball, Linus might say, "The game last night was amazing! It went twelve innings, and then Ramirez hit it out of the park with guys on second and third. He has more RBIs than practically anyone in the league!" Ingrid, who was listening to him, understands not only what was said about last night's game and about Ramirez's RBI statistic but also understands that Linus really loves the sport of baseball.

The second part of active listening is responding to the speaker. Specifically, letting the speaker know you heard him and you understand his feelings. For example, Ingrid might say to Linus, "That game sounds really exciting. It sounds like baseball is something you like a lot. Is Ramirez your favorite player?"

The third part of active listening involves noting cues such as hesitation, inflection, facial expressions, body posture, hand movements, eye movements, and breathing. These cues can give a listener more information about a speaker's feelings, and if the cues send mixed messages, the listener can ask for clarification. For example, while Linus answers Ingrid's question, she might notice that he is leaning forward and gesturing with his hands while he talks. She might notice that he is smiling as well. All these cues would reinforce for Ingrid the knowledge that Linus is a big baseball fan.

The last part of active listening involves testing for understanding. The listener paraphrases what the speaker said and clarifies any misunderstandings before the conversation continues. This allows both the speaker and the listener to know that the message of the conversation was properly delivered and received. For example, after Linus tells Ingrid that Ramirez is his favorite player of all time because of his batting average and his low error rate, Ingrid asks him to explain what a batting average is. He explains both terms, and she asks, "So, he's a great player because he doesn't strike out very often and because he is a great fielder who hardly ever makes mistakes?"

"Yeah," Linus says. "Exactly."

Shinya Kubota, Norio Mishima, and Shoji Nagata (2004) have proposed an adaptation of active listening for group processing. They recommend a group process for developing active-listening skills. This process has two steps, the first of which is role play. When engaging in a role play, students gather in groups of four or five. One person acts as the speaker, one acts as an active listener, one acts as a passive listener, and the others act as observers. The speaker chooses a topic of conversation, and both the active listener and the passive listener listen to the speaker for a preset amount of time while the observers watch both the listeners and the speakers. The active listener is allowed to ask questions for clarification but must not ask so many questions that the speaker is interrupted. The listeners must also be careful not to change the topic that the speaker has chosen, and they should not make comments or give advice.

For example, a speaker might choose the topic of which colleges she will be applying to and why. She begins by listing the colleges she is interested in and then discussing her reasons for applying to each. The active listener asks the speaker to repeat the list of colleges or to elaborate on one of the reasons she discussed, but the listener may not offer a suggestion of another school or tell her which college he thinks would be the best one for her to attend.

The second part of the process is the discussion, and it begins after the preset amount of time for the speaker and listeners is up. During the discussion, the observers tell the listeners about the behaviors they saw that appeared to make the speaker more or less comfortable. For example, after observing a speaker and two listeners, an observer might note that the speaker appeared to be more comfortable when the listeners were looking directly at her and nodding rather than when one or both of them was looking across the room or at the papers in front of them. All observers report on what they saw, and then the speaker responds to the comments of the observers. Finally, the listeners can offer thoughts or ideas as well. All participants should engage in active listening while the discussion is taking place.

The following vignette depicts a teacher using this active listening and speaking strategy in the classroom.

*Mr. Alan has put his students into small groups. They draw straws to see who will be the speaker, the active listener, the passive listener, and the observers in each group. With their roles set, he says, "For the next four minutes you will be in character, so remember the rules for each role." He starts the stopwatch, and the groups begin.*

*Kendall is the speaker in her group, and she uses the four minutes to talk about the whaling problem in Japan and other parts of the world. It is an issue she is passionate about. When the time is up, Kevin, one of the observers, says, "I noticed that when someone asked you a question, you seemed more comfortable talking. Before that, it felt like you were giving a lecture, but when Mona started asking you questions it seemed like you relaxed. And then it felt more like a conversation."*

*Zora says, "I noticed that while Jimmy was the passive listener, it didn't really seem like he was listening. He looked at the clock a lot, and he picked lint off his shirt. I don't know if Kendall and Mona noticed because they seemed really into the conversation, but it just didn't look like he was really listening to me."*

*After the observers have finished speaking, Kendall says she thinks they are right about what they observed: "I did feel nervous until Mona began asking questions. When she did that, it felt like she was really interested, and that made it a lot easier to talk."*

*Finally, Mona and Jimmy respond. Mona says she never knew about the whaling issue and was really interested to learn about it. Jimmy says the observers were probably right. He says, "I have a game today, and I tend to be distracted on game days. I thought I was listening, but maybe I wasn't."*

## Controversy and Conflict Resolution

Ultimately, the goal of developing skills for understanding and interacting with others is to more effectively address controversies and conflicts. As discussed in chapter 2 (page 33), a controversy occurs when someone's beliefs contradict another person's, and the two seek to reach a consensus. A conflict occurs when one person's actions impede another person's (Johnson & Johnson, 2005).

### Steps for Productive Controversy in the Classroom

Johnson and Johnson (1989) provided a detailed six-step process for the productive use of controversy in the classroom.

1. **The students form an initial conclusion based on the information gathered during research on an issue, their experiences, and their current perspectives:** For example, on the topic of whether or not smoking cigarettes should be illegal, a student researches information on the effects of firsthand and secondhand smoke. After reading through the information, the student concludes that the dangers of secondhand smoke alone are serious enough that cigarettes should be outlawed.

2. **The students present their conclusions to their classmates:** For example, the student presents the information on the harm that secondhand smoke causes to peers, and she points out that researchers are not even aware yet of all the harm secondhand smoke causes. "It is illegal to hurt someone else by assaulting them or poisoning them in this country, and secondhand smoke causes exactly that kind of damage," she says. "It is therefore reasonable that cigarettes should be outlawed."

3. **The students are confronted with other conclusions, based on their classmates' information, experiences, and perspectives:** For example, another student has reached the conclusion that cigarettes should not be outlawed. This student challenges the first student by presenting information about how much money in taxes the government makes from the sale of cigarettes and how much money the government must spend in order to arrest, prosecute, and jail those people who are using or selling drugs that

are already illegal in the United States. He says, "Our government would lose a lot of money if cigarettes were to be outlawed, and that means cutting funding for things like education and the military. We already spend so much money fighting the war on drugs as it is, and that cost would vastly increase if cigarettes were illegal. The tax on cigarettes funds too many important things to make them illegal."

4. **The students become uncertain about their initial conclusions:** Hearing the opinions and perspectives of others and hearing more information creates *conceptual conflict.* Conceptual conflict is characterized by a state of uncertainty or disequilibrium. For example, the student who initially concluded that cigarettes should be outlawed might consider the argument of the student who challenged her. "I had only been looking at the health aspects of smoking," she might say. "I hadn't realized that our government would lose so much money in taxes. My uncle used to be a guard at a prison, and I know overcrowding is a really big problem, and making cigarettes illegal could make that problem worse. I'm not sure how I feel about the issue now."

5. **The students search for new information, experiences, and perspectives in response to the conceptual conflict:** The students try to find out more in order to reconcile the disequilibrium and solve the conflict. For example, they might work together in groups and discuss the various pros and cons on the issue. One student might research the costs to the medical community associated with the effects of firsthand and secondhand smoke and point out that should cigarettes be outlawed, that money would not be spent. Another student might point out that the argument of money is fundamentally different from the ethical argument that citizens should not be allowed to harm one another. "I think the ethical obligation to keep citizens safe outweighs the financial problems that would come," he might say. Another student might disagree by saying, "If outlawing cigarettes harms education or the military, then the issue becomes ethical. Students in the United States and soldiers in the military shouldn't have to suffer either."

6. **The students reach a new conclusion based on the whole of their experiences and their exposure to other perspectives and positions:** Discussion and debate take place, and ideally, students reach an agreement. The students' new conclusions are of a higher order and are more creative than their original conclusions. For example, after discussing the issue from a variety of different perspectives, all students agree that the issue is far more complex than they initially believed. After discussing many different possibilities, they decide that the best thing to do is outlaw smoking in all public places and to make the punishment for breaking the law a stiff fine. They agree that by this course of action, fewer people will be exposed to secondhand smoke, but between the taxes on the cigarettes still sold and the money from the fines, the government will not lose money.

The following vignette depicts how a teacher might use the controversy process.

*Ms. Howard's class is discussing the topic of welfare. Cameron has read through all the information presented to him on the topic and has decided that the welfare system ultimately causes more harm than good. He uses statistics and examples of people who have abused the system by not attempting to find jobs or using the money to support substance-abuse habits as justifications for his argument. When the class discusses the issue, he finds that Marilyn (among others) has an opposing opinion.*

*"Poverty is a huge problem in the United States, and telling people to simply get a job isn't a good idea," Marilyn says. "Take the free and reduced lunch program for students. Students using it aren't taking advantage of the system, and many of these kids would be in serious trouble if they didn't at least get that one meal."*

*After taking a day to consider the opposing arguments, Cameron says, "I didn't think about it in terms of the people who really can't help themselves," he says.*

*Marilyn responds, "I agree that an alarming number of people take advantage of the system, and it seems there is no way to monitor it."*

*Cameron and Marilyn and the others in their small group then look for new information and ideas. After discussing the matter further, they find that really they do not disagree; they all think the system should work for people who cannot help themselves and for people who deserve a new start. However, they also think there should be some way to prevent people from taking advantage of the system. They investigate the methods used to test the means available to people who are on welfare as well as welfare that comes from nongovernmental organizations. Finally, they agree that this process should be altered and far more closely monitored, but the problem is where to get the money and the means to do that. They agree that now they can see that welfare is a complex issue fraught with budget and manpower flaws, and there is no easy solution to fixing what is wrong while preserving what is good.*

## Ways to Handle Conflict

Johnson and Johnson (2005) also provided a systemic approach to conflict. They noted that when deciding how to handle conflict, a student must be aware of how important the conflict issue is and how important the relationship with the disputant is. They outlined five different ways to handle conflict, depending on the importance of the conflict issue and the relationship with the disputant.

1. **Problem-solving negotiations:** This conflict strategy is used when both the goal and the relationship are important. This is the ideal way to solve conflict. In problem-solving negotiation, participants focus on the problem instead of the person, manage emotions skillfully, take the easy conflicts first, build trust between disputants, and keep a sense of humor.

2. **Smoothing:** This conflict strategy is used when the relationship is of high importance and the goal is of low importance. This is not the best way to solve a conflict because one

person gives up his or her goals in order to facilitate the other person's needs being met. Smoothing might not harm a relationship, but it means someone must make a sacrifice.

3. **Forcing or win-lose negotiation:** When the goal is important and the relationship with the disputant is not of importance, this strategy can be used. In win-lose negotiation, one person is forced to give up his or her goals for the sake of the other person. This is not a recommended way to solve most conflicts as it often causes animosity and hard feelings.

4. **Compromising:** This conflict strategy is used when both the goal and the relationship are of moderate importance. In compromising, both parties sacrifice something in the goal and the relationship. Many times this strategy is used when there isn't time for problem-solving negotiation. Compromising is not an ideal way to solve a conflict, however, as often no one is satisfied with the results.

5. **Withdrawing:** When neither goal nor relationship is important, this strategy can be used. Withdrawing is not recommended as an effective conflict-resolution technique because one person gives up both his or her goals and the relationship with the other person. However, sometimes withdrawing can work as a temporary method that gives both people time to calm down before implementing another strategy to solve the conflict.

Problem-solving negotiation is the most effective way to solve a conflict because it regards highly both the relationship between the two people in conflict and their individual goals. Table 7.1 presents Johnson and Johnson's (2005) strategy for problem-solving negotiation.

## Table 7.1: Problem-Solving Negotiation

| Steps | Rationale |
|---|---|
| State the goal. | Problem-solving negotiation requires that disputants are open and honest about what they want. Each person needs to know what he or she wants and be able to describe it. |
| State feelings. | Resolution of conflicts requires that feelings be openly recognized and expressed. Rejected and unrecognized feelings create bias, block positive feelings, reduce self-control, and interfere with cognitive processing. |
| State reasons for wants and feelings. | Moving beyond positions to the underlying reasons for wants and feelings helps separate interests from positions and helps differentiate interests so that integrative agreements may be identified. |
| Reverse perspectives. | Higher-level cognitive reasoning, accurate communication, and identifying integrative agreements depend on being able to view the problem from both perspectives simultaneously. |
| Create three or more potential agreements that maximize joint outcomes. | In order to maximize joint outcomes (as opposed to reaching only a barely acceptable agreement), it is necessary to identify a variety of potential agreements from which to choose the one that appears to be most advantageous to all parties. |
| Settle on one agreement and shake. | Each alternative agreement needs to be evaluated to determine whether it is fair to all parties. The agreement must maximize joint outcomes and strengthen participants' future ability to work together and resolve conflicts constructively. |

Source: Adapted from Johnson & Johnson, 2005.

To illustrate the use of problem-solving negotiation, consider the following vignette.

> *Two of Mr. Rainier's students were caught fighting in the school's parking lot. They must both spend their lunch periods inside, and since he is in the building during that time, he decides to sit with them. He asks them exactly how the fight started.*
>
> *"He called me a name for the last time, and I punched him," Reece says.*
>
> *"I wasn't even talking to you," Andy says.*
>
> *"There was no one else there. You were talking to me and you know it," Reece says.*
>
> *Mr. Rainier tells them to calm down. "Reece, you said he called you a name for the last time. Has he called you names before?" Reece says that Andy has, and Andy admits it is true, however, he claims to have been joking. Mr. Rainier says, "So, when you hit him, you wanted him to stop calling you names. Is that right?" Reece says it is. Mr. Rainier asks Andy why he has been calling Reece names.*
>
> *Andy responds, "I call everyone names, not just him. It's just a joke."*
>
> *Mr. Rainier knows the conflict process will take some time, so he asks Andy to consider why he thinks calling people names is funny when clearly other people do not. "Think about what you're getting out of it and what it is you really want," he says.*
>
> *The next day, Mr. Rainier continues the process with Reece and Andy separately; he knows that if Andy is going to be honest, he won't do it with Reece in the room, at least initially.*

## Strategies to Address Anger

Perhaps the ultimate conflict resolution strategy is to allow other people to feel angry without reacting. Johnson and Johnson (2005) discuss how to deal with someone else's anger. They begin with three generalizations students should keep in mind whenever they encounter an angry person.

1.  **Give others the right to feel angry:** Everyone has the right to express anger, just as he or she has the right to express joy, grief, sadness, and hurt. It is important to remember that anger is not aggressiveness. Aggressiveness is an attempt to dominate, to thwart, to control, and sometimes to embarrass or humiliate. Anger is just an emotion that speaks of frustration and sometimes sadness. Someone is often feeling sad or hurt when he or she expresses anger, and it is important to keep this in mind. Also, it is better if someone expresses anger (in a healthy way) than hides it.

2.  **Do not get angry back:** Many times people can be tempted into anger just by being around someone who is angry, but losing tempers will only escalate the situation.

3.  **Recognize that the temptation to use aggression is a sign that the person is feeling weak or vulnerable:** Many times people get angry because they do not know what else

to do; they are frustrated. Help them cool off or take a break rather than escalating the situation by becoming angry as well.

These generalizations are best presented to students and discussed in class. The teacher might provide examples from his or her own life depicting times when these generalizations were employed or should have been employed. For example, a teacher might tell students about a time her husband was really angry when he lost his job after a large company bought out his small company. She might say that he had every right to be angry but that he sometimes snapped at her during that time as well. Though she was tempted, she did not retaliate because she knew it would do no good, and she knew that he also felt helpless and scared about finding another job.

With an understanding of the three generalizations in place, students can be presented with the remaining seven elements of Johnson and Johnson's (2005) strategy for dealing with anger. These are depicted in table 7.2.

## Table 7.2: Dealing With Anger

| Element | Example |
|---|---|
| Focus attention on the task, not the anger. | Two students who are involved in a conflict over who should be the captain of a flag football team each state his reason for thinking he would be the best captain as opposed to yelling personal insults and then getting into a fight. |
| Explain the situation. | One student confronted by another who believes he has been insulted stops the confrontation and explains that he didn't mean to insult anyone; he was only making a joke. |
| Verbalize goals and feelings. | A student who is involved in a conflict with another student over which of them did more work on a group project takes some time alone to talk to herself. She discovers that she really feels angry with the other student for another reason. She verbalizes why she feels angry before speaking with the other student again. |
| Use affection. | One student sees the other person he is in a conflict with begin to cry; he backs off, stops the verbal confrontation, and pats the other person on the back. |
| Teach the person to express anger in words. | An older sibling teaches a younger sibling words she can use to describe feelings of anger or frustration. This way, she does not have to resort to having a temper tantrum. |
| Be a good model. | A student makes a well-timed joke to de-escalate a conflict; he is being a good model. |
| Seek help if necessary. | Two students who are in a conflict regarding the score of a game find that they cannot find a solution on their own, so they seek the help of other students who have been watching. |

Source: Johnson & Johnson, 2005.

Again, teachers should describe each of these steps and provide examples for students. Once students have an understanding of the seven action steps in the strategy, they can practice one or more of the steps in their lives. The strategy is simply too robust for students to practice multiple elements simultaneously. While practicing one or two steps, students would apply them to specific situations in their lives and examine the results. Journaling is a highly useful tool to this end. The following vignette depicts how this might work.

*Ms. Anthony's students have been introduced to the seven steps. Her students continually journal about conflicts in their lives and about how they use the steps as necessary when those conflicts arise.*

*Thisbe writes about the first step, focusing on the task instead of the anger. She writes that it is easier for her to be a good model and show affection and explain the situation when she is not the one who is angry. However, when she is angry, it is very hard for her to focus on anything else. Recently, however, she and her brother got into a fight about who was going to take the car, and she was able to stop herself from yelling and insulting him and instead ask him where he was going. "It turned out he was going to the gym, which is not too far from my friend's house. I told him I would drop him off at the gym and pick him up if I could take the car and go to lunch with my friend," she writes. "It was a small conflict, but I was still able to focus on the task, so that's good."*

## Summary

This chapter has outlined strategies for teaching the conative skill of understanding and interacting with others. Particularly important to developing this skill is the ability to see an issue or a problem from multiple perspectives. Once students have perspective-taking ability, they can begin to interact responsibly by demonstrating assertiveness, developing a sense of social responsibility, and becoming active listeners and speakers. Finally, in the tight-knit global community of the 21st century, learning to negotiate and resolve conflict is a key to effective communication and developing an understanding of others.

# Chapter 7: Comprehension Questions

1. Why are perceptions so powerful?

2. In what situations is perspective analysis likely to be most effective?

3. What is the difference between conflict and controversy?

4. How does controversy improve students' reasoning and perspective-taking skills?

# Chapter 8

# ASSESSMENT

As described in chapter 2, research has shown us that assessment is an important part of the teaching and learning process. More specifically, assessment becomes a powerful instructional tool when it is used to help students. It can help them articulate clear goals they wish to reach by the end of some interval of time, and it can provide them with feedback regarding their current status. Many researchers and theorists have discussed just how to do this in an academic subject area (see Brookhart, 2004; Brookhart & Nitko, 2007; Stiggins, Arter, Chappuis, & Chappuis, 2006; Wiliam & Leahy, 2007). However, using assessments to help students set goals and monitor their progress toward those goals for cognitive and conative skills like those described in this book has not been widely addressed.

At Marzano Research Laboratory, we have taken a very specific approach to assessing both academic content as well as cognitive and conative skills. Our recommendations are described here and addressed in several works (Marzano, 2009, 2010; Marzano & Pickering, 2011).

## Beginning With a Scale

There is little disagreement that assessments should focus on specific aspects of information and skills (Graham & Perin, 2007; Locke & Latham, 1990; Marzano, 2010; Marzano & Haystead, 2008; Tubbs, 1986; Tyler, 1949a, 1949b). We go a step further and recommend that teachers begin by designing a specific rubric or scale that describes levels of performance and understanding regarding specific 21st century skills. To illustrate, consider table 8.1.

**Table 8.1: Five-Value Scale**

| Score 4.0 | More complex learning goal |
| --- | --- |
| Score 3.0 | Target learning goal |
| Score 2.0 | Simpler learning goal |
| Score 1.0 | With help, partial success at score 2.0 content and score 3.0 content |
| Score 0.0 | Even with help, no success |

Source: Marzano, 2009.

The scale in table 8.1 is the generic form for all scales provided in *Teaching and Assessing 21st Century Skills*. Notice that it has five values. To understand the five values of the scale, it is best to start with the score of 3.0. This score represents the level of proficiency that is the target for instruction—the target learning goal. Typically, this means that the student can demonstrate proficiency independently with no major errors or omissions. The score value of 4.0 represents performance above the target level. Typically, score 4.0 proficiency represents application of the target goal in a way that demonstrates unique inferences about its use. Score 2.0 represents performance toward the basic aspects of the goal that are usually prerequisites to demonstrate score 3.0 competence. At this level, the student has an understanding of basic elements of the goal, but cannot independently demonstrate proficiency. Score 1.0 proficiency does not require new content. Rather, it signifies that a student cannot demonstrate proficiency on any of the learning goals independently, but with help and prompting, he or she can perform some aspects of it. Finally, the score value of 0.0 indicates that even with help and prompting, the student has no success at executing the skill. In summary, the score values of 2.0, 3.0, and 4.0 represent different levels of proficiency relative to the learning goal, but score values 1.0 and 0.0 do not. Instead, for students who cannot demonstrate proficiency on their own, these score values represent whether they can execute parts of the skill with help.

Table 8.1 (page 175) is the generic form of the scale. Table 8.2 presents a scale for the cognitive skill of identifying common logical errors in reasoning from chapter 3 (page 44).

## Table 8.2: Scale for Identifying Common Logical Errors

| Score 4.0 | The student applies the strategy in unusual situations or identifies logical errors that go beyond those that were explicitly taught.<br>No major errors or omissions regarding the score 4.0 content |
|---|---|
| Score 3.0 | The student analyzes appropriate information for common logical errors.<br>No major errors or omissions regarding the score 3.0 content |
| Score 2.0 | The student can describe situations in which it is beneficial to analyze information for common logical errors.<br>He or she can describe or recognize the various common logical errors that have been taught, including those of faulty logic, attack, weak reference, and misinformation.<br>No major errors or omissions regarding the score 2.0 content |
| Score 1.0 | With help, partial success at score 2.0 content and score 3.0 content |
| Score 0.0 | Even with help, no success |

Again, to understand the scale, we begin with the score 3.0 content. At this level, the student analyzes appropriate information for common logical errors with no major errors or omissions. For example, the student recognizes the fact that if information is designed to persuade the reader or listener and has implications for future behavior, it is probably important to analyze it for common logical errors. The student then carries out the analysis with no major errors or omissions. At score 2.0, the student recognizes or recalls the common logical errors that have been taught and even describes situations in which it might be useful to apply this knowledge. However, at score 2.0 the student does not actually apply this strategy independently, as described in score 3.0; the ability to actually apply this knowledge comes with practice. Typically, at the score 2.0 level, the student has not yet engaged in extensive practice.

At the score 1.0 level, the student cannot do anything articulated at the score 2.0 level independently, although he or she can do so with some help from the teacher. For example, the student might not be able to describe the usefulness of the overall strategy independently, but he or she can do so with the benefit of clues and hints that the teacher provides. Likewise, the student cannot independently recognize or recall the logical errors that are important to the strategy but can do so when the teacher provides assistance. At score 0.0 status, the student cannot demonstrate anything at the score 2.0 level even with help from the teacher. Finally, at score 4.0, the student can apply the strategy in unique situations not directly addressed in class.

Some teachers prefer a scale with half-point values. This is depicted in table 8.3.

## Table 8.3: Scale With Half-Point Values

| Score 4.0 | The student applies the strategy in unusual situations or identifies logical errors that go beyond those that were explicitly taught. <br> No major errors or omissions regarding the score 4.0 content |
|---|---|
| Score 3.5 | In addition to score 3.0 performance, partial success at score 4.0 content |
| Score 3.0 | The student analyzes appropriate information for common logical errors. <br> No major errors or omissions regarding the score 3.0 content |
| Score 2.5 | No major errors or omissions regarding score 2.0 content, and partial success at score 3.0 content |
| Score 2.0 | The student can describe situations in which it is beneficial to analyze information for common logical errors. <br> He or she can describe or recognize the various common logical errors that have been taught, including those of faulty logic, attack, weak reference, and misinformation. <br> No major errors or omissions regarding the score 2.0 content |
| Score 1.5 | Partial success at score 2.0 content, and major errors or omissions at score 3.0 content |
| Score 1.0 | With help, partial success at score 2.0 content and score 3.0 content |
| Score 0.5 | With help, partial success at score 2.0 content, but not at score 3.0 content |
| Score 0.0 | Even with help, no success |

As depicted in table 8.3, the half-point values provide a finer determination of student performance on a specific learning goal. For example, score 3.5 indicates that the student is able to independently execute the strategy for analyzing logical errors, and is partially successful at applying the same strategy to unusual situations or with logical errors beyond those explicitly taught.

### Scales for the 21st Century Skills

The previous chapters have described two broad categories of 21st century skills: cognitive and conative skills. Each of these broad categories involves a number of more specific skills. These are listed in table 8.4.

Table 8.4 lists nineteen specific skills across the two broad categories. Reproducible scales for each of these are presented in appendix B (page 201). Teachers are free to use these as presented or make adaptations as needed.

## Table 8.4: Specific Cognitive and Conative Skills

| Cognitive Skills | Conative Skills |
|---|---|
| **Analyzing and utilizing information** | **Understanding and controlling oneself** |
| • Navigating digital sources | • Becoming aware of the power of interpretations |
| • Identifying common logical errors | • Cultivating useful ways of thinking |
| • Generating conclusions | • Avoiding negative ways of thinking |
| • Presenting and supporting claims | |

Continued on next page →

| Cognitive Skills | Conative Skills |
|---|---|
| **Addressing complex problems and issues**<br>• Focus<br>• Divergent and convergent thinking<br>• A problem-solving protocol<br>**Creating patterns and mental models**<br>• Identifying basic relationships between ideas<br>• Creating graphic representations<br>• Drawing and sketching<br>• Generating mental images<br>• Conducting thought experiments<br>• Performing mental rehearsal | **Understanding and interacting with others**<br>• Perspective taking<br>• Responsible interaction<br>• Controversy and conflict resolution |

## How to Use the Scales

As explained in chapter 2, the optimum approach to assessment of 21st century skills is to examine student progress over time. To this end, students should track their progress as depicted in figure 8.1. (See chapter 3, pages 52–61, for a discussion of probabilistic and deductive conclusions.)

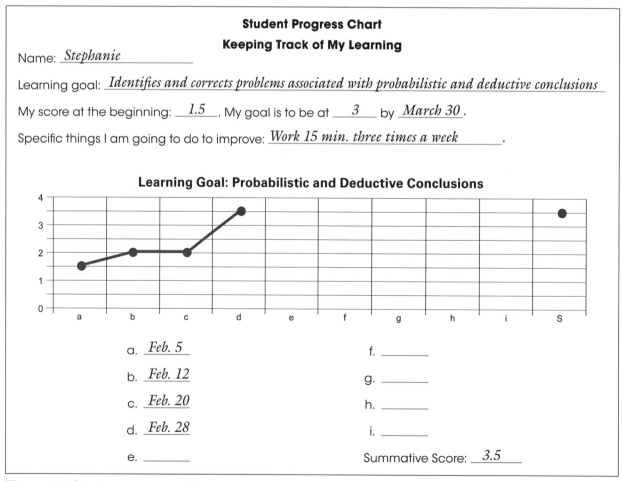

**Student Progress Chart**
**Keeping Track of My Learning**

Name: *Stephanie*

Learning goal: *Identifies and corrects problems associated with probabilistic and deductive conclusions*

My score at the beginning: *1.5*. My goal is to be at *3* by *March 30*.

Specific things I am going to do to improve: *Work 15 min. three times a week* .

**Learning Goal: Probabilistic and Deductive Conclusions**

a. *Feb. 5*          f. _____

b. *Feb. 12*         g. _____

c. *Feb. 20*         h. _____

d. *Feb. 28*         i. _____

e. _____           Summative Score: *3.5*

**Figure 8.1: Student progress chart.**

Source: Adapted from Marzano, 2010.

Note that the scores depicted in figure 8.1 cover a four-week period of time during which four scores were recorded. As described in the book *Formative Assessment and Standards-Based Grading* (Marzano, 2010), this is at the core of formative assessment—students can see their progress over time. There are a number of ways these scores can be assigned: traditional tests, teacher observation and perception, teacher-designed tasks, and student self-analysis.

### Traditional Tests

Traditional tests have their place in the realm of assessing 21st century skills (see Brookhart, 2010), albeit a very circumscribed place. By definition, traditional tests employ selected-response items such as multiple choice, fill in the blank, true or false, and the like. They can be quite effective at assessing some 2.0 content for the various scales for each 21st century skill in appendix B (page 201). Recall from the previous discussion that score 2.0 content is usually informational in nature. Specifically, score 2.0 content usually involves an ability to recognize or recall the important details that are used in the execution of the learning goal. For example, to execute the skill of responsible interaction, a student must be able to describe or recognize the elements of interacting responsibly. A teacher might design a traditional selected-response test for the elements of responsible interaction that have been directly taught in class. For example, figure 8.2 contains a traditional assessment for the four major types of behavior commonly exhibited during interaction.

---

**Directions:** Match the type of behavior to the situation described.

A. Passive

B. Aggressive

C. Passive-aggressive

D. Assertive

1. Maddie is a little worried about her friendship with Jen. Ever since Leah, a new student, started going to their school, Jen has been spending all her time with Leah and hasn't wanted to hang out with Maddie. When Maddie sees Jen walking home from school, she catches up to her and asks if she would mind if she walks with her. Jen says that is fine, and Maddie takes the opportunity to tell Jen how she is feeling and to suggest that maybe Leah, Jen, and she could go to a movie together sometime. She also lets Jen know that she would still like to spend time just with Jen, and they make plans to eat lunch together once a week.

   How can Maddie's behavior be best described?

2. Darcy and Jeff are playing basketball after school with two other friends. They are on the same team, and when Darcy gets the ball, Jeff calls for it. "Pass, pass, I've got the shot!" he says. Instead, Darcy dribbles to the basket and shoots, but she misses the basket by a few inches. Jeff runs over to her and yells, "What's the matter with you? I totally had that shot! If you were smart, you just would have passed me the ball, and we'd be winning. Now we're going to lose, and it's completely your fault! How can you be so stupid?"

   How can Jeff's behavior be best described?

3. Laila's group is discussing the best way to divide up the work for their presentation next Wednesday. Justin says, "I'll make the slides for the presentation." Derrick volunteers to type the notes. "I guess I'll just do the pictures then," says Laila. "You're probably better than I am on the computer, and the pictures are hard to mess up anyway, so what harm can I do?"

   How can Laila's behavior be best described?

4. Jean gives her friend Tara a ride to school each morning because Tara hates taking the bus. However, Tara has started to be habitually late, making Jean wait for her, and sometimes making

---

**Figure 8.2: Assessment for the four major types of behavior.**

Continued on next page →

both of them late for school. Jean tells Tara, "If you can be ready on time, I'm happy to give you a ride to school. But from now on, if I come and you're not ready, I am going to leave your house at 7:15. That way, I can get to school on time; you can ride with me if you're willing to be ready on time. If you aren't ready, you'll have to ride the bus or get a ride from someone else."

How can Jean's behavior be best described?

5. Jenna is angry because her sister, Leigh, has forgotten to walk the dog for the past two days, and their mom has asked Jenna to do it. On Saturday, Jenna deliberately skips her chores before she goes to her friend's house, and when she sees her sister at the park, she doesn't speak to her. Later that day, when her mom asks her why she didn't do her chores, Jenna says, "What? Oh, I thought you'd just make Leigh do them. That's how things seem to work around here."

How can Jenna's behavior be best described?

6. Rodney is sitting by himself at lunch. Jake sees this and goes over to invite him to come and sit with him and his friends. Rodney says, "No, thanks. Nobody ever wants to sit with me. I'm boring, and my jokes are dumb. You and your friends are probably having a great time, and I'd just mess things up. You probably only came over here because you felt bad for me."

How can Rodney's behavior be best described?

7. Maria and Emily are working on a mural for their art class. Maria has sketched out the basic areas, and today they are meeting to start painting. Emily starts painting in the area that Maria marked out for her, but after about five minutes, Maria says, "You know what, why don't you work on a different part? That area needs to be really good, and I can do it after I'm done with what I'm working on now. Why don't you just start filling in some of the background where you can't mess anything up."

How can Maria's behavior be best described?

8. Tom is at a restaurant with his girlfriend, and he thinks she is flirting with their waiter. He feels angry and jealous, but instead of telling her and talking about it, he gets very quiet and refuses to talk to her at all on the way home. She asks him what is wrong, and he says, "If you don't know, that's not my fault." The next day, they are supposed to drive together to her gymnastics meet after school, but he hangs out with his friends in the gym until it's too late for them to make it on time.

How can Tom's behavior be best described?

**Answers:** 1—D; 2—B; 3—A; 4—D; 5—C; 6—A; 7—B; 8—C

### Teacher Observation and Perception

A very straightforward way to assign scores to students using the scales in appendix B (page 201) is for the teacher to record his or her perceptions of students on a weekly or semiweekly basis. Teacher observations or perceptions are best used with score 3.0 and 4.0 content since they involve independent student behavior. To illustrate, a teacher might assign scores weekly or biweekly to each student in the class, focusing on a small set of skills. It would be impractical and even counterproductive to try to address all of the skills in table 8.4 (page 177) during a single year. Rather, an individual teacher would select a small set of skills that fit well with the content. Perhaps one of these skills would be addressed throughout the entire year. Others might be addressed only within a specific quarter, trimester, or semester. For example, a teacher might select the problem-solving protocol (described in chapter 4, page 87) as a focus for the entire year. In that case, students would be tracking their progress on the skill every quarter. In addition to this yearlong focus, the teacher might select the skill of perspective taking (described in chapter 7, page 153) for emphasis during the first trimester. During that trimester, students would track their progress on this skill along with the problem solving. During the second trimester, the teacher would continue the emphasis on problem solving but replace the skill of perspective taking with the skill of focus (addressed in chapter 4, page 71). Students would continue to track their progress on problem solving but would stop tracking progress on perspective taking in lieu of focus.

During the third trimester, the teacher would identify another skill to replace focus and continue the emphasis on problem solving.

When assigning scores on a weekly or biweekly basis, a teacher would simply take a few minutes at the end of the class period or at the end of the day on Friday (let's say) to assign each student a score on the skills appropriate to that trimester based on the teacher's recollection of the students' behavior over the previous week or two weeks. As mentioned previously, teacher observation and perception are probably not the best vehicles for assessing score 2.0 content as it is difficult to observe or perceive a student's understanding of information. Consequently, teacher observation and perception might be used in conjunction with traditional tests. That is, once students have demonstrated score 2.0 competence through traditional tests, teacher observation and perception are then employed.

In addition to systematically recording scores based on perceptions every week or every other week, a teacher might record scores for specific students when those students have done something that demonstrates a specific level of performance on a specific skill. For example, on a given day, a particular student might demonstrate score 3.0 status on a problem-solving strategy. At the end of the class period, the teacher would record a score of 3.0 for this student but not for any others. Scores recorded this way are more situational than systematic.

To keep track of these scores it is useful to have a separate tracking sheet like that in table 8.5 (page 182). Note that table 8.5 has enough room to keep track of four different 21st century skills for each student. Scores would simply be added sequentially, moving from top left to the bottom and top right to the bottom. If the teacher used only weekly or biweekly scores, every student in class would have the same number of entries (unless some students were absent the entire week or two weeks). If the teacher also entered situation-based scores for students, those students would have more scores than others. For example, note the third score for Steph under divergent and convergent thinking. It is a 3.0 with a circle around it. The circle means that a score was assigned for Steph but not for the other students. It might be the case that the teacher observed Steph doing something in class that indicated a score 3.0 status. Also notice the incomplete score (Inc.) for Tammy on divergent and convergent thinking. Tammy either was not present for the assessment or did not complete it. A score of 0.0 is never assigned if a student misses or does not complete an assessment (for a complete discussion of this issue, see Marzano, 2010). At the end of the grading period, a teacher would assign a score for each student in the box in the bottom right-hand corner of each cell. This score represents the final status or the summative score for each student at the end of the grading period.

### Teacher-Designed Tasks

In some situations, a teacher might design a specific task that requires students to use a 21st century skill that is the focus of instruction. For example, for the general skill of using the problem-solving protocol from chapter 4 (page 87), a teacher might present students with the following task (figure 8.3, page 183).

Scores for teacher-designed tasks would be entered along with scores for teacher observation and perception.

### Student Self-Analysis

A final way to assess 21st century skills is through student self-analysis or student self-assessment. As the name indicates, students record self-perceptions of their status on a particular 21st century skill.

**Table 8.5: Teacher Tracking Sheet**

| | Divergent and convergent thinking | Controversy and conflict resolution | Perspective taking | Navigating digital sources |
|---|---|---|---|---|
| **Steph** | 2.5, 3.0, 2.5, (3.0), 3.0 | 2.0, 3.0, 3.0 | 1.5, 1.0, 2.0 | 1.5, Inc., 2.0 |
| **Tammy** | 2.5, Inc., 3.0 | 2.5, 1.5, 3.5 | 1.0, 2.0, 2.5 | 2.0, 3.0, 3.5, 3.5 |
| **Jed** | 3.0, 2.5, 3.0 | (2.5), 3.0, 2.0 | (2.5), 1.5, 1.5, 2.0 | (3.0), Inc., 2.0 |
| **David** | 0.5, 2.0, 3.0 | 3.0, 2.5, 2.5, 3.0 | 1.5, 3.5, 4.0 | 2.5, 2.5, 2.0 |
| **Noah** | (2.5), 2.0, 2.5, 3.0 | 0.5, 1.5, 2.0 | 2.5, (3.0), 2.5 | 2.5, 2.5, 2.0 |
| **Shawna** | 2.5, 1.5, 2.0 | 2.0, 1.5, 2.0 | 3.5, 2.5, 3.0 | 3.0, 1.5, 1.5, 2.5 |
| **Linea** | 3.0, 1.5, (3.0), 2.5 | 1.5, Inc., 2.0 | 1.5, 2.5, 2.0 | 2.5, 1.5, 3.0, 2.0 |
| **Roger** | 3.0, 2.5, 3.5 | 2.5, 3.5, 4.0 | 3.0, 1.5, 2.5, 3.0 | 2.5, 2.5, 3.0 |
| **Andy** | 2.5, 3.5, 4.0 | 2.0, 2.0, 3.0 | 3.5, 3.0, (2.5), 2.0 | 4.0, 3.0, (4.0), 3.5 |

Source: Adapted from Marzano, 2010.

**Directions:** Select a recurring problem you have been having at school or at home and apply the problem-solving protocol we have been studying. The protocol has eight steps.

Step 1: Determine whether you really have a problem.

Step 2: If you think you really have a problem, take a moment to affirm some positive beliefs.

Step 3: Start talking to yourself about the problem.

Step 4: Start looking for the obstacles in your way. What's missing? What is limiting you?

Step 5: For each of the possible solutions you have identified, determine how likely it is to succeed.

Step 6: Try out the solution you believe has the best chance of success and fits your comfort level for risk.

Step 7: If your solution doesn't work, clear your mind, go back to another solution you have identified, and try it out.

Step 8: If no solution can be found that works, revalue what you are trying to accomplish.

Over the next two weeks, apply these steps to the problem you have selected. In writing, describe how you have addressed each step and then evaluate the overall effectiveness of the strategy in helping you solve this problem.

**Figure 8.3: Sample student task for using the problem-solving protocol.**

Students might score themselves at the same time the teacher scores them. For example, assume that a teacher is entering scores for students every other Friday during the last ten minutes of class. The teacher would assign scores to each student using the teacher tracking sheet depicted in table 8.5 (page 182). At the same time, students would score themselves using the same scale as the teacher and turn in their self-ratings to the teacher. The teacher would compare the students' self-ratings with his or her own ratings.

Discrepancies between teacher and student scores could then be discussed. If a student had a higher self-analysis score than the score the teacher provided, the student would be asked to provide evidence that the higher score was the most accurate.

Some teachers have found that students like to use a generic scale, like the one in table 8.6, to rate themselves.

## Table 8.6: Generic Scale for Student Self-Rating

| Score 4.0 | I can apply the skills in ways that go beyond what we did in class. |
| Score 3.0 | I can use the skills as presented in class without making any big mistakes. |
| Score 2.0 | I understand the important information about the skill, but I can't use it by myself. |
| Score 1.0 | I can't explain much about the skill on my own, but with help I can. |
| Score 0.0 | Even with help, I can't explain anything about the skill. |

As its name implies, the generic scale for student self-rating provides only general descriptions for each score value in the scale. Of course, more specificity can be provided if the teacher reminds students about the specific content associated with score values 2.0, 3.0, and 4.0. As a class activity, the teacher might lead students in a discussion of the specific characteristics of score 2.0, 3.0, and 4.0 content.

## Striving for Clarity and Precision

One way for teachers to reinforce and clarify the nature of 21st century skills for students is to take the scales in appendix B (page 201) and highlight the indicators from score values 2.0, 3.0, and 4.0. This way, students have a sense of where they are but also of what they need to do to improve on such skills. Additionally, parents get more feedback about student progressions. At the elementary level, some teachers provide these highlighted scales as part of their Friday Folders. In middle and high schools, teachers can use the comments section of the electronic grading program to attach the scale with electronic highlights.

One way to ensure consistency among teachers' ratings of students in the same grade level or course is to use a method of inter-rater reliability. Ideally, two teachers would *blind score* (score the students without sharing the rating with anyone else) students on the skill that is the focus for a common task. After both teachers have completed their scoring, they compare the results and discuss and address any discrepancies. If the two teachers cannot agree, a third teacher provides a blind score to see where the judgment is consistent. A school would not have to do this with every task, although that would be ideal. Rather, teachers could randomly select students or do a stratified random sample, in which students are classified into varying groups—by ability or behavior—and then a representative sample is randomly selected. This sample might represent five to ten students in a class of thirty. This is a wonderful activity to use for any type of performance task students complete, and it is also great professional development for teachers during common meeting time. It serves multiple purposes because it allows teachers to become more consistent or reliable in their evaluations of students, and it also ensures that students benefit from multiple perspectives.

## Assigning Summative Scores

In chapter 2 (page 34), we introduced the notion of formative verses summative assessments. In general, formative assessments are used to track progress over time, and summative assessments are used to assign a final score to students at the end of some predefined interval of time such as a quarter or a semester. In this book, we use the terms *formative scores* and *summative scores* as opposed to *formative assessments* and *summative assessments*. The reason for this shift in terminology is described in depth in the book *Formative Assessment and Standards-Based Grading* (Marzano, 2010).

Briefly, a single assessment is almost never a precise measure of a student's status at any point in time. There is error associated with any score. This is particularly the case with scores on 21st century skills as described in *Teaching and Assessing 21st Century Skills*. Consider, for example, scores assigned using teacher observation and perception on a weekly or biweekly basis. While assigning these scores, a teacher might incorrectly recall an individual student's performance over the last week or two weeks. This score would be highly inaccurate for that student at that point in time. However, on another occasion for that same student, a teacher might assign a score that is relatively accurate because he or she correctly recalled a specific instance when the student exhibited characteristics important to the 21st century skill in question. In short, no single assessment can ever be trusted as an accurate representation of a student's status at any point in time. Consequently, the ideal of a single summative assessment at the end of a grading period that is trusted as the final score for students makes little sense. Any single score can be accurate or highly inaccurate. What is more reasonable is to use a student's formative scores over time to construct a summative score at the end of each grading period. To illustrate, reconsider the scores in table 8.5 (page 182) on the teacher tracking sheet. For the skill of divergent and convergent thinking, Steph had the following formative scores: 2.5, 2.5, 3.0, and 3.0.

To assign a summative score to Steph for this skill, the teacher would examine the student's progression of scores over time. The final summative score should represent the student's status at the end of the grading period. In the case of Steph's progression, the first score was a 2.5 and the final score was a 3.0 with a gradual progression of increasing scores throughout the grading period. It is reasonable then for the teacher to assume that the final score of 3.0 is the student's summative score. For the most part, the final score in the series will be the student's summative score when there is a consistent progression from low to high scores. However, there will be cases in which this generalization will not produce the most accurate final score. For example, the final score in a series might be much lower than previous scores simply due to the fact that the student had a bad day when he or she took the final assessment. In all cases, the teacher should use all available information including students' perception of their status to assign summative scores.

## Integrating Students' Summative Scores Into Traditional Grading Practices

Some schools and districts across the country are moving toward report cards that provide more information than overall grades. Rather, scores on specific topics are provided for each subject area. For example, in addition to a grade of A, B, C, D, or F in fifth-grade mathematics, students would receive scores for specific topics. To illustrate, consider figure 8.4.

| **Name:** | Al Backstreet | | | | | | | | | |
| **Address:** | 123 Some Street | | | | | | | | | |
| **City:** | Anytown, MD 80000 | | | | | | | | | |
| **Grade Level:** | 5 | | | | | | | | | |
| **Homeroom:** | Ms. Willis | | | | | | | | | |
| Language Arts | 2.46 | C+ | | Divergent and Convergent Thinking | | | | 3.40 | | A |
| Mathematics | 2.50 | B- | | Controversy and Conflict Resolution | | | | 2.90 | | B+ |
| Science | 2.20 | C | | Perspective Taking | | | | 3.40 | | A |
| Social Studies | 3.10 | A- | | Navigating Digital Sources | | | | 2.70 | | B |
| Art | 3.00 | A- | | | | | | | | |

| | | **0.5** | **1.0** | **1.5** | **2.0** | **2.5** | **3.0** | **3.5** | **4.0** |
|---|---|---|---|---|---|---|---|---|---|
| **Language Arts** | | | | | | | | | |
| *Reading:* | | | | | | | | | |
| Word Recognition and Vocabulary | 2.5 | | | | | | | | |
| Reading for Main Idea | 1.5 | | | | | | | | |
| Literary Analysis | 2.0 | | | | | | | | |
| *Writing:* | | | | | | | | | |
| Language Conventions | 3.5 | | | | | | | | |
| Organization and Focus | 2.5 | | | | | | | | |
| Research and Technology | 1.0 | | | | | | | | |
| Evaluation and Revision | 2.5 | | | | | | | | |
| Writing Applications | 3.0 | | | | | | | | |
| *Listening and Speaking:* | | | | | | | | | |
| Comprehension | 3.0 | | | | | | | | |
| Organization and Delivery | 3.0 | | | | | | | | |

**Figure 8.4: Report card for academic and 21st century skills.**          Continued on next page →

| | | 0.5 | 1.0 | 1.5 | 2.0 | 2.5 | 3.0 | 3.5 | 4.0 |
|---|---|---|---|---|---|---|---|---|---|
| Analysis and Evaluation of Oral Media | 2.5 | | | | | | | | |
| Speaking Applications | 2.5 | | | | | | | | |
| *21st Century Skills:* | | | | | | | | | |
| Divergent and Convergent Thinking | 4.0 | | | | | | | | |
| Controversy and Conflict Resolution | 3.5 | | | | | | | | |
| Perspective Taking | 3.5 | | | | | | | | |
| Navigating Digital Sources | 3.0 | | | | | | | | |
| **Average for Language Arts** | 2.46 | | | | | | | | |
| | | | | | | | | | |
| **Mathematics** | | | | | | | | | |
| Number Systems | 3.5 | | | | | | | | |
| Estimation | 3.0 | | | | | | | | |
| Addition/Subtraction | 2.5 | | | | | | | | |
| Multiplication/Division | 2.5 | | | | | | | | |
| Ratio/Proportion/Percent | 1.0 | | | | | | | | |
| *21st Century Skills:* | | | | | | | | | |
| Divergent and Convergent Thinking | 4.0 | | | | | | | | |
| Controversy and Conflict Resolution | 2.0 | | | | | | | | |
| Perspective Taking | 3.5 | | | | | | | | |
| Navigating Digital Sources | 2.0 | | | | | | | | |
| **Average for Mathematics** | 2.5 | | | | | | | | |
| | | | | | | | | | |
| **Science** | | | | | | | | | |
| Matter and Energy | 2.0 | | | | | | | | |
| Forces of Nature | 2.5 | | | | | | | | |
| Diversity of Life | 1.5 | | | | | | | | |
| Human Identity | 3.5 | | | | | | | | |
| Interdependence of Life | 1.5 | | | | | | | | |
| *21st Century Skills:* | | | | | | | | | |
| Divergent and Convergent Thinking | 3.0 | | | | | | | | |
| Controversy and Conflict Resolution | 1.5 | | | | | | | | |
| Perspective Taking | 2.5 | | | | | | | | |

| | | 0.5 | 1.0 | 1.5 | 2.0 | 2.5 | 3.0 | 3.5 | 4.0 |
|---|---|---|---|---|---|---|---|---|---|
| Navigating Digital Sources | 1.0 | | | | | | | | |
| **Average for Science** | 2.2 | | | | | | | | |
| | | | | | | | | | |
| **Social Studies** | | | | | | | | | |
| The Influence of Culture | 3.5 | | | | | | | | |
| Current Events | 3.0 | | | | | | | | |
| Personal Responsibility | 4.0 | | | | | | | | |
| Government Representation | 3.5 | | | | | | | | |
| Human and Civil Rights | 1.5 | | | | | | | | |
| *21st Century Skills:* | | | | | | | | | |
| Divergent and Convergent Thinking | 3.5 | | | | | | | | |
| Controversy and Conflict Resolution | 3.5 | | | | | | | | |
| Perspective Taking | 3.5 | | | | | | | | |
| Navigating Digital Sources | 4.0 | | | | | | | | |
| **Average for Social Studies** | 3.1 | | | | | | | | |
| | | | | | | | | | |
| **Art** | | | | | | | | | |
| Purposes of Art | 3.5 | | | | | | | | |
| Art Skills | 3.0 | | | | | | | | |
| Art and Culture | 2.5 | | | | | | | | |
| *21st Century Skills:* | | | | | | | | | |
| Divergent and Convergent Thinking | 2.5 | | | | | | | | |
| Controversy and Conflict Resolution | 4.0 | | | | | | | | |
| Perspective Taking | 4.0 | | | | | | | | |
| Navigating Digital Sources | 3.5 | | | | | | | | |
| **Average for Art** | 3.0 | | | | | | | | |

Source: Adapted from Marzano & Waters, 2009.

In figure 8.4 (page 185), the top left part of the report card looks quite traditional. This particular student, Al Backstreet, received a C+ in language arts, a B- in mathematics, and so on. These grades were derived from summative scores that were derived from formative scores as described previously. Consider the student's scores for language arts. There were twelve specific language arts topics addressed during the grading period. For reading there were three topics: word recognition and vocabulary, reading for main idea, and literary analysis. Writing involved five topics, and listening and speaking involved four topics. There is a bar graph for each topic representing the student's summative score at the end of the grading period. For example, the student's summative score for word recognition and vocabulary was 2.5. Note that for each bar graph, the base is more darkly shaded than the top part of the graph. The darkly shaded part of the bar graph represents a student's status on the topic at the beginning of the grading period. In figure 8.4 (page 185), the student began the grading period with a score of 1.0 for word recognition and vocabulary but ended the grading period with a summative score of 2.5.

To convert the twelve summative language arts scores to an overall grade for language arts, the conversions reported in table 8.7 were used.

## Table 8.7: Conversion Scale to Traditional Grade

| Average Scale Score Across Multiple Goals | Traditional Grade |
|---|---|
| 3.75–4.00 | A+ |
| 3.26–3.74 | A |
| 3.00–3.25 | A- |
| 2.84–2.99 | B+ |
| 2.67–2.83 | B |
| 2.50–2.66 | B- |
| 2.34–2.49 | C+ |
| 2.17–2.33 | C |
| 2.00–2.16 | C- |
| 1.76–1.99 | D+ |
| 1.26–1.75 | D |
| 1.00–1.25 | D- |
| Below 1.00 | F |

Source: Marzano, 2010.

Also, note that the top right-hand section of the report card provides grades for four 21st century skills: divergent and convergent thinking, controversy and conflict resolution, perspective taking, and navigating digital sources. These four 21st century skills were addressed and assessed in every subject area. However, the scores for the 21st century skills in a particular subject area were not included in the overall grade for a subject area. For example, the average of 2.46 reported for language arts, which translates to a grade of C+, is the average of the summative score for the twelve language arts topics and does not include the summative scores in language arts for the four 21st century skills. The scores for the 21st century skills that were translated into the grades reported in the top right-hand section of the report card were computed by averaging the 21st century scores across the subject areas. For example, the average score of 3.40 for divergent and convergent thinking, which translates to a grade of A, was derived by averaging the student's scores for divergent and convergent thinking across language arts, mathematics, science, social studies, and art.

In this case, the school had decided to address the same four 21st century skills in all classes. Presumably, another set of 21st century skills would be addressed in each class during the next grading period. Another option would be for different subject areas to address different 21st century skills.

Of course, there are many different ways to design report cards and translate summative scores on scales to traditional grades. For a detailed discussion of these various schemes, see *Formative Assessment and Standards-Based Grading* (Marzano, 2010). The point here is that 21st century skills can easily be integrated into current grading and reporting practices.

## Summary

It stands to reason that when teachers teach 21st century skills, they should adequately assess students' understanding of them. This chapter focused on assessing the nineteen cognitive and conative skills we have identified throughout *Teaching and Assessing 21st Century Skills* as being crucial to students' success in the coming years. The chapter presented a five-point scale that can be used in assessing any learning goal, and scales for each of the nineteen skills are included in appendix B (page 201). Traditional selected-response tests are best used with score 2.0 content, while teacher observation, teacher-designed tasks, and student self-analysis can be used in assessing scores 3.0 and above. Finally, we addressed the topic of assigning summative scores and translating those scores into traditional grades.

# Chapter 8: Comprehension Questions

1. What is the role of feedback in a system of assessment?

2. Using the five-point scale described in the chapter, what does a score of 3.0 indicate? 2.0? 4.0? 1.0? 0.0?

3. When might it be appropriate for a teacher to use a traditional, selected-response type of test?

4. What are some constraints that a teacher should be aware of when using teacher observation and perception?

# EPILOGUE

In chapter 1, we noted that this book, *Teaching and Assessing 21st Century Skills*, only addresses a few of the changes that will be necessary in the coming years. As our audience is primarily the classroom teacher, we focus on those cognitive and conative skills teachers can immediately integrate into the classroom. However, there are systemic changes that will most probably take place in the 21st century as well. As Ian McCoog noted, "When we [adults] . . . went to school, the 'three r's' were reading, riting, and rithmetic. . . . This idea has been replaced with the 'three r's' for the 21st century: rigor, relevance, and real world skills" (McCoog, 2008, pp. 2–3). On a large scale, the education system will need to integrate technology into the classroom in a relevant and adaptable way, begin a fundamental accountability shift from the teacher to the student, and discard the time-based structure of the education system in favor of a proficiency-based structure. Briefly, we address these three systemic changes.

## Technology

Whereas students of the 20th century might have spent time away from school playing street games, talking on the phone, reading a book, or watching television, students of the 21st century commonly spend their time away from school listening to an iPod, monitoring text messages on their cell phones, watching television, browsing magazines, and monitoring social websites—all at the same time. Technology is ubiquitous in most 21st century students' lives, and students expect to use it to communicate, create, socialize, and interact. Reaching them requires teachers and schools to embrace a wide variety of technological devices and programs as well. This will require more than just purchasing and installing new gadgets in classrooms. Meaningful professional development is essential for teachers to use technology effectively. As Chris Dede noted, "Learning technologies are not like fire . . . you don't get benefit from them just by standing close to them" (as cited in Cummings, 2007).

Just as we know technology is here to stay, we know that it is a dynamic, ever-changing force in our lives; there will always be new technologies to learn and new frameworks in which to learn them. This can be intimidating for those of us who grew up in a different era, but it is important to remember that technology is, ultimately, only a tool. Teachers do not need to teach technology; rather, teachers need to *use* technology in order to teach the cognitive and conative skills students will need to succeed in the 21st century.

## Shift in Accountability

In a typical 20th century classroom, explicit learning goals were not shared with students. Instead, the teacher presented the information, and students often memorized it in preparation for a quiz or test that the teacher would prepare and grade. Many times, students could not articulate what it was they were learning or why it was important. The teacher calculated the grades and kept them in a grading book. If students did not choose to keep track of their own scores over the grading term, they might not have much of an idea of what their grades would be, and they very likely had little to no idea how much they had learned. As discussed in chapter 1, this system worked because many people left school and worked in heavily managed positions until retirement.

In the 21st century, however, students will need to become accountable for their own learning. Explicit learning goals need to be provided to them so that they understand very clearly what is expected of them and what demonstrating proficiency will look like. They will need to be able to measure and record their own scores on assessments and evaluate their progress. By inviting and teaching students to monitor and manage their education, schools can help them become more accountable for their own learning. In districts where this work has already begun, students are engaged and curious, often planning alternative learning experiences for themselves and sometimes graduating early. For more information on how to implement the structures that support these shifts in accountability, see *Designing and Teaching Learning Goals and Objectives* (Marzano, 2009), *Formative Assessment and Standards-Based Grading* (Marzano, 2010), and *The Highly Engaged Classroom* (Marzano & Pickering, 2011).

## Proficiency-Based System

In the 20th century, most if not all schools in the United States worked on a time-based system. That is, students moved from one grade to the next largely based on age. As students got older, they progressed through grades until graduation at the age of eighteen. In very few instances did students repeat or skip grade levels, and when they did, it was often a great source of stress. Additionally, there was not much room to maneuver between subject areas. That is, if a student excelled in math but struggled with writing, he or she was often frustrated in a language arts course that was moving too quickly and bored in a math course that moved too slowly. Such a system was also difficult for teachers, who had students working at very different levels of proficiency all in one class.

In a proficiency-based system, students only progress to the next level when they have demonstrated proficiency. This means that students are not just passed along from one grade level to the next having earned only Ds. This kind of system ensures that students really are learning as they progress. It also allows for flexibility between subject areas. A student might be at level 2 in language arts, level 5 in mathematics, and level 4 in social studies. Many educators are concerned that this leads to grouping students of different ages together. To some degree this is true, but multiage grouping is not a new concept. In fact, many schools have utilized multiage classes and grouping structures for years with excellent results. When thoughtfully and carefully implemented, these structures can eliminate frustration and ensure high-quality learning experiences for all students.

Once again, we see these systemic changes as mainly the responsibility of school and district leaders. This does not mean that teachers and teacher leaders do not need to educate themselves about the issues of technology, accountability, and proficiency-based systems, but these topics are beyond the scope of this book. Here, our goal has been to provide research-based strategies that teachers can implement in their classrooms to more effectively prepare their students for the challenges of the 21st century.

# APPENDIX A

# ANSWERS TO COMPREHENSION QUESTIONS

# Answers to Chapter 3: Comprehension Questions

1. How might you help students develop keywords to use when searching?

   Using a thesaurus or doing preliminary online research (for example, browsing sites related to their topic) to create a list of related terms are both strategies that students might utilize. Making a list of synonyms, cause-and-effect words, more specific terms, or proper nouns related to the research topic can also provide meaningful keywords for searching.

2. What are the defining features of errors of faulty logic, attack, weak reference, and misinformation?

   Faulty logic is a failure to use proper logic. Attack focuses on irrelevant information. Weak reference means using untrustworthy or unreliable sources. Misinformation is the use of incorrect information or the misapplication of information.

3. Why is it important for students to evaluate both the validity and the truth of deductive conclusions?

   A valid conclusion logically follows its premises. However, if the premises are untrue, then the conclusion may also be untrue. Valid conclusions are not necessarily true.

4. How does the use of qualifiers facilitate students' work as they generate and defend claims?

   Since qualifiers allow for exceptions to a claim, identifying them encourages students to engage in divergent thinking, perspective taking, and logical reasoning as they formulate claims. By identifying situations in which their claim might not be true, students can refine and strengthen their initial claims.

# Answers to Chapter 4: Comprehension Questions

1.  Why is it a good idea to discourage students from multitasking with tasks that require complex thought?

    Because the brain is unable to think about two things at once, multitasking asks one's brain to switch back and forth between multiple tasks. This switching wastes time, and the process of continually activating and deactivating rules for certain tasks can cause performance on both tasks to deteriorate.

2.  What role does self-evaluation play in the process of enhancing focus?

    Self-evaluation is important to ensure that students are able to mentally evaluate the outcome of an activity and move on from a success or a failure to next steps. Evaluating what actions led to success or failure allows one to learn from previous experiences and move on to subsequent projects without feeling overly guilty about failure or overly egotistical about success. Without this step, positive experiences can lead to overly prideful behavior or apathy (resting on one's laurels). Negative experiences, if not left in the past, can hinder future work with challenging problems or activities.

3.  What is the underlying dynamic between convergent and divergent thinking?

    Convergent and divergent thinking are best used cyclically, as options are generated (divergent thinking) and then narrowed (convergent thinking). Often, after engaging in convergent thinking but not reaching a solution to a problem, it is helpful to return to divergent thinking to generate more possibilities or to examine what actions might have prevented a successful outcome to an activity. Convergent thinking can then be used again to decide on a new course of action, and so on.

4.  What is the role of affirmative judgment when students are using convergent thinking?

    Affirmative judgment helps students to maintain a positive perspective while narrowing down a list of possibilities. Instead of looking for options to eliminate, they should focus on identifying the pros and cons of various choices and then looking for the best options.

# Answers to Chapter 5: Comprehension Questions

1. How does parsing sentences into propositions help students identify important relationships between ideas?

   By breaking down sentences into their smallest meaningful ideas, parsing sentences into propositions can help students identify which relationships are essential to the content being studied.

2. Explain the reasoning behind asking students to create mental images. What advantages do mental images have over graphic representations and drawing and sketching?

   Mental images require more mental energy and therefore lead to deeper processing than creating graphic representations, drawing, or sketching. When students create mental images, they must hold them in their working memory while elaborating on them, questioning them, and drawing conclusions from them. The effort required to visualize and manipulate mental images creates a more permanent and more deeply processed record in the brain of the content being studied.

3. How can thought experiments be used to help students gain new perspectives?

   Because thought experiments can challenge current views and create new beliefs, they can be very useful for students who think that their opinion is the truth. Considering a scenario or story in which their current beliefs would logically lead them to act in ways that they would consider unsavory or wrong might help such students to step back and think about other perspectives on the issue.

4. Why can mental practice sometimes be more effective than physical practice?

   For novices, mental practice is less detailed than physical practice, so students can focus on remembering the important aspects and big ideas of their skill without having to worry about making mistakes or practicing incorrectly. For experts, mental practice allows them to focus on and fine-tune specific aspects of a skill that still need improvement.

# Answers to Chapter 6: Comprehension Questions

1. Why are optical illusions a good way to stimulate discussion about perceptions?

   Because optical illusions are usually morally neutral, they allow students to easily acknowledge the truth of a perception different from their own. This allows them to freely discuss both their own and others' perceptions, and it visually illustrates the idea that two people can hold different perspectives and both be right (or wrong).

2. What are the important differences between the growth mindset and the fixed mindset?

   The growth mindset states that any individual is able to get smarter by working harder. It emphasizes effort over innate talent. The fixed mindset states that everyone is born with a certain amount of intelligence, and an individual cannot change that intelligence, no matter what. The differences between the theories are important because they affect how students approach challenging or difficult tasks. A student who believes that she can increase her intelligence is more likely to take on a challenging task because she sees it as an opportunity to learn. A student who believes that her intelligence is fixed may hesitate to take on a difficult task because she sees no benefit from it and is afraid of failing. For a student with a fixed mindset, if a task is not easy, then he explains it by saying that he is not smart enough. For a student with a growth mindset, difficult tasks are simply opportunities to gain intelligence.

3. How can teaching students about resiliency help them to cultivate a sense of self-efficacy?

   Resiliency emphasizes the ability of a person to be successful in spite of his or her circumstances. Students with low self-efficacy see their circumstances as beyond their control. By learning about resiliency, these students will realize that one's circumstances do not always determine one's outcomes, and bad circumstances do not always need to lead to bad outcomes.

4. Why is emotional thinking a negative way of thinking?

   Because involuntary processes in the brain largely control emotions, people who are operating under the influence of emotions often describe themselves as *not thinking*. This lack of control can lead to inappropriate behavior and bad choices. While emotions are unavoidable, students should understand that reacting before they mentally process an event and decide on an appropriate response can be harmful to themselves and others.

# Answers to Chapter 7: Comprehension Questions

1. Why are perceptions so powerful?

   Because many people view their perceptions as reality, they base their actions and decisions on their perceptions. If a person perceives himself to be a popular person, for example, it may cause him to behave in ways that he might not if he perceived himself as a shy person. Perceptions are powerful because they play an important role in governing people's actions and decisions.

2. In what situations is perspective analysis likely to be most effective?

   When considering topics that are controversial, perspective analysis can help students identify the ideas and perceptions that lead them to hold a certain position. By analyzing positions opposed to their own, students may either gain greater confidence in their original position, or they may see that their original position was weak and decide that they actually agree with the opposite position. In some cases, the exercise will cause students to become unsure about which position they agree with, and inspire them to conduct more research on the topic.

3. What is the difference between conflict and controversy?

   Conflict occurs when actions or goals are incompatible. Controversy occurs when ideas are incompatible.

4. How does controversy improve students' reasoning and perspective-taking skills?

   Controversy, when handled appropriately, requires students to defend their own claims about issues and to listen to others defend claims about their positions. Through the evaluation of others' and their own claims, students learn reasoning skills. By listening and speaking respectfully about opposing viewpoints, students become more adept at perspective taking.

# Answers to Chapter 8: Comprehension Questions

1. What is the role of feedback in a system of assessment?

   Feedback allows students to see their past and current progress and helps them articulate goals for the future.

2. Using the five-point scale described in the chapter, what does a score of 3.0 indicate? 2.0? 4.0? 1.0? 0.0?

   Score 3.0 indicates that a student can independently perform a skill or appropriately apply knowledge with no major errors or omissions. Score 2.0 indicates that a student is able to recognize or recall the steps of a skill or factual knowledge about a skill and is even able to describe examples and situations in which the skill or knowledge would be used. Score 4.0 indicates that a student is applying a strategy, skill, or knowledge in unusual situations or identifying types of examples that go beyond those explicitly taught in class. Score 1.0 indicates that with assistance a student can achieve partial success at score 2.0 or score 3.0 content. Score 0.0 indicates that even with help a student has no success with any of the content.

3. When might it be appropriate for a teacher to use a traditional, selected-response type of test?

   Traditional, selected-response types of tests are best used to assess students' grasp of score 2.0 content. Because score 2.0 measures a student's ability to recognize or recall specific facts or information about a skill or topic, multiple-choice, true/false, and fill-in-the-blank questions usually found on traditional tests more easily measure it.

4. What are some constraints that a teacher should be aware of when using teacher observation and perception?

   Teacher observation and perception are best used after students have demonstrated proficiency on score 2.0 content. Because 2.0 content (a student's factual knowledge about a concept or skill) is difficult to observe, teachers are advised to use traditional tests to assess 2.0 content.

# APPENDIX B

# SCALES FOR 21ST CENTURY SKILLS

# Analyzing and Utilizing Information: Navigating Digital Sources

| | |
|---|---|
| **Score 4.0** | The student:<br>• Applies the strategy in unusual situations, employs elements that were not explicitly taught, or both<br>No major errors or omissions regarding the score 4.0 content |
| **Score 3.5** | In addition to score 3.0 performance, partial success at score 4.0 content |
| **Score 3.0** | The student:<br>• Analyzes and evaluates websites for the validity of their content<br>No major errors or omissions regarding the score 3.0 content |
| **Score 2.5** | No major errors or omissions regarding score 2.0 content, and partial success at score 3.0 content |
| **Score 2.0** | The student:<br>• Can describe important considerations to keep in mind when examining websites<br>• Can describe situations in which checking for the validity of information found on the Internet would be important<br>• Can describe or recognize examples of legitimate and illegitimate websites<br>No major errors or omissions regarding the score 2.0 content |
| **Score 1.5** | Partial success at score 2.0 content, and major errors or omissions at score 3.0 content |
| **Score 1.0** | With help, partial success at score 2.0 content and score 3.0 content |
| **Score 0.5** | With help, partial success at score 2.0 content, but not at score 3.0 content |
| **Score 0.0** | Even with help, no success |

# Analyzing and Utilizing Information: Identifying Common Logical Errors

| Score 4.0 | The student:<br>• Applies the strategy in unusual situations, identifies logical errors that go beyond those that were explicitly taught, or both<br>No major errors or omissions regarding the score 4.0 content |
|---|---|
| Score 3.5 | In addition to score 3.0 performance, partial success at score 4.0 content |
| Score 3.0 | The student:<br>• Analyzes appropriate information for common logical errors<br>No major errors or omissions regarding the score 3.0 content |
| Score 2.5 | No major errors or omissions regarding score 2.0 content, and partial success at score 3.0 content |
| Score 2.0 | The student:<br>• Can describe situations in which it is beneficial to analyze information for common logical errors<br>• Can describe or recognize the various common logical errors that have been taught, including those of faulty logic, attack, weak reference, and misinformation<br>No major errors or omissions regarding the score 2.0 content |
| Score 1.5 | Partial success at score 2.0 content, and major errors or omissions at score 3.0 content |
| Score 1.0 | With help, partial success at score 2.0 content and score 3.0 content |
| Score 0.5 | With help, partial success at score 2.0 content, but not at score 3.0 content |
| Score 0.0 | Even with help, no success |

# Analyzing and Utilizing Information: Generating Conclusions

| Score 4.0 | The student:<br><br>• Applies the strategy in unusual situations, addresses issues with probabilistic and deductive conclusions not covered in class, or both<br><br>No major errors or omissions regarding the score 4.0 content |
|---|---|
| Score 3.5 | In addition to score 3.0 performance, partial success at score 4.0 content |
| Score 3.0 | The student:<br><br>• Identifies and corrects problems associated with probabilistic and deductive conclusions<br><br>No major errors or omissions regarding the score 3.0 content |
| Score 2.5 | No major errors or omissions regarding score 2.0 content, and partial success at score 3.0 content |
| Score 2.0 | The student:<br><br>• Can describe situations in which it is important to analyze conclusions<br><br>• Can explain the problems that can occur with probabilistic conclusions and how to avoid them<br><br>• Can explain the problems that can occur with deductive conclusions and how to avoid them<br><br>No major errors or omissions regarding the score 2.0 content |
| Score 1.5 | Partial success at score 2.0 content, and major errors or omissions at score 3.0 content |
| Score 1.0 | With help, partial success at score 2.0 content and score 3.0 content |
| Score 0.5 | With help, partial success at score 2.0 content, but not at score 3.0 content |
| Score 0.0 | Even with help, no success |

# Analyzing and Utilizing Information: Presenting and Supporting Claims

| Score 4.0 | The student: |
|---|---|
| | • Applies the strategy in unusual situations, addresses aspects of claims, grounds, backing, and qualifiers not addressed in class, or both |
| | No major errors or omissions regarding the score 4.0 content |
| Score 3.5 | In addition to score 3.0 performance, partial success at score 4.0 content |
| Score 3.0 | The student: |
| | • When appropriate, generates claims with accompanying grounds, backing, and qualifiers |
| | No major errors or omissions regarding the score 3.0 content |
| Score 2.5 | No major errors or omissions regarding score 2.0 content, and partial success at score 3.0 content |
| Score 2.0 | The student: |
| | • Can describe the basic nature of claims |
| | • Can explain the relationship between grounds and backing |
| | • Can explain the role and function of qualifiers |
| | • Can describe or recognize examples of claims with valid support |
| | No major errors or omissions regarding the score 2.0 content |
| Score 1.5 | Partial success at score 2.0 content, and major errors or omissions at score 3.0 content |
| Score 1.0 | With help, partial success at score 2.0 content and score 3.0 content |
| Score 0.5 | With help, partial success at score 2.0 content, but not at score 3.0 content |
| Score 0.0 | Even with help, no success |

# Addressing Complex Problems and Issues: Focus

| Score 4.0 | The student:<br>• Applies the strategy in unusual situations, addresses aspects of focus or multitasking not covered in class, or both<br>No major errors or omissions regarding the score 4.0 content |
|---|---|
| Score 3.5 | In addition to score 3.0 performance, partial success at score 4.0 content |
| Score 3.0 | The student:<br>• When appropriate, focuses attention on a specific task and avoids distraction<br>No major errors or omissions regarding the score 3.0 content |
| Score 2.5 | No major errors or omissions regarding score 2.0 content, and partial success at score 3.0 content |
| Score 2.0 | The student:<br>• Can describe the basic nature and function of focus<br>• Can describe situations in which it is important to focus<br>• Can describe situations in which multitasking is acceptable and situations in which it would be dangerous<br>• Can describe or recognize facts about multitasking<br>No major errors or omissions regarding the score 2.0 content |
| Score 1.5 | Partial success at score 2.0 content, and major errors or omissions at score 3.0 content |
| Score 1.0 | With help, partial success at score 2.0 content and score 3.0 content |
| Score 0.5 | With help, partial success at score 2.0 content, but not at score 3.0 content |
| Score 0.0 | Even with help, no success |

# Addressing Complex Problems and Issues: Divergent and Convergent Thinking

| Score 4.0 | The student:<br>• Applies the strategy in unusual situations, addresses aspects of convergent or divergent thinking not covered in class, or both<br>No major errors or omissions regarding the score 4.0 content |
|---|---|
| Score 3.5 | In addition to score 3.0 performance, partial success at score 4.0 content |
| Score 3.0 | The student:<br>• When appropriate, employs strategies for convergent and divergent thinking to address complex problems and issues<br>No major errors or omissions regarding the score 3.0 content |
| Score 2.5 | No major errors or omissions regarding score 2.0 content, and partial success at score 3.0 content |
| Score 2.0 | The student:<br>• Can contrast the basic purposes and functions of convergent and divergent thinking<br>• Can recognize or recall examples of convergent and divergent thinking<br>• Can explain the role of convergent and divergent thinking in addressing complex problems and issues<br>No major errors or omissions regarding the score 2.0 content |
| Score 1.5 | Partial success at score 2.0 content, and major errors or omissions at score 3.0 content |
| Score 1.0 | With help, partial success at score 2.0 content and score 3.0 content |
| Score 0.5 | With help, partial success at score 2.0 content, but not at score 3.0 content |
| Score 0.0 | Even with help, no success |

# Addressing Complex Problems and Issues: A Problem-Solving Protocol

| Score 4.0 | The student: |
|---|---|
| | • Applies the strategy in unusual situations, addresses aspects of the strategy not covered in class, or both |
| | No major errors or omissions regarding the score 4.0 content |
| Score 3.5 | In addition to score 3.0 performance, partial success at score 4.0 content |
| Score 3.0 | The student: |
| | • When appropriate, applies the problem-solving protocol to solve problems encountered in life |
| | No major errors or omissions regarding the score 3.0 content |
| Score 2.5 | No major errors or omissions regarding score 2.0 content, and partial success at score 3.0 content |
| Score 2.0 | The student: |
| | • Can describe situations in which the problem-solving protocol would be beneficial |
| | • Can explain the nature and function of the various components of the problem-solving protocol |
| | • Can describe situations in which the problem-solving protocol would be beneficial |
| | No major errors or omissions regarding the score 2.0 content |
| Score 1.5 | Partial success at score 2.0 content, and major errors or omissions at score 3.0 content |
| Score 1.0 | With help, partial success at score 2.0 content and score 3.0 content |
| Score 0.5 | With help, partial success at score 2.0 content, but not at score 3.0 content |
| Score 0.0 | Even with help, no success |

# Creating Patterns and Mental Models: Identifying Basic Relationships Between Ideas

| Score 4.0 | The student:<br>• Applies the strategy in unusual situations, addresses aspects of basic relationships not covered in class, or both<br>No major errors or omissions regarding the score 4.0 content |
|---|---|
| Score 3.5 | In addition to score 3.0 performance, partial success at score 4.0 content |
| Score 3.0 | The student:<br>• When appropriate, analyzes the basic relationships between ideas<br>No major errors or omissions regarding the score 3.0 content |
| Score 2.5 | No major errors or omissions regarding score 2.0 content, and partial success at score 3.0 content |
| Score 2.0 | The student:<br>• Can describe general categories of relationships between ideas<br>• Can recognize relationships between ideas in specific circumstances<br>• Can diagram basic relationships between ideas<br>No major errors or omissions regarding the score 2.0 content |
| Score 1.5 | Partial success at score 2.0 content, and major errors or omissions at score 3.0 content |
| Score 1.0 | With help, partial success at score 2.0 content and score 3.0 content |
| Score 0.5 | With help, partial success at score 2.0 content, but not at score 3.0 content |
| Score 0.0 | Even with help, no success |

# Creating Patterns and Mental Models: Creating Graphic Representations

| Score 4.0 | The student: |
|---|---|
| | • Applies the strategy in unusual situations, addresses aspects of graphic representations not covered in class, or both |
| | No major errors or omissions regarding the score 4.0 content |
| Score 3.5 | In addition to score 3.0 performance, partial success at score 4.0 content |
| Score 3.0 | The student: |
| | • Uses appropriate graphic representations to organize information |
| | No major errors or omissions regarding the score 3.0 content |
| Score 2.5 | No major errors or omissions regarding score 2.0 content, and partial success at score 3.0 content |
| Score 2.0 | The student: |
| | • Can describe situations in which graphic representations would be helpful |
| | • Can explain the purpose of different types of graphic representations |
| | No major errors or omissions regarding the score 2.0 content |
| Score 1.5 | Partial success at score 2.0 content, and major errors or omissions at score 3.0 content |
| Score 1.0 | With help, partial success at score 2.0 content and score 3.0 content |
| Score 0.5 | With help, partial success at score 2.0 content, but not at score 3.0 content |
| Score 0.0 | Even with help, no success |

# Creating Patterns and Mental Models: Drawing and Sketching

| Score 4.0 | The student:<br>• Applies the strategy in unusual situations, addresses aspects of drawing and sketching not covered in class, or both<br>No major errors or omissions regarding the score 4.0 content |
|-----------|------------------------------------------------------------------------------------------------------------------------------------------------------------------------------------------------------|
| Score 3.5 | In addition to score 3.0 performance, partial success at score 4.0 content |
| Score 3.0 | The student:<br>• When appropriate, creates drawings or sketches that accurately organize information<br>No major errors or omissions regarding the score 3.0 content |
| Score 2.5 | No major errors or omissions regarding score 2.0 content, and partial success at score 3.0 content |
| Score 2.0 | The student:<br>• Can describe situations in which drawing or sketching would be beneficial<br>• Can describe or recognize the purpose of specific drawings and the information they present<br>No major errors or omissions regarding the score 2.0 content |
| Score 1.5 | Partial success at score 2.0 content, and major errors or omissions at score 3.0 content |
| Score 1.0 | With help, partial success at score 2.0 content and score 3.0 content |
| Score 0.5 | With help, partial success at score 2.0 content, but not at score 3.0 content |
| Score 0.0 | Even with help, no success |

# Creating Patterns and Mental Models: Generating Mental Images

| Score 4.0 | The student:<br>• Applies the strategy in unusual situations, addresses aspects of mental images not covered in class, or both<br>No major errors or omissions regarding the score 4.0 content |
|---|---|
| Score 3.5 | In addition to score 3.0 performance, partial success at score 4.0 content |
| Score 3.0 | The student:<br>• When appropriate, creates mental images that accurately organize information<br>No major errors or omissions regarding the score 3.0 content |
| Score 2.5 | No major errors or omissions regarding score 2.0 content, and partial success at score 3.0 content |
| Score 2.0 | The student:<br>• Can describe situations in which using mental images would be helpful<br>• Can describe the benefits of mental images over other forms of mental models<br>No major errors or omissions regarding the score 2.0 content |
| Score 1.5 | Partial success at score 2.0 content, and major errors or omissions at score 3.0 content |
| Score 1.0 | With help, partial success at score 2.0 content and score 3.0 content |
| Score 0.5 | With help, partial success at score 2.0 content, but not at score 3.0 content |
| Score 0.0 | Even with help, no success |

# Creating Patterns and Mental Models: Conducting Thought Experiments

| Score 4.0 | The student: |
|---|---|
| | • Applies the strategy in unusual situations, addresses aspects of thought experiments not covered in class, or both |
| | No major errors or omissions regarding the score 4.0 content |
| Score 3.5 | In addition to score 3.0 performance, partial success at score 4.0 content |
| Score 3.0 | The student: |
| | • When appropriate, engages in thought experiments that generate new awarenesses |
| | No major errors or omissions regarding the score 3.0 content |
| Score 2.5 | No major errors or omissions regarding score 2.0 content, and partial success at score 3.0 content |
| Score 2.0 | The student: |
| | • Can explain the basic principles behind thought experiments |
| | • Can describe situations in which thought experiments would be revealing or beneficial |
| | • Can recognize thought experiments that others have conducted |
| | No major errors or omissions regarding the score 2.0 content |
| Score 1.5 | Partial success at score 2.0 content, and major errors or omissions at score 3.0 content |
| Score 1.0 | With help, partial success at score 2.0 content and score 3.0 content |
| Score 0.5 | With help, partial success at score 2.0 content, but not at score 3.0 content |
| Score 0.0 | Even with help, no success |

# Creating Patterns and Mental Models: Performing Mental Rehearsal

| Score 4.0 | The student:<br>• Applies the strategy in unusual situations, addresses aspects of mental rehearsal not covered in class, or both<br>No major errors or omissions regarding the score 4.0 content |
|---|---|
| Score 3.5 | In addition to score 3.0 performance, partial success at score 4.0 content |
| Score 3.0 | The student:<br>• When appropriate, uses mental rehearsal to practice a specific skill<br>No major errors or omissions regarding the score 3.0 content |
| Score 2.5 | No major errors or omissions regarding score 2.0 content, and partial success at score 3.0 content |
| Score 2.0 | The student:<br>• Can explain the basic principles behind mental rehearsal<br>• Can describe situations in which mental rehearsal would be beneficial<br>• Can recognize examples of people who have benefited from mental rehearsal<br>No major errors or omissions regarding the score 2.0 content |
| Score 1.5 | Partial success at score 2.0 content, and major errors or omissions at score 3.0 content |
| Score 1.0 | With help, partial success at score 2.0 content and score 3.0 content |
| Score 0.5 | With help, partial success at score 2.0 content, but not at score 3.0 content |
| Score 0.0 | Even with help, no success |

# Understanding and Controlling Oneself: Becoming Aware of the Power of Interpretations

| Score 4.0 | The student: |
|-----------|--------------|
| | • Applies the strategy in unusual situations, addresses aspects of interpretations not covered in class, or both |
| | No major errors or omissions regarding the score 4.0 content |
| Score 3.5 | In addition to score 3.0 performance, partial success at score 4.0 content |
| Score 3.0 | The student: |
| | • When appropriate, manages his or her interpretations in a way that produces positive outcomes |
| | No major errors or omissions regarding the score 3.0 content |
| Score 2.5 | No major errors or omissions regarding score 2.0 content, and partial success at score 3.0 content |
| Score 2.0 | The student: |
| | • Can describe the basic characteristics of misperceptions |
| | • Can describe situations in which different interpretations might lead to misunderstanding or conflict |
| | • Can describe or recognize his or her own interpretations |
| | • Can explain a basic process for managing interpretations |
| | No major errors or omissions regarding the score 2.0 content |
| Score 1.5 | Partial success at score 2.0 content, and major errors or omissions at score 3.0 content |
| Score 1.0 | With help, partial success at score 2.0 content and score 3.0 content |
| Score 0.5 | With help, partial success at score 2.0 content, but not at score 3.0 content |
| Score 0.0 | Even with help, no success |

# Understanding and Controlling Oneself: Cultivating Useful Ways of Thinking

| | |
|---|---|
| **Score 4.0** | The student: <br> • Applies the strategy in unusual situations, addresses aspects of useful ways of thinking not covered in class, or both <br> No major errors or omissions regarding the score 4.0 content |
| **Score 3.5** | In addition to score 3.0 performance, partial success at score 4.0 content |
| **Score 3.0** | The student: <br> • Actively cultivates one or more of the useful ways of thinking <br> No major errors or omissions regarding the score 3.0 content |
| **Score 2.5** | No major errors or omissions regarding score 2.0 content, and partial success at score 3.0 content |
| **Score 2.0** | The student: <br> • Can describe the fixed versus growth mindset and how they each affect people's thinking <br> • Can describe the defining characteristics of resilience and how it affects people's thinking <br> • Can describe the defining characteristics of creating positive possible selves and how they affect people's thinking <br> • Can describe the defining characteristics of an optimistic explanatory style and how it affects people's thinking <br> No major errors or omissions regarding the score 2.0 content |
| **Score 1.5** | Partial success at score 2.0 content, and major errors or omissions at score 3.0 content |
| **Score 1.0** | With help, partial success at score 2.0 content and score 3.0 content |
| **Score 0.5** | With help, partial success at score 2.0 content, but not at score 3.0 content |
| **Score 0.0** | Even with help, no success |

# Understanding and Controlling Oneself: Avoiding Negative Ways of Thinking

| | |
|---|---|
| **Score 4.0** | The student:<br>• Applies the strategy in unusual situations, addresses aspects of emotional thinking or worry not covered in class, or both<br>No major errors or omissions regarding the score 4.0 content |
| **Score 3.5** | In addition to score 3.0 performance, partial success at score 4.0 content |
| **Score 3.0** | The student:<br>• When appropriate, recognizes and manages his or her emotional thoughts and worry<br>No major errors or omissions regarding the score 3.0 content |
| **Score 2.5** | No major errors or omissions regarding score 2.0 content, and partial success at score 3.0 content |
| **Score 2.0** | The student:<br>• Can recognize or recall examples of negative thinking<br>• Can describe the basic nature and pitfalls of emotional thinking<br>• Can describe the basic nature and pitfalls of worry<br>• Can describe some basic strategies for addressing emotional thinking and worry<br>No major errors or omissions regarding the score 2.0 content |
| **Score 1.5** | Partial success at score 2.0 content, and major errors or omissions at score 3.0 content |
| **Score 1.0** | With help, partial success at score 2.0 content and score 3.0 content |
| **Score 0.5** | With help, partial success at score 2.0 content, but not at score 3.0 content |
| **Score 0.0** | Even with help, no success |

# Understanding and Interacting With Others: Perspective Taking

| | |
|---|---|
| **Score 4.0** | The student:<br><br>• Applies the strategy in unusual situations, addresses aspects of perspective taking not covered in class, or both<br><br>No major errors or omissions regarding the score 4.0 content |
| **Score 3.5** | In addition to score 3.0 performance, partial success at score 4.0 content |
| **Score 3.0** | The student:<br><br>• When appropriate, examines his or her perspective on an issue and contrasts it with other perspectives<br><br>No major errors or omissions regarding the score 3.0 content |
| **Score 2.5** | No major errors or omissions regarding score 2.0 content, and partial success at score 3.0 content |
| **Score 2.0** | The student:<br><br>• Can describe the basic characteristics of perspective taking<br><br>• Can describe situations in which it would be beneficial to see one issue from different perspectives<br><br>• Can describe a basic process for analyzing perspectives<br><br>No major errors or omissions regarding the score 2.0 content |
| **Score 1.5** | Partial success at score 2.0 content, and major errors or omissions at score 3.0 content |
| **Score 1.0** | With help, partial success at score 2.0 content and score 3.0 content |
| **Score 0.5** | With help, partial success at score 2.0 content, but not at score 3.0 content |
| **Score 0.0** | Even with help, no success |

# Understanding and Interacting With Others: Responsible Interaction

| Score 4.0 | The student: |
|---|---|
| | • Applies the strategy in unusual situations, addresses aspects of responsible interaction not covered in class, or both |
| | No major errors or omissions regarding the score 4.0 content |
| Score 3.5 | In addition to score 3.0 performance, partial success at score 4.0 content |
| Score 3.0 | The student: |
| | • When appropriate, takes steps to ensure that he or she is interacting responsibly with others |
| | No major errors or omissions regarding the score 3.0 content |
| Score 2.5 | No major errors or omissions regarding score 2.0 content, and partial success at score 3.0 content |
| Score 2.0 | The student: |
| | • Can describe the basic characteristics of passive, aggressive, passive-aggressive, and assertive behavior and how they affect interactions |
| | • Can describe basic techniques for effective listening and speaking |
| | • Can describe situations in which responsible interaction is necessary |
| | No major errors or omissions regarding the score 2.0 content |
| Score 1.5 | Partial success at score 2.0 content, and major errors or omissions at score 3.0 content |
| Score 1.0 | With help, partial success at score 2.0 content and score 3.0 content |
| Score 0.5 | With help, partial success at score 2.0 content, but not at score 3.0 content |
| Score 0.0 | Even with help, no success |

# Understanding and Interacting With Others: Controversy and Conflict Resolution

| Score 4.0 | The student: |
|---|---|
| | • Applies the strategy in unusual situations, addresses aspects of controversy and conflict not covered in class, or both |
| | No major errors or omissions regarding the score 4.0 content |
| Score 3.5 | In addition to score 3.0 performance, partial success at score 4.0 content |
| Score 3.0 | The student: |
| | • When appropriate, applies strategies that lessen or diminish the negative effects of controversy and conflict |
| | No major errors or omissions regarding the score 3.0 content |
| Score 2.5 | No major errors or omissions regarding score 2.0 content, and partial success at score 3.0 content |
| Score 2.0 | The student: |
| | • Can describe the basic characteristics of controversy and conflict |
| | • Can recognize or recall examples of controversy and conflict |
| | • Can describe basic strategies for controversy and conflict |
| | No major errors or omissions regarding the score 2.0 content |
| Score 1.5 | Partial success at score 2.0 content, and major errors or omissions at score 3.0 content |
| Score 1.0 | With help, partial success at score 2.0 content and score 3.0 content |
| Score 0.5 | With help, partial success at score 2.0 content, but not at score 3.0 content |
| Score 0.0 | Even with help, no success |

# REFERENCES AND RESOURCES

21st Century Fluency Project. (2010, June 10). InfoWhelm and information fluency [Video file]. Accessed at www.youtube.com/watch?v=7ECAVxbfsfc on January 6, 2011.

Aaseng, N. (1990). *Close calls: From the brink of ruin to business success.* Minneapolis, MN: Lerner.

Abrami, P. C., Bernard, R. M., Borokhovski, E., Wade, A., Surkes, M. A., Tamim, R., et al. (2008). Instructional interventions affecting critical thinking skills and dispositions: A stage 1 meta-analysis. *Review of Educational Research, 78*(4), 1102–1134.

Abrams v. United States, 250 U.S. 616 (1919). Accessed at http://caselaw.lp.findlaw.com/scripts/getcase.pl?navby=case&court=us&vol=250&invol=616 on April 15, 2011.

Adversity Advantage. (n.d.). *About Paul Stoltz and Erik Weihenmayer.* Accessed at www.adversity advantage.com/weihenmayer.html on January 7, 2011.

Albanese, M. A., & Mitchell, S. (1993). Problem-based learning: A review of literature on its outcomes and implementation issues. *Academic Medicine, 68,* 52–81.

Albert, T. (Producer), & Ramis, H. (Director). (1993). *Groundhog day* [Motion picture]. United States: Columbia.

Amabile, T. M. (1983). *The social psychology of creativity.* New York: Springer-Verlag.

Anderson, D. K. (Producer), & Lasseter, J. (Director). (2006). *Cars* [Motion picture]. United States: Walt Disney.

Anderson, L., & Krathwohl, D. (Eds.). (2001). *A taxonomy for learning, teaching, and assessing: A revision of Bloom's taxonomy of educational objectives.* New York: Addison-Wesley Longman.

Andrews, V. (2000, June 26). Can you teach resilience? *MedicineNet.com.* Accessed at www.medicinenet.com/script/main/art.asp?articlekey=50812 on January 7, 2011.

Apatow, J. (Producer), & McKay, A. (Director). (2004). *Anchorman: The legend of Ron Burgundy* [Motion picture]. United States: DreamWorks.

Arnold, B. (Producer), Guggenheim, R. (Producer), & Lasseter, J. (Director). (1995). *Toy story* [Motion picture]. United States: Pixar.

Ashman, H. (Producer), Musker, J. (Producer), & Clements, R. (Director). (1989). *The little mermaid* [Motion picture]. United States: Walt Disney.

Atchley, P., & Dressel, J. (2004). Conversation limits the functional field of view. *Human Factors, 46,* 664–673.

AuWerter, S. (2006, June 16). Costly credit-card tricks. *SmartMoney.* Accessed at www.smartmoney .com/personal-finance/debt/costly-credit-card-tricks-19642 on January 12, 2011.

Barell, J. (2010). Problem-based learning: The foundation for 21st century skills. In J. Bellanca & R. Brandt (Eds.), *21st century skills: Rethinking how students learn* (pp. 175–199). Bloomington, IN: Solution Tree Press.

Baum, C. (Producer), Meyers, N. (Producer), Rosenman, H. (Producer), & Shyer, C. (Director). (1991). *Father of the bride* [Motion picture]. United States: Sandollar.

Benard, B. (2004). *Resiliency: What we have learned.* San Francisco: WestEd.

Berg, A. E. (2002). *The impossible just takes a little longer: Living with purpose and passion.* New York: HarperCollins.

Berlin, P. (2006, July 13). A contrite Zidane apologizes to the world. *The New York Times,* p. D1.

Bloom, B. S., Englehart, M. D., Furst, E. J., Hill, W. H., & Krathwohl, D. R. (Eds.). (1956). *Taxonomy of educational objectives: The classification of educational goals—Handbook 1, cognitive domain.* New York: David McKay.

Bodow, S. (Writer), & O'Neil, C. (Director). (2010a). Rick Perry pt. 2 [Television series episode]. In R. Albanese, J. Lieb, & J. Stewart (Executive producers), *The daily show with Jon Stewart.* New York: Comedy Central.

Bodow, S. (Writer), & O'Neil, C. (Director). (2010b). Rod Blagojevich [Television series episode]. In R. Albanese, J. Lieb, & J. Stewart (Executive producers), *The daily show with Jon Stewart.* New York: Comedy Central.

Bradley, P. (2006). *Fake websites—Social, political, religious, tourism and more.* Accessed at www.philb .com/fakesites2.htm on January 7, 2011.

Bradley, P. (2010). *Fake websites—Scientific and commercial.* Accessed at www.philb.com/fakesites.htm on January 7, 2011.

Brookhart, S. (2004). *Grading.* Upper Saddle River, NJ: Pearson Education.

Brookhart, S. (2010). *How to assess higher-order thinking skills in your classroom.* Alexandria, VA: Association for Supervision and Curriculum Development.

Brookhart, S., & Nitko, A. (2007). *Assessment and grading in classrooms.* Upper Saddle River, NJ: Pearson Education.

Brooks, J. L. (Producer), Mark, L. (Producer), Sakai, R. (Producer), & Crowe, C. (Director). (1996). *Jerry Maguire* [Motion picture]. United States: TriStar Pictures.

Brophy, J. E. (2004). *Motivating students to learn* (2nd ed.). Mahwah, NJ: Erlbaum.

Brown, J. R. (1991). *The laboratory of the mind: Thought experiments in the natural sciences.* New York: Routledge.

Camber, R., & Nathan, S. (2010, February 12). British fashion icon Alexander McQueen commits suicide days after death of his beloved mother. *Mail Online.* Accessed at www.dailymail.co.uk/news/article-1250249/Alexander-McQueen-commits-suicide.html on January 7, 2011.

Carroll, J. (2010, August 29). BP internal report said to find engineers misread Gulf well test results. *Bloomberg.* Accessed at www.bloomberg.com/news/2010–08–29/bp-internal-report-said-to-find-engineers-misread-gulf-well-test-results.html on January 7, 2011.

Centers for Disease Control and Prevention. (1982). Current trends smoking and cancer. *MMWR Weekly, 31*(7), 77–80. Accessed at www.cdc.gov/mmwr/preview/mmwrhtml/00000206.htm on January 14, 2011.

Chomsky, N. (1965). *Aspects of the theory of syntax.* Cambridge, MA: MIT Press.

Clark, H. H., & Clark, E. U. (1977). *Psychology and language.* San Diego, CA: Harcourt Brace Jovanovich.

Clay, R. A. (2009). Mini-multitaskers. *Monitor on Psychology, 40*(2), 38.

Clijsters wins after controversial ending. (2009, September 15). Accessed at http://sports.espn.go.com/sports/tennis/usopen09/news/story?id=4468762 on April 25, 2011.

Colvin, G. (1999). *Defusing anger and aggression: Safe strategies for secondary school educators.* Eugene, OR: IRIS Media.

Common Ground. (n.d.). *Active, authentic learning.* Accessed at www.nhep.com/curriculum.php on January 7, 2011.

Conflict Resolution Education. (n.d.). *Classroom activities on perspective taking.* Accessed at www.creducation.org/resources/perception_checking/classroom_activities_on_perspective_taking.html on January 7, 2011.

Considine, D. M. (2002). *Media literacy across the curriculum.* Washington, DC: Cable in the Classroom. Accessed at www.medialit.org/reading-room/media-literacy-across-curriculum/ on January 7, 2011.

Coyle, D. (2009). *The talent code.* New York: Bantam Books.

Csikszentmihalyi, M. (1988). Introduction. In M. Csikszentmihalyi & I. S. Csikszentmihalyi (Eds.), *Optimal experience: Psychological studies of flow in consciousness* (pp. 3–14). New York: Cambridge University Press.

Csikszentmihalyi, M. (1990). *Flow: The psychology of optimal experience.* New York: Harper & Row.

Cummings, J. S. (Speaker). (2007). *Chris Dede on emerging technologies and neomillennial learning styles* [Audio recording]. Boulder, CO: EDUCAUSE. Accessed at www.educause.edu/blog/jcummings/ChrisDedeonEmergingTechnologie/166539 on January 7, 2011.

Daily Beast. (2010, April 1). Stars who were bullied [Web log post]. Accessed at www.thedailybeast.com/blogs-and-stories/2010–04–01/stars-who-were-bullied on January 7, 2011.

Darling-Hammond, L. (2010). New policies for 21st century demands. In J. Bellanca & R. Brandt (Eds.), *21st century skills: Rethinking how students learn* (pp. 33–49). Bloomington, IN: Solution Tree Press.

de Bono, E. (1969). *The mechanism of mind*. London: Penguin.

de Bono, E. (1999). *Six thinking hats*. New York: Back Bay Books.

Dede, C. (2010). Comparing frameworks for 21st century skills. In J. Bellanca & R. Brandt (Eds.), *21st century skills: Rethinking how students learn* (pp. 51–75). Bloomington, IN: Solution Tree Press.

Diaz, J. (2009). Becoming a writer. *O, the Oprah Magazine*. Accessed at www.oprah.com/spirit/Junot-Diaz-Talks-About-What-Made-Him-Become-a-Writer on January 7, 2011.

Dingli, S. (2001). *Action research final report: Brief literature review*. Msida, Malta: Edward de Bono Programme for the Design and Development of Thinking. Accessed at www.um.edu.mt/__data/assets/pdf_file/0017/55052/LIT.pdf on January 7, 2011.

Disabled World. (2008a, April 6). *Famous people with club feet or foot*. Accessed at www.disabled-world.com/artman/publish/famous-clubfoot.shtml on January 7, 2011.

Disabled World. (2008b, January 17). *Famous people with epilepsy*. Accessed at www.disabled-world.com/artman/publish/epilepsy-famous.shtml on January 7, 2011.

Disney, W. (Producer), & Geronimi, C. (Director). (1959). *Sleeping beauty* [Motion picture]. United States: Walt Disney.

Disney, W. (Producer), Geronimi, C. (Director), Jackson, W. (Director), & Luske, H. (Director). (1950). *Cinderella* [Motion picture]. United States: Walt Disney.

Dochy, F., Segers, M., Van den Bossche, P., & Gijbels, D. (2003). Effects of problem-based learning: A meta-analysis. *Learning and Instruction, 13,* 533–568.

Documentary Educational Resources. (2011). Accessed at www.der.org on March 24, 2011.

Doherty, P. C., & Zinkernagel, R. M. (1996). *Autobiography*. Accessed at http://nobelprize.org/nobel_prizes/medicine/laureates/1996/doherty-autobio.html on January 7, 2011.

Doidge, N. (2007). *The brain that changes itself: Stories of personal triumph from the frontiers of brain science*. New York: Penguin Books.

Doran, L. (Producer), & Forster, M. (Director). (2006). *Stranger than fiction* [Motion picture]. United States: Columbia.

Dougy Center. (1999). *35 ways to help a grieving child*. Portland, OR: Author.

Dougy Center. (2003). *Helping the grieving student: A guide for teachers*. Portland, OR: Author.

Duchesne, S., Larose, S., Guay, F., Tremblay, R. E., & Vitaro, F. (2005). The transition from elementary to high school: The pivotal role of family and child characteristics in explaining trajectories of academic functioning. *International Journal of Behavioral Development, 29,* 409–417.

Duchesne, S., Vitaro, F., Larose, S., & Tremblay, R. E. (2008). Trajectories of anxiety during elementary-school years and the prediction of high school noncompletion. *Journal of Youth and Adolescence, 37,* 1134–1146.

Dux, P. E., Ivanoff, J., Asplund, C. L., & Marois, R. (2006). Isolation of a central bottleneck of information processing with time-resolved fMRI. *Neuron, 52,* 1109–1120.

Dweck, C. S. (2000). *Self-theories: Their role in motivation, personality, and development.* New York: Psychology Press.

Dweck, C. S., & Molden, D. C. (2005). Self-theories: Their impact on competence motivation and acquisition. In A. J. Elliot & C. S. Dweck (Eds.), *Handbook of competence and motivation* (pp. 122–140). New York: Guilford Press.

Eby, D. (n.d.). *Creativity and flow psychology.* Accessed at http://talentdevelop.com/articles/Page8 .html on January 7, 2011.

Edwards, J. (1988). *The direct teaching of thinking skills, CoRT 1: An evaluative case study.* Unpublished doctoral dissertation, James Cook University, North Queensland, Australia.

Edwards, J., & Baldauf, R. B., Jr. (1983). Teaching thinking in secondary science. In W. Maxwell (Ed.), *Thinking: The expanding frontier* (pp. 129–138). Philadelphia: Franklin Institute Press.

Edwards, J., & Clayton, J. (1989, August). *Observing a thinking skills classroom.* Paper presented at the Fourth International Conference on Thinking, San Juan, Puerto Rico.

Ekman, P. (1994). Moods, emotions, and traits. In P. Ekman & R. J. Davidson (Eds.), *The nature of emotion: Fundamental questions* (pp. 56–58). New York: Oxford University Press.

Erickson, L. (2010). Conceptual designs for curriculum and higher-order instruction. In R. Marzano (Ed.), *On excellence in teaching* (pp. 169–192). Bloomington, IN: Solution Tree Press.

Erickson, T. (2008). *Plugged in: The generation Y guide to thriving at work.* Boston: Harvard Business School Press.

Erwin, J. C. (2004). *The classroom of choice: Giving students what they need and getting what you want.* Alexandria, VA: Association for Supervision and Curriculum Development.

Essley, R. (2008). *Visual tools for differentiating reading and writing instruction: Strategies to help students make abstract ideas concrete and accessible.* New York: Scholastic.

Facts about forks. (n.d.). Accessed at www.interestingfacts.org/fact/facts-about-forks on January 7, 2011.

Farah, M. J. (1989). The neural basis of mental imagery. *Trends in Neurosciences, 12,* 395–399.

Finke, R. A. (1980). Levels of equivalence of mental images and perception. *Psychological Review, 87,* 113–132.

Finke, R. A. (1985). Theories relating mental imagery to perception. *Psychological Bulletin, 98,* 236–259.

Finke, R. A., & Shephard, R. N. (1986). Visual functions of mental imagery. In K. R. Boff, L. Kaufman, & J. P. Thomas (Eds.), *Handbook of perception and human performance* (pp. 37–55). New York: Wiley.

Fleming, A. (1992). *What, me worry? How to hang in when your problems stress you out.* New York: Atheneum.

Foerde, K., Knowlton, B. J., & Poldrack, R. A. (2006). Modulation of competing memory systems by distraction. *Proceedings of the National Academy of Sciences, 103*(31), 11778–11783. Accessed at www.poldracklab.org/Publications/pdfs/Proc%20Natl%20Acad%20Sci%20USA%202006%20 Foerde-1.pdf on January 7, 2011.

Frey, N., Fisher, D., & Gonzalez, A. (2010). *Literacy 2.0: Reading and writing in 21st century classrooms.* Bloomington, IN: Solution Tree Press.

Gallese, V., Fadiga, L., Fogassi, L., & Rizzolatti, G. (1996). Action recognition in the premotor cortex. *Brain, 119,* 593–609.

Gardner, H. (2010). Five minds for the future. In J. Bellanca & R. Brandt (Eds.), *21st century skills: Rethinking how students learn* (pp. 9–31). Bloomington, IN: Solution Tree Press.

Garmezy, N. (1974). Children at risk: The search for the antecedents of schizophrenia—Part II, ongoing research programs, issues, and intervention. *Schizophrenia Bulletin, 1*(9), 55–125.

Georgia College Counseling Services. (n.d.). *Test anxiety quiz.* Accessed at www.gcsu.edu/counseling /docs/Test_Anxiety_Quiz.doc on January 6, 2011.

Gilmore, D. K. L. (2009). *Cora cooks pancit.* Walnut Creek, CA: Shen's Books.

Gladwell, M. (2008). The uses of adversity: Can unprivileged outsiders have an advantage? *The New Yorker, 84*(36), 36.

The global seed vault. (n.d.). Accessed at www.interestingfacts.org/fact/the-global-seed-vault on January 7, 2011.

Goleman, D. (1995). *Emotional intelligence: Why it can matter more than IQ.* New York: Bantam Books.

Google. (2011). Google history. Accessed at www.google.com/intl/en/corporate/history.html#2000 on January 7, 2011.

Graham, S., & Perin, D. (2007). *Writing next: Effective strategies to improve writing of adolescents in middle and high schools—A report to Carnegie Corporation of New York.* Washington, DC: Alliance for Excellent Education. Accessed at www.all4ed.org/publications/WritingNext/WritingNext.pdf on January 7, 2011.

Grimm, J., & Grimm, W. (1903). Cinderella. In E. H. L. Turpin (Ed.), *Grimm's fairy tales* (pp. 156–167). New York: Maynard, Merrill, & Company.

Grouios, G. (1992). Mental practice: A review. *Journal of Sport Behavior, 15*(1), 42. Accessed at http:// psycnet.apa.org/psycinfo/1992-26532-001 on January 7, 2011.

Gustafson, D. K. (2007). Children's worries and anxiety, experience of life stress, and coping responses in the context of social-economic adversity. *Dissertation Abstracts International, 68*(02), 1305A. (UMI No. 3252519) Accessed at http://proquest.umi.com/pqdlink?did=1276405821&Fmt=14 &VType=PQD&VInst=PROD&RQT=309&VName=PQD&TS=1285103130&clientId=79356 on January 7, 2011.

Haberman, C. (2005, September 27). Feet and minds need a chance to wander. *The New York Times,* p. B1. Accessed at http://query.nytimes.com/gst/fullpage.html?res=9A05E0D61530F934A157 5AC0A9639C8B63 on April 25, 2011.

Hagstrom, R. G. (1999). *The Warren Buffett portfolio: Mastering the power of the focus investment strategy*. New York: Wiley.

Hallowell, E. M. (2005). Overloaded circuits: Why smart people underperform. *Harvard Business Review, 83*(1), 54–62.

Halpern, D. F. (1984). *Thought and knowledge: An introduction to critical thinking*. Hillsdale, NJ: Erlbaum.

Halpern, D. F. (1998). Teaching critical thinking for transfer across domains: Dispositions, skills, structure training, and metacognitive monitoring. *American Psychologist, 53*(4), 449–455.

Hargreaves, A. (2010). Leadership, change, and beyond the 21st century skills agenda. In J. Bellanca & R. Brandt (Eds.), *21st century skills: Rethinking how students learn* (pp. 327–348). Bloomington, IN: Solution Tree Press.

Harter, S. (1999). *The construction of the self*. New York: Guilford Press.

Harwood, C., Cumming, J., & Hall, C. (2003). Imagery use in elite youth sport participants: Reinforcing the applied significance of achievement goal theory. *Research Quarterly for Exercise and Sport, 74*(3), 292–300.

Hattie, J. (2009). *Visible learning: A synthesis of over 800 meta-analyses relating to achievement*. New York: Routledge.

Hattie, J., & Timperley, H. (2007). The power of feedback. *Review of Educational Research, 77*, 81–112.

Haystead, M. W., & Marzano, R. J. (2009). *Meta-analytic synthesis of studies conducted at Marzano Research Laboratory on instructional strategies*. Englewood, CO: Marzano Research Laboratory. Accessed at www.marzanoresearch.com/documents/Instructional_Strategies_Report_9_2_09.pdf on January 7, 2011.

Head Jammer. (2010, May 17). Top ten funny things kids say [Web log post]. Accessed at http://thedadjam.com/toddler/top-ten-funny-things-kids-say/ on January 7, 2011.

Hembree, R. (1988). Correlates, causes, effects, and treatment of test anxiety. *Review of Educational Research, 58*(1), 47–77.

Hiltz, S. R. (2000). *Computers and society: Lecture 1—History and theoretical perspectives* [Lecture notes]. Accessed at http://cpe.njit.edu/dlnotes/login/CIS/CIS350/notes/Lecture1.pdf on January 7, 2011.

Ho, T. (2009, August 13). From paralysis to inspiration rise: Morris Goodman overcame a plane crash to chart an even more fulfilling life. *Investor's Business Daily*, p. A3.

Horn Book. (2011). *Asian and Pacific American books*. Accessed at www.hbook.com/resources /books/asianpacific.asp on March 24, 2011.

Horton, P. B., McConney, A. A., Gallo, M., Woods, A. L., Senn, G. J., & Hamelin, D. (1993). An investigation of the effectiveness of concept mapping as an instructional tool. *Science Education, 77*(1), 95–111.

Hutson, M. (2009). Going through the motions. *Psychology Today, 42*(1), 49.

Hyerle, D. (1991). Expand your thinking. In A. L. Costa (Ed.), *Developing minds: Programs for teaching thinking* (pp. 16–26). Alexandria, VA: Association for Supervision and Curriculum Development. Accessed at www.thinkingfoundation.org/research/journal_articles/pdf/developing-minds-hyerle .pdf on January 7, 2011.

Hyerle, D. (2009). *Visual tools for transforming information into knowledge* (2nd ed.). Thousand Oaks, CA: Corwin Press.

Ialongo, N., Edelson, G., Werthamer-Larsson, L., Crockett, L., & Kellam, S. (1995). The significance of self-reported anxious symptoms in first-grade children: Prediction to anxious symptoms and adaptive functioning in fifth grade. *Journal of Child Psychology and Psychiatry and Allied Disciplines, 36,* 427–437.

Jacobs, J. (1890). *English fairy tales.* London: David Nutt.

Jacobson, T. (Producer), & Hughes, J. (Director). (1986). *Ferris Bueller's day off* [Motion picture]. United States: Paramount.

Jean, A. (Writer), Reiss, M. (Writer), & Moore, R. (Director). (1991). Stark raving dad [Television series episode]. In J. L. Brooks, M. Groening, A. Jean, I. Maxtone-Graham, & M. Selman (Executive producers), *The Simpsons.* Los Angeles, CA: Fox Broadcasting.

Jeannerod, M. (1994). The representing brain: Neural correlates of motor intention and imagery. *Behavioral and Brain Sciences, 17,* 187–202.

Jeannerod, M. (1995). Mental imagery in the motor context. *Neuropsychologia, 33,* 1419–1432.

Jobs for the Future. (2005). *Education and skills for the 21st century: An agenda for action.* Boston: Author. Accessed at www.jff.org/sites/default/files/ActionAgenda.pdf on January 7, 2011.

Johnson, D. W., & Johnson, R. T. (1979). Conflict in the classroom: Controversy and learning. *Review of Educational Research, 49*(1), 51–69.

Johnson, D. W., & Johnson, R. T. (1989). *Cooperation and competition: Theory and research.* Edina, MN: Interaction Book Company.

Johnson, D. W., & Johnson, R. T. (2005). *Teaching students to be peacemakers* (4th ed.). Edina, MN: Interaction Book Company.

Johnson, D. W., & Johnson, R. T. (2007). *Creative controversy: Intellectual challenge in the classroom* (4th ed.). Edina, MN: Interaction Book Company.

Johnson, D. W., & Johnson, R. T. (2009). Energizing learning: The instructional power of conflict. *Educational Researcher, 38*(1), 37–51.

Johnson, D. W., & Johnson, R. T. (2010). Cooperative learning and conflict resolution: Essential 21st century skills. In J. Bellanca & R. Brandt (Eds.), *21st century skills: Rethinking how students learn* (pp. 201–219). Bloomington, IN: Solution Tree Press.

Johnson, D. W., Johnson, R. T., & Stanne, M. B. (2000). *Cooperative learning methods: A meta-analysis.* Minneapolis: University of Minnesota. Accessed at www.tablelearning.com/uploads/File/EXHIBIT -B.pdf on January 7, 2011.

Johnson-Laird, P. N. (1983). *Mental models.* Cambridge, MA: Harvard University Press.

Johnson-Laird, P. N., & Byrne, R. M. J. (1991). *Deduction*. Hillsdale, NJ: Erlbaum.

Just, M. A., Keller, T. A., & Cynkar, J. A. (2008). A decrease in brain activation associated with driving when listening to someone speak. *Brain Research, 1205,* 70–80. Accessed at www.distraction.gov /research/PDF-Files/carnegie-mellon.pdf on January 7, 2011.

Kagan, S., & Kagan, M. (2009). *Kagan cooperative learning*. San Clemente, CA: Kagan.

Kamp, D. (2010, June 30). Nurturing New York's oysters. *The New York Times*, p. D1.

Kang, O. R. (2002). *A meta-analysis of graphic organizer interventions for students with learning disabilities*. Unpublished doctoral dissertation, University of Oregon.

Kay, K. (2010). 21st century skills: Why they matter, what they are, and how we get there. In J. Bellanca & R. Brandt (Eds.), *21st century skills: Rethinking how students learn* (pp. xiii–xxxi). Bloomington, IN: Solution Tree Press.

Kersey, C. (1998). *Unstoppable: 45 powerful stories of perseverance and triumph from people just like you*. Naperville, IL: Sourcebooks.

Kevin's story. (2011). Accessed at www.kevinsaunders.com/about.php#story on January 7, 2011.

Kim, A. H., Vaughn, S., Wanzek, J., & Wei, S. (2004). Graphic organizers and their effects on the reading comprehension of students with LD: A synthesis of research. *Journal of Learning Disabilities, 37*(2), 105–118.

Kintsch, W. (1974). *The representation of meaning in memory*. Hillsdale, NJ: Erlbaum.

Klauer, S. G., Dingus, T. A., Neale, V. L., Sudweeks, J. D., & Ramsey, D. J. (2006). *The impact of driver inattention on near-crash/crash risk: An analysis using the 100-car naturalistic driving study data* [Tech. Rep. No. DOT HS 810 594]. Springfield, VA: National Technical Information Service. Accessed at www.nsc.org/safety_road/Distracted_Driving/Documents/The%20Impact%20of %20Driver%20Inattention%20on%20Near-Crash.pdf on March 30, 2011.

Knapp, K. (2010, July 6). Triathlete's clear sense of purpose—though blind, his competitive edge is sharp. *The Times*. Accessed at www.nj.com/mercer/index.ssf/2010/07/triathletes_clear_sense _of_pur.html on January 7, 2011.

Kubota, S., Mishima, N., & Nagata, S. (2004). A study of the effects of active listening on listening attitudes of middle managers. *Journal of Occupational Health, 46,* 60–67.

Kuiper, E., Volman, M., & Terwel, J. (2005). The web as an information resource in K–12 education: Strategies for supporting students in searching and processing information. *Review of Educational Research, 75*(3), 285–328.

Kushner, D. (Producer), & Lisberger, S. (Director). (1982). *Tron* [Motion picture]. United States: Walt Disney.

Landmark School Outreach Program. (n.d.). *Test preparation*. Accessed at www.landmarkoutreach .org/documents/TestPrep_Strategies.pdf on January 7, 2011.

Larson, C. E., & LaFasto, F. M. (1989). *Teamwork: What must go right/what can go wrong*. Newbury Park, CA: SAGE.

Lavery, L. (2008). *Self-regulated learning for academic success: An evaluation of instructional techniques.* Unpublished doctoral dissertation, University of Auckland, New Zealand.

Lemke, C. (2010). Innovation through technology. In J. Bellanca & R. Brandt (Eds.), *21st century skills: Rethinking how students learn* (pp. 243–272). Bloomington, IN: Solution Tree Press.

Lemke, M., Sen, A., Pahlke, E., Partelow, L., Miller, D., Williams, T., et al. (2004). *International outcomes of learning in mathematics literacy and problem solving: PISA 2003 results from the U.S. perspective.* Washington, DC: Department of Education, National Center for Education Statistics. Accessed at http://nces.ed.gov/pubs2005/2005003.pdf on June 16, 2011.

Leu, D. J., Jr. (2002). Internet workshop: Making time for literacy. *The Reading Teacher, 55,* 466–472.

Levinson Medical Center for Learning Disabilities. (2010). *Dyslexic? You're not alone . . . .* Accessed at www.dyslexiaonline.com/famous/famous.htm on January 7, 2011.

Li, Y. (2005). *A thousand years of good prayers: Stories.* New York: Random House.

Locke, E. A., & Latham, G. P. (1990). *A theory of goal setting and task performance.* Englewood Cliffs, NJ: Prentice Hall.

Lord, C. G., & Taylor, C. A. (2009). Biased assimilation: Effects of assumptions and expectations on the interpretation of new evidence. *Social and Personality Psychology Compass, 3*(5), 827–841.

Loukopoulos, L. D., Dismukes, R. K., & Barshi, I. (2009). *The multitasking myth.* Burlington, VA: Ashgate.

Markus, H., & Nurius, P. (1986). Possible selves. *American Psychologist, 41*(9), 954–969.

Marzano, R. J. (1992). *A different kind of classroom: Teaching with dimensions of learning.* Alexandria, VA: Association for Supervision and Curriculum Development.

Marzano, R. J. (2003). *Classroom management that works: Research-based strategies for every teacher.* Alexandria, VA: Association for Supervision and Curriculum Development.

Marzano, R. J. (2007). *The art and science of teaching: A comprehensive framework for effective instruction.* Alexandria, VA: Association for Supervision and Curriculum Development.

Marzano, R. J. (2009). *Designing and teaching learning goals and objectives.* Bloomington, IN: Marzano Research Laboratory.

Marzano, R. J. (2010). *Formative assessment and standards-based grading.* Bloomington, IN: Marzano Research Laboratory.

Marzano, R. J., & Brown, J. L. (2009). *A handbook for the art and science of teaching.* Alexandria, VA: Association for Supervision and Curriculum Development.

Marzano, R. J., Gaddy, B. B., Foseid, M. C., Foseid, M. P., & Marzano, J. S. (2005). *A handbook for classroom management that works.* Alexandria, VA: Association for Supervision and Curriculum Development.

Marzano, R. J., Hagerty, P., Valencia, S., & DiStefano, P. (1987). *Reading diagnosis and instruction: Theory into practice.* Englewood Cliffs, NJ: Prentice Hall.

Marzano, R. J., & Haystead, M. W. (2008). *Making standards useful in the classroom.* Alexandria, VA: Association for Supervision and Curriculum Development.

Marzano, R. J., & Kendall, J. S. (2007). *The new taxonomy of educational objectives* (2nd ed.). Thousand Oaks, CA: Corwin Press.

Marzano, R. J., & Kendall, J. S. (2008). *Designing and assessing educational objectives: Applying the new taxonomy.* Thousand Oaks, CA: Corwin Press.

Marzano, R. J., & Marzano, J. S. (2010). The inner game of teaching. In R. Marzano (Ed.), *On excellence in teaching* (pp. 345–367). Bloomington, IN: Solution Tree Press.

Marzano, R. J., & Pickering, D. J. (with Heflebower, T.). (2011). *The highly engaged classroom.* Bloomington, IN: Marzano Research Laboratory.

Marzano, R. J., Pickering, D. J., & Pollock, J. E. (2001). *Classroom instruction that works: Research-based strategies for increasing student achievement.* Alexandria, VA: Association for Supervision and Curriculum Development.

Marzano, R. J., & Waters, T. (2009). *District leadership that works: Striking the right balance.* Bloomington, IN: Solution Tree Press.

Marzano, R. J., Zaffron, S., Zraik, L., Robbins, S. L., & Yoon, L. (1995). A new paradigm for educational change. *Education, 116*(2), 162–173.

Marzano Research Laboratory. (n.d.). *Appendix B: What is an effect size?* Accessed at www.marzanoresearch.com/documents/AppendixB_DTLGO.pdf on January 7, 2011.

Mathews, A. (1990). Why worry? The cognitive structure of anxiety. *Behavior Research and Therapy, 28,* 455–468.

Mayer, R. E. (1997). Multimedia learning: Are we asking the right questions? *Educational Psychologist, 32,* 1–19.

Mayer, R., & Anderson, R. B. (1991). Animations need narrations: An experimental test of a dual-coding hypothesis. *Journal of Educational Psychology, 83*(4), 484–490.

Mayerowitz, S. (2010, August 10). Steven Slater, JetBlue flight attendant out on bail. Accessed at http://abcnews.go.com/US/steven-slater-jetblue-flight-attendant-bail-emergency-slide/story?id=11367793 on April 25, 2011.

McCain, T., & Jukes, I. (2001). *Windows on the future: Education in the age of technology.* Thousand Oaks, CA: Corwin Press.

McCaul, K. D., & Mullens, A. B. (2003). Affect, thought, and self-protective health behavior: The case of worry and cancer screening. In J. Suls & K. A. Wallston (Eds.), *Social psychological foundations of health and illness* (pp. 137–168). Malden, MA: Blackwell.

McCoog, I. J. (2008). *21st century teaching and learning.* Accessed at www.eric.ed.gov/PDFS/ED502607.pdf on January 7, 2011. (ERIC Document Reproduction Service No. ED502607)

Moore, A. S. (2010, July 25). Failure to communicate. *The New York Times,* p. ED20. Accessed at www.nytimes.com/2010/07/25/education/edlife/25roommate-t.html?ref=edlife on January 7, 2011.

Moore, D. W., & Readence, J. E. (1984). A quantitative and qualitative review of graphic organizer research. *Journal of Educational Research, 78*(1), 11–17.

Morris, T., Spittle, M., & Watt, A. P. (2005). *Imagery in sport.* Champaign, IL: Human Kinetics.

Mortenson, G., & Relin, D. O. (2006). *Three cups of tea: One man's mission to fight terrorism and build nations . . . one school at a time.* New York: Penguin.

Morton Grove Public Library's Webrary. (2007). *Asian Americans: Chinese Americans.* Accessed at www.webrary.org/kids/jbibasianamericans.html on March 24, 2011.

Müller-Lyer, F. C. (1889). Optische Urteilstäuschungen. *Dubois–Reymonds Archive für Anatomie und Physiologie, Supplement Volume,* 263–270.

Myers, W. D. (2008). *Sunrise over Fallujah.* New York: Scholastic Press.

Nadler, R. (2009). What was I thinking? Handling the hijack. *Business Management, 16.* Accessed at www.busmanagement.com/article/What-Was-I-Thinking-Handling-the-Hijack on January 7, 2011.

Nafisi, A. (2003). *Reading Lolita in Tehran: A memoir in books.* New York: Random House.

National Geographic. (2011). *Ladybug.* Accessed at http://animals.nationalgeographic.com/animals /bugs/ladybug/ on January 18, 2011.

National Leadership Council for Liberal Education and America's Promise. (2007). *College learning for the new global century.* Washington, DC: Association of American Colleges and Universities. Accessed at www.aacu.org/leap/documents/GlobalCentury_final.pdf on January 7, 2011.

Nemours Foundation/KidsHealth, Department of Health Education and Recreation, & National Association of Health Education Centers. (2005). *KidsHealth KidsPoll—Coping poll: Summary of findings.* Jacksonville, FL: KidsHealth. Accessed at www.nahec.org/KidsPoll/stress/Stress _Summary_of_Findings.pdf on January 7, 2011.

Nemours Foundation/KidsHealth, Department of Health Education and Recreation, & National Association of Health Education Centers. (2007). *KidsHealth KidsPoll—What do kids worry about? (2007) Summary of findings.* Jacksonville, FL: KidsHealth. Accessed at http://kidshealth.org /media/kidspoll/related/worry_summary_of_findings_(07)_CE.pdf on January 7, 2011.

Nesbit, J. C., & Adesope, O. O. (2006). Learning with concept and knowledge maps: A meta-analysis. *Review of Educational Research, 76*(3), 413–448.

Nickerson, R. S. (1999). Enhancing creativity. In R. J. Sternberg (Ed.), *Handbook of creativity* (pp. 392–430). Cambridge, England: Cambridge University Press.

North Central Regional Educational Laboratory, & Metiri Group. (2003). *enGauge 21st century skills: Literacy in the digital age.* Chicago: North Central Regional Educational Laboratory. Accessed at www.metiri.com/features.html on January 7, 2011.

November, A. (2010a). *Empowering students with technology* (2nd ed.). Thousand Oaks, CA: Corwin Press.

November, A. (2010b). Technology rich, information poor. In J. Bellanca & R. Brandt (Eds.), *21st century skills: Rethinking how students learn* (pp. 275–283). Bloomington, IN: Solution Tree Press.

Novotney, A. (2009, August 8). When it comes to well-being, you've got to be carefully taught [Web log post]. Accessed at http://apaconvention.typepad.com/apaconvention/2009/08/kids-need -a-lesson-in-wellbeing.html on January 7, 2011.

Ophir, E., Nass, C., & Wagner, A. D. (2009). Cognitive control in media multitaskers. *Proceedings of the National Academy of Sciences, 106,* 15583–15587. Accessed at www.pnas.org/content /106/37/15583.full.pdf+html on January 7, 2011.

Organisation for Economic Co-operation and Development. (2005). *The definition and selection of key competencies: Executive summary.* Paris: Author. Accessed at www.oecd.org/dataoecd/47/61 /35070367.pdf on January 7, 2011.

Orlick, T. (2008). *In pursuit of excellence: How to win in sport and life through mental training* (4th ed.). Champaign, IL: Human Kinetics.

O'Shaughnessy, J. (2009). *Interpretation in social life, social science, and marketing.* New York: Routledge.

Oyserman, D., Terry, K., & Bybee, D. (2002). A possible selves intervention to enhance school involvement. *Journal of Adolescence, 25,* 313–326.

Pajares, F. (1996). Self-efficacy beliefs in academic settings. *Review of Educational Research, 66,* 543–578.

Parnes, S. J. (1961). Effects of extended effort in creative problem solving. *Journal of Educational Psychology, 52,* 117–122.

Parnes, S. J., & Meadow, A. (1959). Effects of brainstorming instruction on creative problem solving by trained and untrained subjects. *Journal of Educational Psychology, 50,* 171–176.

Partnership for 21st Century Skills. (2003). *Learning for the 21st century: A report and mile guide for 21st century skills.* Washington, DC: Author. Accessed at http://web.archive.org /web/20031002142253/www.21stcenturyskills.org/downloads/P21_Report.pdf on January 7, 2011.

Partnership for 21st Century Skills. (2009). *P21 framework definitions.* Washington, DC: Author. Accessed at www.p21.org/documents/P21_Framework_Definitions.pdf on January 7, 2011.

Pekrun, R. (2009). *Student emotions.* Accessed at www.education.com/reference/article/student -emotions/ on January 7, 2011.

Perkins, D. (1981). *The mind's best work.* Cambridge, MA: Harvard University Press.

Perkins, D. (1995). *Outsmarting the IQ.* New York: Free Press.

Perkins, D. N. (1984). Creativity by design. *Educational Leadership, 42,* 18–25.

Perkins, D. N. (1985). *Where is creativity?* Paper presented at the University of Iowa Second Annual Humanities Symposium, Iowa City, Iowa.

Perkins, D. N. (1989). Selecting fertile themes for integrated learning. In H. H. Jacobs (Ed.), *Interdisciplinary curriculum: Design and implementation* (pp. 67–76). Alexandria, VA: Association for Supervision and Curriculum Development.

Peter D. Hart Research Associates/Public Opinion Strategies. (2005). *Rising to the challenge: Are high school graduates prepared for college and work? A study of recent high school graduates, college instructors, and employers.* Washington, DC: Author. Accessed at www.achieve.org/files/pollreport_0.pdf on January 7, 2011.

Phan, T. (2003). Life in school: Narratives of resiliency among Vietnamese-Canadian youths. *Adolescence, 38*(151), 555–566.

Pickering, D. (2010). Teaching the thinking skills that higher-order tasks demand. In R. Marzano (Ed.), *On excellence in teaching* (pp. 145–166). Bloomington, IN: Solution Tree Press.

Pintrich, P. R., & De Groot, E. (1990). Motivational and self-regulated learning components of classroom academic performance. *Journal of Educational Psychology, 82*(1), 33–50.

Polson, P. G., & Jeffries, R. (1985). Instruction in general problem-solving skills: An analysis of four approaches. In J. W. Segal, S. F. Chipman, & R. Glaser (Eds.), *Thinking and learning skills: Relating instruction to research* (pp. 417–456). Hillsdale, NJ: Erlbaum.

Portis, A. (2007). *Not a box.* New York: HarperCollins.

Prensky, M. (2001). Digital natives, digital immigrants. *On the Horizon, 9*(5), 1–6. Accessed at www.marcprensky.com/writing/Prensky%20-%20Digital%20Natives,%20Digital%20Immigrants%20-%20Part1.pdf on January 7, 2011.

Puccio, G. J., Mance, M., & Murdock, M. C. (2011). *Creative leadership: Skills that drive change* (2nd ed.). Thousand Oaks, CA: SAGE.

Quote Garden. (2010). *Quotations about worrying.* Accessed at www.quotegarden.com/worry.html on January 7, 2011.

Ramachandran, V. S. (2006). *Mirror neurons and the brain in the vat.* Accessed at www.edge.org/3rd_culture/ramachandran06/ramachandran06_index.html on January 12, 2011.

Rideout, V. J., Foehr, U. G., & Roberts, D. F. (2010). *Generation M2: Media in the lives of 8- to 18-year olds.* Menlo Park, CA: Kaiser Family Foundation. Accessed at www.kff.org/entmedia/upload/8010.pdf on January 7, 2011.

Rizzolatti, G., & Craighero, L. (2004). The mirror-neuron system. *Annual Review of Neuroscience, 27,* 169–192. Accessed at www.kuleuven.be/mirrorneuronsystem/readinglist/Rizzolatti%20&%20Craighero%202004%20-%20The%20MNS%20-%20ARN.pdf on January 12, 2011.

Rizzolatti, G., Fadiga, L., Gallese, V., & Fogassi, L. (1996). Premotor cortex and the recognition of motor action. *Cognitive Brain Research, 3,* 131–141.

Rockefeller, K. (2007). *Visualize confidence: How to use guided imagery to overcome self-doubt.* Oakland, CA: New Harbinger.

Rogers, C. R., & Farson, R. E. (1957/2007). Active listening. In J. S. Osland, M. E. Turner, D. A. Kolb, & I. M. Rubin (Eds.), *The organizational behavior reader* (8th ed., pp. 279–290). Upper Saddle River, NJ: Pearson.

Rosenthal, A. K., & Lichtenheld, T. (2009). *Duck! Rabbit!* San Francisco: Chronicle Books.

Rowe, H. (1985). *Problem solving and intelligence.* Hillsdale, NJ: Erlbaum.

Rubin, L. (1996). *The transcendent child: Tales of triumph over the past.* New York: Basic Books.

Rubinstein, J. S., Meyer, D. E., & Evans, J. E. (2001). Executive control of cognitive processes in task switching. *Journal of Experimental Psychology: Human Perception and Performance, 27*(4), 763–797.

Rural Learning Center. (n.d.). *MCCR: How it all began.* Accessed at www.rurallearningcenter.org /MCCR-HowItAllBegan.html on January 7, 2011.

Russell, B., & Branch, T. (1979). *Second wind.* New York: Ballantine.

Sadoski, M., & Paivio, A. (2001). *Imagery and text: A dual coding theory of reading and writing.* Mahwah, NJ: Erlbaum.

Sanchez-Burks, J., Bartel, C., & Blount, S. (2009). Performance in intercultural interactions at work: Cross-cultural differences in response to behavioral mirroring. *Journal of Applied Psychology, 94,* 216–223.

Schloat, A. W. (1999). *Expressing anger: Healthy vs. unhealthy.* Mt. Kisco, NY: Human Relations Media.

Schumacher, E. H., Seymour, T. L., Glass, J. M., Fencsik, D. E., Lauber, E. J., Kieras, D. E., et al. (2001). Virtually perfect time sharing in dual-task performance: Uncorking the central cognitive bottleneck. *Psychological Science, 12*(2), 101–108.

Schunk, D. H. (1984). Self-efficacy perspective on achievement behavior. *Educational Psychologist, 19,* 48–58.

Schunk, D. H., & Pajares, F. (2005). Competence perceptions and academic functioning. In A. J. Elliot & C. S. Dweck (Eds.), *Handbook of competence and motivation* (pp. 85–104). New York: Guilford Press.

Scieszka, J. (1996). *The true story of the three little pigs.* New York: Puffin.

Scott, G., Leritz, L. E., & Mumford, M. D. (2004). The effectiveness of creativity training: A quantitative review. *Creativity Research Journal, 16*(4), 361–388.

Seattle Public Library. (2010). *Asian-American.* Accessed at www.spl.org/default.asp?pageID=audience _teens_bmm_readinglist&cid=1182355348339 on March 24, 2011.

Seckel, A. (2004). *Masters of deception: Escher, Dali and the artists of optical illusion.* New York: Sterling.

Seckel, A. (2006). *The ultimate book of optical illusions.* New York: Sterling.

Seibert, A. (2005). *The resiliency advantage: Master change, thrive under pressure, and bounce back from setbacks.* San Francisco: Berrett-Koehler.

Seipp, B. (1991). Anxiety and academic performance: A meta-analysis of findings. *Anxiety Research, 4,* 27–41.

Seligman, M. E. P. (2006). *Learned optimism: How to change your mind and your life.* New York: Vintage Books.

Shannon, G. (2005). *White is for blueberry.* New York: Greenwillow Books.

Shapiro, L. E. (1994). *The anger control tool kit.* King of Prussia, PA: Center for Applied Psychology.

Shea, P. D. (2003). *Tangled threads: A Hmong girl's story.* New York: Clarion Books.

Shepard, R. N. (1990). *Mind sights: Original visual illusions, ambiguities, and other anomalies, with a commentary on the play of mind in perception and art.* New York: Freeman.

Sheskey, B. (2010). Creating learning connections with today's tech-savvy student. In H. H. Jacobs (Ed.), *Curriculum 21: Essential education for a changing world* (pp. 195–209). Alexandria, VA: Association for Supervision and Curriculum Development.

Silver, J. (Producer), Wachowski, A. (Director), & Wachowski, L. (Director). (1999). *The matrix* [Motion picture]. United States: Warner Bros.

Small, G., & Vorgan, G. (2008). *iBrain: Surviving the technological alteration of the modern mind.* New York: HarperCollins.

Snow, R. E., & Jackson, D. N. (1993). *Assessment of conative constructs for educational research and evaluation: A catalogue* (CSE Tech. Rep. No. 354). Los Angeles: National Center for Research on Evaluation, Standards, and Student Testing. Accessed at www.cse.ucla.edu/products/Reports/TECH354.pdf on January 7, 2011.

Sternberg, R. J. (1987). Most vocabulary is learned from context. In M. G. McKeown & M. E. Curtis (Eds.), *The nature of vocabulary acquisition* (pp. 89–105). Hillsdale, NJ: Erlbaum.

Sternberg, R. J., & Lubart, T. I. (1999). The concept of creativity: Prospects and paradigms. In R. J. Sternberg (Ed.), *Handbook of creativity* (pp. 3–15). Cambridge, England: Cambridge University Press.

Stevie Nicks in her own words. (n.d.). *Destiny: Stevie Nicks in her own words.* Accessed at www.inherownwords.com/destiny.htm on January 7, 2011.

Stewart, V. (2010). A classroom as wide as the world. In H. H. Jacobs (Ed.), *Curriculum 21: Essential education for a changing world* (pp. 97–114). Alexandria, VA: Association for Supervision and Curriculum Development.

Stiggins, R., Arter, J., Chappuis, J., & Chappuis, S. (2006). *Classroom assessment for student learning: Doing it right—Using it well.* Princeton, NJ: Merrill Prentice Hall.

Strobel, J., & van Barneveld, A. (2009). When is PBL more effective? A meta-synthesis of meta-analyses comparing PBL to conventional classrooms. *The Interdisciplinary Journal of Problem-Based Learning, 3*(1), 44–58.

Sullins, E. S. (1991). Emotional contagion revisited: Effects of social comparison and expressive style on mood convergence. *Personality and Social Psychology Bulletin, 17*(2), 166–174.

Sunburst. (1999). *Student workshop: Angry? Ten ways to cool off—Grades: K–2.* Pleasantville, NY: Author.

Tapscott, D. (2009). *Grown up digital: How the Net generation is changing your world.* New York: McGraw-Hill.

Taylor, M. (1999). *Faraway home.* Dublin, Ireland: O'Brien Press.

Tennessee Department of Education. (n.d.). *"Test-time" strategies for students, parents, and teachers.* Accessed at www.state.tn.us/education/assessment/doc/tsteststrategies.pdf on January 7, 2011.

Tesla, N. (1919/2007). *My inventions: The autobiography of Nikola Tesla.* New York: Cosimo.

Titchener, E. B. (1915). *A beginner's psychology.* New York: Macmillan.

Tittle, P. (2005). *What if . . . collected thought experiments in philosophy.* New York: Pearson.

Toulmin, S., Rieke, R., & Janik, A. (1981). *An introduction to reasoning.* New York: Macmillan.

Trilling, B., & Fadel, C. (2009). *21st century skills: Learning for life in our times.* San Francisco: Jossey-Bass.

Tubbs, M. E. (1986). Goal setting: A meta-analytic examination of the empirical evidence. *Journal of Applied Psychology, 71*(3), 474–483.

Tyler, R. W. (1949a). *Basic principles of curriculum and instruction.* Chicago: University of Chicago Press.

Tyler, R. W. (1949b). *Constructing achievement tests.* Chicago: University of Chicago Press.

Ungerleider, S. (2005). *Mental training for peak performance: Top athletes reveal the mind exercises they use to excel.* Harlan, IA: Rodale.

U.S. Department of Labor, Secretary's Commission on Achieving Necessary Skills. (1991). *What work requires of schools: A SCANS report for America 2000.* Washington, DC: Author. Accessed at http://wdr.doleta.gov/SCANS/whatwork/whatwork.pdf on January 7, 2011.

Vásquez, O. V., & Caraballo, J. N. (1993, August). *Meta-analysis of the effectiveness of concept mapping as a learning strategy in science education.* Paper presented at the Third International Seminar on the Misconceptions and Educational Strategies in Science and Mathematics Education, Ithaca, NY.

Vega, V. (2009, July). *Media-multitasking: Implications for learning and cognitive development in youth.* Paper presented at the Seminar on the Impacts of Media Multitasking on Children's Learning and Development, Palo Alto, CA. Accessed at http://multitasking.stanford.edu/Multitasking BackgroundPaper.pdf on January 7, 2011.

Wagner, T. (2008). *The global achievement gap: Why even our best schools don't teach the new survival skills our children need—and what we can do about it.* New York: Basic Books.

Wallis, C. (2006, March 27). gen M: The multitasking generation. *Time, 167*(13), 48–55. Accessed at www.time.com/time/magazine/article/0,9171,1174696,00.html on April 25, 2011.

Way, T. (n.d.). *Dihydrogen monoxide FAQ.* Accessed at www.dhmo.org/facts.html on January 7, 2011.

Weinberg, R. (2009). 30: Tyson bites Holyfield's ear in rematch. Accessed at http://sports.espn.go.com/espn/espn25/story?page=moments/30 on April 25, 2011.

Wiliam, D., & Leahy, S. (2007). A theoretical foundation for formative assessment. In J. H. McMillan (Ed.), *Formative classroom assessment* (pp. 29–42). New York: Teachers College Press.

Williams, M. (2005). *Brothers in hope: The story of the lost boys of Sudan.* New York: Lee & Low Books.

Williams, P., & Rowlands, I. (2007). *Information behaviour of the researcher of the future: The literature on young people and their information behaviour—Work package II.* London: CIBER. Accessed at www.ucl.ac.uk/infostudies/research/ciber/downloads/GG%20Work%20Package%20II.pdf on January 7, 2011.

Willis, J. (2006). *Research-based strategies to ignite student learning.* Alexandria, VA: Association for Supervision and Curriculum Development.

Wulf, G., Horstmann, G., & Choi, B. (1995). Does mental practice work like physical practice without information feedback? *Research Quarterly for Exercise and Sport, 66*(3), 262–267.

Yankelovich, D. (2000). The magic of dialogue. *National Head Start Bulletin, 68,* 13–14.

# INDEX